Teaching Young Children a Second Language

Teaching Young Children a
Second Language

Tatiana Gordon

TEACHING YOUNG CHILDREN

Doris Pronin Fromberg and Leslie R. Williams

Series Editors

Westport, Connecticut
London

Library of Congress Cataloging-in-Publication Data

Gordon, Tatiana, 1956–
    Teaching young children a second language / Tatiana Gordon.
       p.   cm.—(Teaching young children, ISSN 1554–6004)
    Includes bibliographical references and index.
    ISBN 0–275–98604–7 (alk. paper)
    1. English language—Study and teaching (Primary)—Foreign speakers.
    2. Second language acquisition.   I. Title.
    PE1128.A2G654   2007
    428.2′4–dc22   2006025922

British Library Cataloguing in Publication Data is available.

Library of Congress Catalog Card Number: 2006025922
ISBN-10: 0–275–98604–7
ISBN-13: 978–0–275–98604–9
ISSN: 1554–6004

First published in 2007

Praeger Publisher, 88 Post Road West, Westport, CT 06881
An imprint of Greenwood Publishing Group, Inc.
www.praeger.com

Printed in the United States of America

The paper used in this book complies with the
Permanent Paper Standard issued by the National
Information Standards Organization (Z39.48–1984).

10 9 8 7 6 5 4 3 2 1

Contents

Series Foreword

After the Native American Indians, the United States is a country of immigrants. For immigrants, the English language is the conduit to help them grow into the social, cultural, and economic life of the United States. For young children, the task of learning English as a second language can be a relatively seamless task when they have opportunities to play with other children who speak English. Young immigrant children also can learn the conventions of English during the primary grades from adults who use reliable strategies that provide opportunities for the children to feel successful and valued. With respect to adult intervention, this book makes an important distinction between what young children are ready to learn and what is reasonable to expect them to learn. Indeed, this book illustrates the critical importance of the interaction of language and thought, an embodiment of Vygotsky's outlook.

In this book, Dr. Tatiana Gordon has shared a sensitive perspective about the experience of young immigrant children who are learning English as a second language. Her own wealth of experience as a second language learner with long and significant experience as a successful teacher of English as a second language to young immigrant children and their teachers enriches the reader's knowledge base. She has provided many experiences for young children that will entice them to active engagement in learning English. Beyond the practical aspects, she has provided an important sense of context in a multicultural society that helps the prospective and practicing teacher to understand why particular approaches are worthwhile. She has made theoretical understandings drawn from sociocultural and linguistic sources connect to many lively practices that embody caring about children, practices that help them retain the potential joys of childhood which are their birthright.

This is a rich source book that helps the reader learn how to teach English to young immigrant children. At the same time, it addresses important issues about the place of second language learning in early childhood. The concept of the young child showing the way to adults in the family as a repository of the family's aspirations for becoming part of the fabric of life in the United States is a weighty one. The reader comes to see the young English language learner as an achiever but also as an important lever in her/his family. This book is a page turner, with wonderful textures to savor and images to touch the heart.

Doris Pronin Fromberg and Leslie R. Williams

Preface

If you are about to read this book, you are probably interested in education of young second language learners. Maybe you are about to become a teacher of English as a Second Language (ESL). Or perhaps you are a mainstream classroom teacher and have immigrant children who are learning to speak English in your classroom. Or possibly you are a parent or an administrator who would like to learn more about young immigrant children's second language development.

If education of young language learners is of interest to you, you most probably would like to find out about young immigrants' lives and language learning. What do these children experience when they come to the United States? How can a teacher account for children's immigration experiences in the classroom? What is known about the dynamics of immigrant families? What can a teacher of young immigrant children do to involve immigrant parents in their children's education? What processes take place in the brain of a young language learner? How can a teacher account for these neurological processes? And more generally speaking—what second language teaching strategies work with primary grade children? What can a teacher do to help young language learners speak, read, and write in English?

This book examines how current research answers these and related questions. The first three chapters offer an overview of recent sociological and ethnographic studies of children's immigration and examine research of various aspects of children's second language development. The book's second half summarizes some of the most important methodological

concerns that pertain to teaching young language learners. While reca-
pitulating research findings, the book illustrates the discussion of theoretical principles with samples of good practice. Practical recommendations
contained on these pages flow directly from the classroom. The book describes innovative second language lessons developed and implemented
by ESL teachers who work with language learners enrolled in primary
grades.

This book has a special concern. It looks into ways of rendering primary grade ESL instruction more cognitively enriching. Obviously, it is
not easy to provide intellectually stimulating lessons to young children
who are not fully proficient in English. The book examines research and
action research work of those educators who are trying to deal with the
challenge of helping children grow intellectually while they are learning
a second language. Cognitively enriching second language lessons contained in this book have been developed by teacher learners and alumni of
the MS TESOL program at Hofstra University in Hempstead, New York.

Acknowledgments

I owe a debt of deep gratitude to my teachers who have inspired me with their love of language, their methodological and linguistic expertise, and their teaching skill. My special thanks go to my role models— Nancy Cloud, Frank Horowitz, JoAnne Kleifgen, Lyubov Krikunova, Maxine Levy, Elizabeth Lewis, Raymond Piotrovsky, Svetlana Ruhman, Vera Tarasova, and many others.

I extend my heartfelt thanks to my students about whom I was thinking when writing this book. Their ideas, questions, and enthusiasm have been a source of inspiration. I also thank from the bottom of my heart those Hofstra alumni who generously contributed their lesson ideas to this book.

The naming of instructional strategies is a difficult matter. It is an important one too, because it seems that you teach more consciously and more creatively when you have some kind of taxonomy for what you do. I thank Annette Ezekiel for helping me come up with the names for the teaching strategies described in this book and also for translating the Sholom Aleichem epigraph into English.

I deeply appreciate the work of Ellen Craig who helped me put this volume together. Without Ellen's help the project would not have been completed.

Finally, I thank Doris Fromberg and Leslie Williams for editing the book. I do appreciate all their insightful comments, helpful suggestions, countless revisions, and also occasional proddings.

CHAPTER 1

Language Minority Children in the United States

In order to teach immigrant children effectively, second language teachers need to understand who their students are. Why do immigrant children leave their home countries and what are their journeys to the United States like? How do young children adjust to the new culture? What sort of dynamics prevail in immigrant families? What are young immigrants' schooling experiences like? This chapter addresses these and other related questions that are of interest to second language teachers.

Before talking about today's young language learners, however, the chapter offers some discussion of the past of children's immigration to the United States. This short detour is meant to provide the readers with a historical perspective on the problems that today's immigrant children confront. Certain parallels between the past and the present of immigrant children in the United States are too important to be ignored. In fact, it seems impossible to contemplate solutions to the problems that young immigrants are experiencing today without having some understanding of the history of children's immigration.

Immigrant Children in Historic Perspective

Irish Immigrant Children

God keep all the mothers who rear up a child,
And also the father who labors and toils.

Trying to support them he works night and day,
And when they are reared up, they then go away.[1]

This nineteenth-century Irish poem describes the pain of the Irish parents who often raised their children only to see them leave for the United States. A historian of Irish immigration, Kerby Miller, remarks that immigrating to the United States became a way of life in Ireland, and that emigration of the younger generation from Ireland was dreaded but also thought of as inevitable. Miller cites nineteenth-century observers who said that Irish children were "brought up with the idea of probably becoming emigrants trained to regard life 'in the country' as a transitory matter, merely a period of waiting until the time shall come for them to begin life 'over there.'"[2] Emigrating children were the subject matter of many a song and ballad sung at the American Wake, a farewell party for those departing for America.

The biggest wave of Irish immigrants crossed the Atlantic during the years of *an Gorta Mor*, the Great Famine of the 1840s and 1850s. When for a number of successive years the blight destroyed the potato crop, a famine of horrific proportions ravaged the country. Children were the famine's first victims. Contemporaries describe little boys and girls haggard and emaciated, with drawn adult-like features, too weak to cry. Because the starving children tried to eat grass, their lips were smeared with green. There were accounts of mothers who were so affected by the apathy caused by the famine that they stopped taking care of their offsprings. Nearly a million people died of starvation and diseases during the Irish potato famine, reducing the country's population by one-third. The famine also triggered emigration of unprecedented proportions. During the years following the famine, almost two million people emigrated to America.

Most of the Irish immigrants who came to the United States in the 1840s and 1850s were peasants and children of peasants. Having at last completed the cross-Atlantic journey in disease-ridden "coffin ships" and finding themselves on the American shore, the uneducated, illiterate Irish immigrants could count on only the hardest and least desirable, menial jobs. It was the Irish immigrants who dug the Erie Canal, laid railroad across the prairies, mined coal, and worked in textile factories. Irish men built bridges and constructed steel skeletons for skyscrapers, and Irish women worked as domestic servants. Irish children worked as well, helping out in family stores, at factories, and on farms. In Miller's words, the Irish built the United States.

Irish Americans were the first mass migrants to the United States and the first large immigrant group that settled in big cities (rather than on farmland) where they were observed by fellow Americans. The Irish were also the first immigrant group to ignite a public debate and a virulent *nativist* (anti-immigrant) sentiment. Middle-class Bostonians, New Yorkers, and Philadelphians who took pride in their values and their institutions were shocked by the ways of the newcomers. The squalor of the shantytowns inhabited by the Irish, the newcomers' tendency to huddle together, recreating the life of the Old Country on North American soil caused alarm and dismay. The Irish were perceived to be unfit to live in a civilized, democratic society and were stereotyped as undisciplined, lazy, impetuous, and prone to criminal behavior.

Protestants believed that Catholicism was the root of the Irish problem. There existed a common perception in the nineteenth-century United States that because their primary allegiance was to the pope, Roman Catholics were incapable of making independent decisions essential for living in a republic. These feelings were deep-seated. The memories of escaping from the "popish" trappings of the Anglican Church were still fresh in people's minds, and the fact that Catholic France had been North America's ally during the Revolutionary War did not seem to sway opinion in the United States.

Historian John Higham writes that even children were embroiled in nativist hostility: "Middle class boys growing up in the American town of the late nineteenth century battled incessantly with roughneck Irish gangs from the other side of the tracks."[3] Higham quotes a memoir of Henry Seidel Canby who wrote, "No relations except combat were possible or thought of between our gangs and the 'micks' ... They were still an alien, and had to be shown their place."[4]

The Irish immigrants' perception of the harsh reality of immigration inspired a poem that had an admonition addressed to would-be young immigrants:

Go back to Ireland, my modest young girl;
Listen to me, little lad, and head for home,
Where you'll have a pound and sixpence on fair day
And freedom for a carefree dance together on the dew.[5]

Chinese Immigrant Children

Swallows and magpies flying in glee
Greetings for New Year

Daddy has gone to Gold Mountain
To earn money,
He will earn gold and silver
Ten thousand taels.
When he returns,
We will build a house and buy farmland.[6]

This is a lullaby that Chinese mothers sang to their children in nineteenth-century China. Discovery of gold in California brought hope to the citizens of the once prosperous but now impoverished and civil-strife-ridden middle kingdom. Excitement about the prospect of emigration was particularly great in the southern Guandong province whose sea-faring residents were known in China for their restless, adventurous, and entrepreneurial spirit. Before long, Guandong husbands, fathers, and sons started obtaining counterfeit papers to leave for California. There were only men among those first Chinese emigrants because ancient custom forbade women to leave their homes.

Once the men from Guandong found themselves in the bachelor gold prospector communities of California, they were hired to do traditional female jobs, such as cooking and laundry washing. After the gold rush subsided, Chinese Americans moved inland where they worked as laborers, often taking low-paying and dangerous jobs. For instance, when working on the construction of the Central Pacific Railroad, Chinese Americans who had earned experience working with explosives when creating fireworks in their home country, were engaged in blasting ways across cliffs.

Since the tax-paying Chinese immigrants did not enjoy any political rights, including the right to vote and to testify in court, they were—in the words of an immigration historian Iris Chang—"locked out of the entire political process"[7] and had no incentive to mix with mainstream residents of the United States. In urban centers, they moved to segregated Chinatowns, where they lived in overcrowded, unsanitary tenements, saving whatever money they could to send back home. Chinatowns' poverty was compounded by other social problems. In the almost exclusively male bachelor societies of the Chinatowns, prostitution and gambling were common. Another distinguishing feature of Chinatowns was their governance. Chinatowns were controlled by the "Six Companies," the influential and rich business organizations that oversaw virtually every aspect of economic and social life in Chinese communities in America.

The residents of Chinatowns were viewed with vehement resentment by the white populations. Chinese immigrants were perceived as pests—strange, subhuman creatures who infected and polluted the white population. The cartoons of that period often depicted the Chinese as mice-eating, queue-wearing creatures who should be driven out of the country. The common view held was that the Chinese were "inassimilable," unable to appreciate and adopt the North American culture.[8]

Even the very few children of Chinatown bachelor societies became victims of anti-Chinese sentiments. In October 1871, when anti-Chinese riots swept through San Francisco's Chinatown, a little Chinese boy was seized by the rioters and hanged.[9] Not only adult native-born Americans but also children were perpetrators of racism. Huie Kin recalls his life in the 1870s' San Francisco: "Children spit upon us as we pass by and call us rats." Another memoirist J.S. Look remembers that as he and fellow Chinese Americans "walked along the street of San Francisco often the small American boys would throw rocks at us."[10] The *New York Times* (1880) reported an incident when Cheng Lanbing "was pelted with stones and hooted at by young ruffians" on the streets of New York. The episode was all the more striking given Cheng's status—Cheng was a Chinese minister to the United States, a position similar to that of an ambassador.

In 1881, a bill was introduced in Congress to bar Chinese immigration for the next twenty years. John F. Miller, a senator from California in charge of the bill, compared Chinese immigrants to "inhabitants from another planet" and argued that the Chinese were "machine-like . . . of obtuse nerve, but little affected by heat or cold, wiry, sinewy, with muscles of iron . . . like beasts." In Miller's view, the Chinese immigrants were unfit for the land "resonant with the sweet voices of flaxen-haired children."[11] The Chinese Exclusion Act was signed into law in 1882.

European Immigrant Children

> What if you just—one, two, three—picked up and left for America? Then what?
> —Shalom Aleihem, *Tevye the Milkman*

From the 1860s until the 1920s, the United States was affected by profound demographic, social, and economic changes. As the country's population was growing, its landscape was quickly transforming from rural to urban. Throughout these years, the wave of immigration was steadily mounting. From 1860 until 1920, more than twenty million immigrants, most of whom were from southern and eastern Europe, entered the United States. In any given year, beginning from 1860 through 1920, one out of seven residents was foreign born.

Today, one sees the fruit of the labors of these European immigrants all over the northeastern United States. Immigrants constructed the "rust belt,"[12] the areas of the now abandoned and dilapidated factories which were at one time booming centers of production. In the words of Roger Daniels, a historian of American immigration, European immigrants "made these factories go and provided the human raw material that transformed the United States into a great industrial power."[13]

Even though children under fourteen could not be legally employed, immigrant children worked alongside adults. Children as young as eight years old worked at factories and stores. When government inspectors arrived, underage workers were simply hidden from view. Children worked with adults in tenement dwellings converted into sweatshops and on the streets of American cities. Young "newsies" sold newspapers, young street vendors peddled matches and shoelaces, and young bootblacks waited for customers in the parks and on street corners. Even though government inspectors tried hard to eliminate truancy, dropping out of school by young children was very common. Immigrant families could not have possibly survived without the children providing their share of income.[14]

The United States both welcomed European immigrants and repelled them. On the one hand, business owners supported immigration (because of the cheap workforce it provided), and numerous volunteers assisted immigrants in their adjustment process. On the other hand, citizens viewed newcomers with unprecedented dismay or animosity. Immigrant families' very way of life seemed uncivilized and degraded. Recent farmers settled in the tenements of urban slum areas inhabited by the former fellow residents of their home villages and towns. In these overcrowded immigrant quarters, dirty children roamed the streets, garbage was thrown out the windows, and buckets were emptied in the backyards, creating foul cesspools. An even greater cause of resentment was immigrants' involvement in labor movements. Political trials against European immigrant radicals were the first "red scare" in America.

Anti-immigrant feelings acquired the veneer of rational thinking when the pseudo-scientific discipline of eugenics caught nativists' attention. The unprecedented scientific discoveries of the nineteenth century gave American people an avid appetite for science. Americans who had witnessed the making of the light bulb (to name just one wonder of the Gilded Age) shared the sense of radiant optimism about the power of science to improve their lives and cure social ills. So when in 1900 the genetic research of Gregor Mendel was rediscovered by scientists, eugenicists with a characteristic penchant for grand naïve theorizing proclaimed that they had found the way toward the betterment of human society. The answer lay in encouraging the genetically best stock to reproduce and in curtailing the reproduction of the genetically unfit. The intellectual influence of eugenicists in the nineteenth century was enormous. A historian reports that in

1910 "the general magazines carried more articles on eugenics than on the question of slums, tenements, and living standards combined."[15] Eugenicists spread their doctrine by organizing "better babies" and "fitter families" contests, where children were displayed at county fairs like prize animals.

The influence of eugenics grew even more when Lewis H. Terman, a professor from Stanford University, developed the so-called Stanford-Binet Test, claiming it was a tool for measuring human intelligence. Terman believed that a single score obtained after a short testing procedure would enable teachers to sort out the smart children from the slow ones. He wrote proudly about IQ testing: "The forty-minute test has told more about the mental ability of this boy [a testee] than the intelligent mother had been able to learn in eleven years of daily and hourly observation."[16]

In 1912, in the first mass testing exercise in American history, almost two million men were tested to determine if they were fit for the battlefield. The results "revealed" that the members of Mediterranean races, Jews, and Slavs were of inferior intelligence when compared to the members of the Nordic race.

Once the testing results became available, a campaign to stop immigration of the "genetically undesirable" southern and eastern Europeans acquired new momentum. A Harvard-based Immigration Restriction League, which was made of prominent Harvard graduates, extolled the virtues of the Anglo-Saxon race and lamented the pernicious influence of southern and eastern European genes that brought stupidity, anarchy, and degradation to the American soil. Nativists argued that immigrants from southern and eastern Europe should be stopped from coming to the United States. Said Carl C. Brigham, a proponent of psychometrics, "Immigration should not only be restrictive but highly selective.... The really important steps are those looking toward the prevention of the continued propagation of defective strains in the present population."[17]

The lobbying by the Immigration Restriction League and other organizations yielded results. In 1924, Congress passed the Johnson Reed Act, which set restrictive quotas on the numbers of immigrants who could come to the United States. The law determined American immigration policy for decades until it was repealed in 1965.

Mexican Immigrant Children

While the 1924 Johnson Reed National Origins Act effectively curtailed European immigration, it created a workforce void, particularly palpable because of the economic boom of the 1920s. This void was filled by

Mexicans and Mexican immigrants who traveled North in response to the job demand. The history of Mexicans in the United States, however, started a hundred years earlier, in the 1800s. It was as a history of the conquered people.

In 1848, after the bloody Mexican war, the territories that are now known as the Southwest were seized by the United States. Among the members of the diverse group that lived in that part of Mexico were *Mestizos* (individuals of mixed Spanish and Indian ancestry) and *Indios* (Native Americans), affluent landowning *Californios*, and impoverished *peons*. After 1848, these former Mexicans came under the dominion of another nation and became Mexican Americans.

The treaty of Guadalupe Hidalgo signed by the warring parties in 1848 guaranteed Mexicans who lived on the conquered land all the civil liberties enjoyed by other Americans. But equality of rights existed only on paper. In actuality, Mexican Americans were relegated to the position of second-class citizens. The Mexican land ownership tradition was overridden by American laws, and most *Mexicanos* eventually lost their land. Ironically, they continued to toil this land, making an enormous contribution to American agriculture. Mexican American migrant farm workers, Mexican *braceros* (hired farmers brought to America under contract during World War II), and Mexican illegal immigrants put food on the tables of Americans. They grubbed brush and cactus, dug irrigation canals, leveled land, and planted and harvested crops. Working for abysmally low wages, Mexican Americans and Mexicans have, in the words of historians, subsidized United States' agriculture.[18]

Mexicans have been subject to racism and discrimination, which remained largely unchallenged until the Civil Rights movement of the 1960s. In a book entitled *They Called Them Greasers*, Arnoldo De Leon, a historian of immigration, writes that Mexicans were alternatively described by Anglos as evil and wicked, docile and tractable, vicious and treacherous, and indolent and lethargic.[19]

A sphere where anti-Mexican discrimination was felt particularly acutely from the early days of Mexican American history was the school system. While Mexican American children were considered white *de jure*, *de facto*, they were segregated and subjected to substandard education. Segregated education was justified as being in the best interest of Mexican American children. An argument was made that it was better to school Mexican children in separate facilities, because segregation spared them from competition with their more able Anglo peers. It was also pointed out that Mexican American children needed to be taught English and "Americanized" before they could mix with Anglo children. Mexican American children's bilingualism was held suspect and was believed to be responsible for their academic problems; children who spoke two languages were seen as "alingual" or "bicultural illiterates," proficient in neither English nor Spanish. Children's home culture was perceived by some educators and educational administrators to be conducive to apathy and laziness—antithetical to the active, hard work-oriented Anglo culture. This is how a 1938 study explains why Mexican American children lagged behind in school:

> The Mexicans, as a group, lack ambition. The peon of Mexico has spent so many generations in a condition of servitude that a lazy acceptance of his lot has become a racial characteristic.[20]

Reforming education became one of the major causes of the Mexican American Civil Rights movement, also known as the Chicano movement or *movimiento*. (Notably, the term "Chicano" has not been embraced by all Mexican Americans and is a subject of considerable controversy. The term is used here, because it was a self-appellation of choice of Mexican American civil rights leaders.) Chicano leaders demanded that schools' curricula be reformed to account for the Mexican American culture and that Spanish language be accorded a place in the classroom. (Chapter 2 of this book that deals with language rights and immigration policies describes the ways in which the Civil Rights movement of the 1960s and the Chicano movement challenged and changed the situation of Mexican American children in American schools.)

Immigrant Children Today

> We got on a plain. My mom said, "Sleep. We are going to a Soul."
> I slept for many hours. Then I woke up, and we got off the plain. I saw that everybody looked different. I asked my mom, "Where are we?" She said, "New York."
>
> —Jimmy, 8 years old

The beginning of the third millennium is an exciting period to be an educator of young English Language Learners, since our time is characterized by immigration of historic proportions. The sheer number of immigrants (children and adults) coming to the United States is staggering and can be compared only to the influx of immigrants at the beginning of the twentieth century. Today, 11 percent of Americans are immigrants, a figure not much below the 15 percent of the turn of the century. The absolute number of immigrants (31 million) is the highest it has ever been.

If the children who are being born into immigrant families are added into the equation, the figure is even more impressive. All in all, one out of five residents today is either an immigrant or a child of a recent immigrant.[21] Every fifth school-age child is an immigrant.[22]

While the influx of immigrant children is comparable to the one that transformed the United States at the beginning of the century, many parameters of immigration have changed. Immigrant families at the turn of the century came mostly from Europe; the vast majority of today's immigrants—over half of them—are Hispanic. Asian immigrants are the second largest minority group, comprising a little more than a quarter of the immigrant community. Sizeable groups of immigrant children hail from the Caribbean countries, the Middle East, and Eastern Europe.

Immigrants' residential patterns have also been changing. Until recently, immigrant families mostly concentrated in the "gateway" cities, such as New York, Los Angeles, Miami, Houston, and Chicago. Over the last decade, however, this trend has changed. Immigrant children now live not only in the south of the United States, including North Carolina, Georgia, Arkansas, and Tennessee, but also in the Midwestern states, such as Iowa, where the immigrant community has doubled since the 1990s. Another new trend is enrollment of "right off the boat" immigrant children in suburban schools. Bypassing the once common pattern of settling in big cities and moving to suburban homes at a later time, more and more immigrant families leapfrog to the suburbs right after their arrival in the United States.

Another distinguishing trait of modern immigration has to do with immigrants' educational backgrounds and their participation in the economy. Among today's first and second generations of immigrant parents are highly educated individuals (such as computer programmers from India and scientists from China), as well as those who have had very little formal schooling (some Cambodian refugees and Mexican farm workers). This disparity of educational backgrounds creates an hourglass economy in which some immigrant parents take advantage of better-paying jobs and a relatively affluent lifestyle while others make do with low-end positions and enjoy very few opportunities for upward mobility.

Immigrant Children's Passage to America

Immigration experiences begin with a journey. Immigrant children's passages to the United States are as diverse as their cultural backgrounds. Some families leave their home countries motivated by a desire to better their economic situation, while others flee to the United States seeking asylum from political strife. Some children come to the United States after a relatively peaceful and short journey. Others experience protracted and hazardous passages. There are Puerto Rican children, United States citizens, who arrive on the mainland after a short airplane trip and those children who may come from South and Central America as undocumented immigrants. Some undocumented immigrant children come from as far away as Nicaragua, El Salvador, Honduras, and Guatemala, making illegal crossings of multiple borders on their way to the United States. Among young Asian immigrants, there are "parachute" children, unaccompanied youngsters who have been sent to the United States by their affluent Taiwanese parents (so that the younger generation could avoid the cutthroat competition of Taiwanese colleges) and children of "astronauts fathers," Hong Kong businessmen who live and run their businesses in Hong Kong while supporting their families who reside in the United States. There are also Asian immigrants who were brought to the United States by "snakeheads" (human cargo smugglers) in food containers or leaky boats, and South Asian children who have come to this country after having spent months or even years in refugee camps.[23]

The journey of children who have fled their countries to escape civil strife may have been particularly harsh. These children may have witnessed murder or fled their countries in conditions of great danger. There are young children who come to the United States after having stayed in refugee transit camps. For many months and sometimes even years, children from Vietnam, Laos and Cambodia have lived in camp facilities located in Hong Kong, Thailand, Indonesia, and Philippines.[24] Children who experienced refugee camps have suffered the deprivations, the hazards, the tedium, and the unpredictability of camp life.

The passage to America is especially traumatic for the young children who come to this country as undocumented immigrants. Consider an example of a Mexican family. For months or even years the parents worked for a few dollars a day, putting away money to save the thousands of dollars needed to pay a "coyote," a smuggler who takes illegal immigrants across the Mexico American border. Children left their hometowns and villages often not knowing where their families were headed or why they were going there. They waited with their parents in the towns south of the United States-Mexico border for an opportune moment to cross. In a little Mexican border town that has been growing by the day because of the booming industry of people smuggling, children stayed in shabby guest houses waiting for their parents to stock up on the goods necessary for the hazardous crossing: plastic water jugs, toilet paper, can openers, and canned food.

Then the time came when children and adults embarked on the journey across the Arizona desert. Following trailheads marked with articles of clothing hanging from a bush or a tree on the Mexican side of the border, or using outlines of mountains and high voltage transmission wires as landmarks on the United States side of the border, coyotes took their "pollos" (chickens) across the desert. Travelers had to brave the scorching desert sun and freezing nighttime cold, rattle snakes and dehydration. Greater dangers, however, were presented by people. There are border bandits who prey on illegal immigrants. Coyotes sometimes demand more money than they had originally bargained for. Gun-toting United States vigilantes, who believe that the government has been inefficient in dealing with the illegals, roam Arizona, Texas, and New Mexico borders intent on protecting their property. Since "La migra" (immigration authorities) have cracked down on illegal immigrants in their efforts to tighten borders, border patrols equipped with helicopters, powerful projectors, and night-vision goggles are working hard to stop illegal entrants.[25]

Of course, a passage to a new life is not only traumatizing for children; it is also enriching. Wide-eyed with curiosity, children take in new impressions of the journey—perhaps the first one in their lives. "Mom, how come there are no leaves on the trees?"[26] asked a little boy from Guyana when riding in a car to his new home in the suburbs. "Daddy can speak cat language!" enthusiastically proclaimed a little immigrant TV viewer while his father translated a dialogue between two cartoon cats from English into Russian.

Children from impoverished countries are amazed by the abundance of food; those from rural areas marvel at the tall buildings. The feeling of elation and excitement is described by immigration psychologists to be a typical initial reaction to the new home. The kind of welcome that is given to the new immigrants largely determines their experiences in the United States. Whether children are made to feel welcome in the schools and in their neighborhoods, whether they find themselves in an accepting environment, has a great affect on their emotional and academic welfare in the United States.

Unwelcoming Attitudes

It should be noted that today, just as in the past, immigrant children and their parents are confronted with nativism. Alongside with welcoming and supportive attitudes, there are manifestations of indifference and downright hostility. Members of communities affected by abrupt demographic changes are particularly prone to be resentful of newcomers whether they are adults or young children. "I want our schools to be the way they used to be," is the phrase heard by researchers in areas which experience an influx of Mexican immigrants.[27]

Immigrant children of color interviewed by scholars of immigration are particularly likely to tell stories of the racist and nativist sentiments that they have experienced in the United States and of the situations when they feel like second-class citizens. "Most Americans think that we are stupid," said a ten-year-old Haitian girl to a researcher. "Most Americans think we are members of gangs," echoed a nine-year-old Central American girl.[28]

In some instances, nativism can be more insidious. There are bitter testimonies by Asian Americans who say that they and their children are perceived as foreigners, even though they are American citizens and even though their American lineage may go back as many as six generations. *Perpetual foreigner* status of Asian Americans seems to be deeply entrenched in the U.S. culture; in the words of sociologist Mia Tuan, "an assumption of foreignness stubbornly clings to them [Asian ethnics]," because "whiteness . . . is equated with being American; Asianness is not."[29]

Little children as well as adults experience first-hand what it means to be a perpetual foreigner. The *New York Times* describes an incident when Megan Higoshi, a young Japanese American girl scout was selling cookies at a local mall in Southern California. Megan politely asked a male shopper if he would like to buy some cookies. "I only buy from American girls," responded the man.[30]

The "model minority" myth which dates back to the 1960s, when media juxtaposed common patterns of academic achievement of Asian Americans and African Americans, complicates the issue even further. The model minority reputation takes away the public attention from anti-Asian discrimination. Moreover, because of the inflated reputation for unfailing academic success, Asian American children who are not part of the "cream of the crop" have difficulty in getting help whenever they experience emotional, social, or academic problems.

Stereotyping of language minority cultures by the media is also a covert form of nativism. Not only adult immigrants will cringe at the condescending clichés, or mocking portrayal of their culture. Immigrant children too will feel shocked by these misrepresentations. Eleven-year-old Vinesh Viswanathan from India describes his reaction in his letter to the *San Francisco Chronicle*:

One time when I finished eating my dinner, I decided to sit on the couch and watch television. I decided to watch a popular show called "The Simpsons." While I was watching one part of "The

Simpsons," I became very angry. One of the characters, Homer, made fun of my culture's god, Ganesha, because of his elephant head. Homer asked the Indian store-owner about the picture of Ganesha. He said, "What do you feed him, peanuts?" This provided my schoolmates a good weapon to use to ridicule me the following day at school. I was so depressed that I came home complaining to my mom about how unfair life is."[31]

Adjusting to the New Environment

Amidst the attitudes that range from friendliness and acceptance to open hostility and even aggression, young children begin their adaptation to the new culture, learning to live in an environment that, more often than not, is different from the one they experienced at home.

Some losses may seem insignificant to adults but are very real to children. Psychologists report that children miss the sights, sounds, and smells of their home countries.[32] An immigrant boy from Afghanistan described missing the sound of a bell tied to the harness of a donkey that delivered water in his native village. A little girl missed having classes outdoors, in the shade of a tree, the way she used to have in her home country, The Dominican Republic. Muslim children fondly recall the sense of belonging and of oneness with others which they used to experience when an entire large community celebrated the month of Ramadan.

One of the greatest changes that children experience is separation from family members. In many cases, children leave their extended families, grandparents, aunts and uncles, back home. In some instances, immigrant children become reunited with their parents after a period of prolonged separation. (Often, parents leave first and do not send for their children until later.) A little Haitian American girl, Danticat, who was left behind by her mother with her loving aunt in Haiti, recalled that she felt she was "my mother's daughter and Tante Atie's child."[33] Similar situations are described by Harvard-based sociologist Mary Waters in her study of immigrant children from the Caribbean region. Waters notes that mothers from that region leave children at home (often with a grandmother or aunt), make the passage to America, find jobs, settle in the new country, and only then send for their sons and daughters. While at home in Haiti, remarks Waters, children do not feel disturbed by the fact that they are looked after by the members of their extended family, since this practice is quite common and acceptable in the region. However, once children are in the United States, they often begin to view the experiences of separation from their mothers through an American cultural lens and begin to feel angry and resentful.[34] Researchers note that it is not uncommon for a child to "act out" upon the reunification with their parents as "a way to 'punish' parents for leaving him behind."[35]

One of the greatest changes that children must adjust to is the change in their home environment. Children who grew up in little towns and villages and enjoyed the luxury of being able to play outside and roam neighborhoods with friends, suddenly find themselves cooped up in small apartments. Carola Suarez-Orozco and Marcelo Suarez-Orozco write in their study of immigrant children that their subjects experience "a significant loss of freedom because immigrant parents are often very concerned about crime in their new neighborhoods."[36] Not being able to leave home at any time creates the sense of being "shut up" or *encerramiento* as Spanish-speaking children put it. Young immigrant children are so unhappy about staying home alone that they will often tell their teachers that they did not enjoy a weekend or a school break and would much rather be at school with their peers.

Undocumented children constitute a relatively small group of the overall immigrant population, but it is important to recognize their adaptation experiences, because these happen to be particularly harsh. Researchers report that many undocumented children feel hunted and remain guarded with their teachers and other school personnel. There is evidence that illegal immigrants, for fear that their children may be apprehended, severely constrain their children's activities.[37] The Suarez-Orozcos tell of incidents when parents give inaccurate information to school officials, preventing schools from contacting families in an emergency.

Limited Parent Availability

Children adjusting to a new culture are in need of parental guidance. Immigrant parents, however, are often unable to provide this much needed attention. The pressures of making a living in a new country put great demands on the time of the adults. In their efforts to earn a living, send remittances back home, or pay for other family members' passage to the United States, immigrant parents often need to take on multiple jobs and spend a lot of their time away from home.

Consider the example of Juana, an immigrant from El Salvador. Two of Juana's children did not see a lot of their mother. Juana left her war wrecked country where there was no economic or educational future for her two children and came to the United States leaving her husband behind, so that the children could "become somebody."[38] Like many other Central American parents who are ready to make every possible sacrifice to assure that their children do well in American school,[39] Juana plunged into hard work. Having only seventh grade education and no English language skills, she took a job as a maid. Juana often worked six days a week from 6 am till sundown. To get to the homes of her employers from the inner city where she lived with her children, Juana had to take two or even three buses, which was particularly hard to do in wintertime.[40] Even though Juana was unable to spend a lot of time with her children, her dream came true when her younger son got into a prestigious American University.

The hectic schedule of a Chinese American, Mrs. A. Ying, is described in a study of Chinese garment workers.[41] Mrs. Ying lives with her husband and two children in Brooklyn, New York. Her fellow workers think that she is lucky to have the help from her mother-in-law, but for Mrs. Ying the pressure of pleasing the elderly woman is often taxing. Mrs. Ying's day begins at 7 a.m. She dresses her children, deferentially discusses the shopping list with her mother-in-law, takes one of her children to childcare and then rushes to her job in Chinatown. At work, Mrs. Ying tries to work as fast as she can (as a "headless fly" in her own words), devoting as little time as possible for snacks or a visit to the restroom. At 5 p.m. she leaves work, does some grocery shopping and takes a subway home. At home she does some sewing to earn extra money. She stays up till after midnight, waiting for her husband to come home from his job in a restaurant. She then dutifully serves him a bowl of soup cooked with medicinal herbs, which residents of Canton believe to be indispensable for one's health, and goes to bed at 1 a.m.

The mother and father of M.K., a seven-year-old Korean boy, are always at home; but they also have little time for M. The K.'s run a small mom-and-pop style store, a business that requires a tremendous amount of their time. While Mr. K. manages the store, Mrs. K. waits on customers at the cash register. Even though the K's have lived in the United States for six years, they are—because of the nature of their business—isolated from the mainstream American culture. When at home, Mr. and Mrs. K. speak Korean to their children, while the children respond in English. Is the pressure of running a mom-and-pop store going to result in the K's alienation from their children—a pattern observed by researchers in many Korean American families?[42]

Often, because of the stress of adjusting to life in a new country, parents are unavailable to children not only physically but also emotionally. A problem that is particularly likely to make immigrant parents feel distraught and depressed is that of *downward mobility*. Because of the lack of English language skills, limited cultural competence or the need for professional retraining, immigrant children's parents often find themselves in social and professional positions well below those they enjoyed in their home countries. A former Salvadorian office worker has to take a house-cleaning job, a Middle Eastern engineer runs a family store, a Russian concert pianist works as a visiting nurse. This loss of social and professional clout cannot but affect emotional well-being of immigrant adults and has a negative effect on their interaction with children.

Culture Shock, Cultural Incompetence, and Role Reversal

Whether they do or do not speak English, whether their jobs are socially isolating or positioned in the midst of the mainstream culture, whether they are quick to maintain their professional and social status or are affected by downward mobility, most immigrant parents experience some adjustment problems. First comes the culture shock, an uncomfortable feeling that every element of the new environment is strange and unfamiliar. The culture shock is compounded by the realization of one's own cultural inaptitude. Immigrant parents need to master innumerable skills that are taken for granted by native-born Americans. Dialing a phone number, signing a child up for school, attending a parent-teacher conference may be challenges in the life of an immigrant. An adult Mexican American immigrant sums up the experience by saying, "I became an infant again. I had to learn all over again to eat, to speak, to dress, and what was expected of me."[43] Psychologists who study immigrants refer to this state of mind as *cultural incompetence* and *cultural disorientation*.

Often in immigrant families with children taking less time than do adults to learn some English, children and adult roles become switched. In this situation of *role reversal* children find themselves taking care of adults. Immigrant children often have to provide translations, call service agencies, interpret confusing situations—in short, look after their parents. Psychologists report that children tend to resent the role reversal and miss the time when they could securely entrust themselves to the care of their parents.

An Iranian American author, Firoozeh Dumas, poignantly summarizes her childhood perception of the role reversal: "At an age when most parents are guiding their kids toward independence, my mother was hanging on to me for dear life."[44]

Unlike adults, children are fairly quick to learn the ways of the new country. Yet even they experience some degree of culture shock and cultural disorientation. Life of a child ceases to be predictable in a new culture. Behavior of others is no longer habitual and ceases to go unnoticed.

Various aspects of day-to-day existence that the child used to take for granted back home strike the attention of a young newcomer. The way adults and children act and interact, talk or look, the way adults praise or admonish and the way children play may seem unusual, discomforting, or jarring.

Adjustment to School

The most difficult cultural frontier that the immigrant child needs to cross is that of the classroom. Immigrant children are full of excitement, nervousness, and apprehension about what awaits them in the new school. The realities of adjusting to new educational environment may be very harsh for some of them. This is how a Vietnamese girl describes the sense of confusion and isolation that she experienced as a nine-year-old, fresh-off-the-boat immigrant:

> You don't know anything. You don't even know what to eat when you go to the lunchroom. The day I started school all the kids stared at me like I was from a different planet. I wanted to go home with my dad, but he said I had to stay. I was very shy and scared. I didn't know where to sit or eat or where the bathroom was or how to eat the food. I felt that all around me activities were going on as if I were at a dance but no one danced with me and I was not a part of anything. I felt so out of place that I felt sick.[45]

Children have to deal with the stress of standing out physically. Children who hail from countries whose population is predominantly Asian or Black become for the first time aware of their skin color or other physical characteristics when they come to the United States. This is how a Chinese American woman describes what it felt like to find herself in the predominantly white community of Fresno, California:

> You look at my kindergarten picture, and there were like a couple of whites, and most were nonwhite. And you go to my first grade picture, and me and one other Chicano, a Mexican kid, was in the picture, and the rest were white. So that was the biggest contrast. So it did something to me. I think it made me insecure because I was very self-conscious of how I was physically. That I was different, physically, from everybody else.[46]

Not knowing a game that everybody plays, not having seen a cartoon that everybody has seen, or wearing an outfit that makes you stand out may be the source of embarrassment or even trauma for a young child. A Russian American writer Gary Shteyngart recollects his first days in an American school:

> I was wearing my very fine Russian fur coat, made out of a bear or an elk or some other fierce woodland animal, when my first grade teacher took me aside and said, "You can't wear that anymore. We don't dress like that here." The dear secretaries at the Hebrew school I attended started a little clothing drive for me, a gathering of the Batman and Green Lantern T-shirts their sons had outgrown, so that I could look half-way normal on the playground.[47]

One cannot help noticing that the embarrassment felt by the child is still experienced as real and acute by the adult, a successful, acclaimed novelist.

Often immigrant children have to deal with the taunting and teasing by other children. There are also animosities between the immigrant children of different ethnic backgrounds and rifts within ethnic groups, as when second or third generation immigrant children distance themselves from the ones who are FOB (Fresh off the Boat). Researchers of immigrant children point out that teachers and school administrators are not effective in dealing with these incidents and too often dismiss them as a prank or a phase.[48]

School and Home Culture Mismatch

Adjusting to the school culture may be particularly challenging when the culture of the school clashes with an immigrant child's home culture. The dissonance between the American culture and those of the children's homes is referred to by experts in multicultural education as the *mismatch between school and home culture*.

Outside the security of their homes, language minority children often deal with adults who find their behavior inappropriate, unusual, and incomprehensible, because it is at odds with the expectations which North Americans have for children's conduct. Second language teachers engage in a lifetime of cross-cultural ethnographic studies to make sense of their new students' behavior patterns and to understand how they can be accounted for within the value system of the children's home cultures. But no matter how much teachers know about their students, cultural puzzles continue.

Examples of misunderstandings that stem from the home and school culture mismatches are numerous. For instance, a little Cambodian boy was in the state of emotional turmoil when another child patted him on the head. His teachers did not understand his reaction until they learned that in Vietnam, Cambodia and some other Asian cultures the head is considered to be the seat of the child's soul and is not to be touched. A teacher was about to mistakenly report a case of child abuse when noticing red marks on a child's skin, because she was not aware of the custom of coining, a folk remedy of rubbing a coin into the skin, believed in some Asian cultures to relieve symptoms of a cold and other illnesses.[49] Even though these misunderstandings are quite dramatic, they are not very hard to resolve, because they originate from the cultural norms of which both parties involved are aware and which they can describe.

The task of dealing with a cultural mismatch becomes quite difficult when educators and immigrants deal with culture-specific values and behaviors which members of a culture "'know' but may have not been able to articulate."[50] We all have such unanalyzed, unregistered principles and behavior patterns that we find only natural or self-evident. It takes careful ethnographic analysis to uncover, describe and analyze these culture specific norms and actions. Consider some examples of cultural mismatches described in recent studies.

Preschool aged Asian children may strike their new teachers as being immature and demanding. By the same token, young Asian students may come across as being unusually quiet, reticent, and almost morose.[51] These behavior patterns, which may cause American teachers to be concerned, make sense within the context of traditional Asian cultures. Ethnographic studies of Asian socialization practices report that in traditional Asian families, very young children are "not expected to know any better" and are thus not held accountable for their disruptive behavior.[52] As children grow up, however, they are expected to value social harmony, oneness with the group and being in step with others. In the more traditional Asian cultures, excessive talkativeness in older children is frowned upon and is perceived as a sign of immaturity. Children are brought up to respect restraint and composure, as well as to employ indirect communication styles; they are expected to learn to read situations for clues and understand the needs of others, even if those needs are not stated directly. In the words of psychologist Sam Chan, "Early on, children are taught to observe nonverbal cues that guide behaviors in social interactions; moreover, they are scolded (e.g., "Have you no eyes!") and feel ashamed if they lack ability to meet someone's needs that were not articulated."[53] Psychologist May Tung makes a similar observation, saying that Chinese children "are not encouraged to 'speak up.' Instead, they are told to *ting hua*, literally, listen to the speech/talk/words of elders."[54]

During a parent-teacher conference attended by Asian parents, a teacher may discover that her students' parents do not seem to welcome the praise that she bestows on the child. Father and mother may keep dismissing the teacher's praise of their daughter's performance and then keep telling their daughter to "try harder." This behavior, so unlike the behavior of parents in the United States who are quick to acknowledge their children's accomplishments can be understood in light of the family values and interaction patterns common in traditional Asian families. Researchers report that, in Asian cultures, it is common for individuals to derive strengths and protection from their families. In traditional Asian families, children are seen as family extensions. While parents are expected to make every possible sacrifice to ensure their children's success (in the words of a Chinese philosopher Mencius, "A good mother is ready to move three times to give children a good education"), the children's duty is to do well in school and to make their parents proud. Says Chan,

> Whereas the family sacrifices and mobilizes its resources to provide an environment conducive to academic achievement, the child, in turn, is expected to work hard and receive high grades. Within this context, overt rewards, contingent praise, and personal credit are generally not given for positive achievements or behaviors because they [the achievements] are expected.[55]

A different example of the home school culture clash may involve Middle Eastern children. Virginia-Shirin Sharifzadeh, an Iranian American scholar, believes that Middle Eastern children may strike American teachers as being overly dependent and lacking in autonomy. Sharifzadeh explains that in the Middle Eastern culture interdependence is valued over independence, based upon the belief that the bond between individuals is crucial for dealing with the adversities of life. Thus, while American parents encourage their children to be independent, Middle Eastern parents focus on fostering the bond between the children and the people in their environment. Says Sharifzadeh,

> Middle Eastern mothers ... do not press for their children to eat, bathe, or put on their clothes independently at an early age. Thus, Middle Eastern children may differ from American children in the chronology of self-help skills. This should not be interpreted as a deficiency in the child but as a difference in parental attitude toward the child's independence.[56]

Sharifzadeh mentions that because Middle Eastern parents generally prefer to see their children grow as interdependent members of the family, children may be encouraged to socialize with adult family members and stay up late at night at family functions. Sharifzadeh notes that a Middle Eastern child's not paying attention at school on a certain day may well have been the result of socializing the night before.

The very language used by teachers to commend or critique children's work, to give directions, and to discipline may strike children as being unusual or strange and may cause confusion, because they may be rooted in disparate value systems. A Russian American father was shocked when he heard the American teacher tell her class, "Boys, and girls, what do you do when someone is bothering you?" and the children responded in unison "Tell the teacher!" The concept of a teacher as somebody who formulates the rules (often with the help of the children) and then proceeds to enforce them is foreign to many Russian-speaking parents. In Russian schools, popular teachers may be an object of almost exalted reverence with the children and parents. However, quite often the teachers are seen as adversaries, figures of oppression, whose rule children like to challenge. In a culture where children bond together against the teacher, telling on your peers is seen as a shameful act.[57]

A teacher in the United States may feel that her Korean American students are overburdened with after-school curricular activities. Every day after their regular school hours, children attend all manner of after-school classes, including additional English as a Second Language (ESL) and math, as well as lessons in Korean language. Korean parents' efforts to provide their children with the best education available can be understood in the context of the role of education throughout Korean history. As far back as 788 A.D., Korea adopted the Chinese examination system whereby passing a highly rigorous civil service examination provided the sole route to a coveted civil service career. The value placed on education as the means for obtaining upward mobility is still deeply ingrained in the Korean culture.[58]

One of the biggest cultural disconnects cited in scores of studies of immigrant communities is the way families discipline their children. Many Haitian, Vietnamese, Mexican and Cambodian parents (to name just a few immigrant groups) feel that because, in the United States, they cannot use corporal punishment, their authority over their children erodes. These parents are frightened when they observe their children "Americanize," that is adopt the ways of communicating with adults that the more traditional patriarchal cultures perceive as being disrespectful and stemming from the overly permissive and licentious American culture. Immigrant parents may feel disempowered by American child-rearing practices.

Reports a Harvard-based sociologist Mary Waters: "That the state can dictate that a parent cannot beat a child is seen by these parents as a real threat to their ability to raise their children correctly."[59]

Cultural Rift at Home

Making sense of being different, reinventing oneself, reconciling the two realities, the one of the home and the one of the school, is a puzzle that immigrant children set about to solve. For some children the transition from the old home culture to the new American culture is relatively smooth and easy. It is important to bear in mind, however, that even the children who are confidently bilingual and bicultural may have difficulty reconciling their two cultural selves. Indian American writer Mitra Kalita captures the complexity of the bicultural life in her book about the Indian American communities in suburban New Jersey:

> I became two Mitras. The one at home spoke Asamese, ate with her little hands, and slept tucked between two parents in a king-size bed. The one in school spoke in a thick Long Island accent, dreamed of a family past as storied as Laura Ingalls Wilder's, and vacillated between the black Cabbage Patch Kid and the white one, settling on the latter. I grew distressed if my two worlds collided, as they inevitably did.[60]

As time goes on and children adapt to the new culture, some immigrant families may experience a different type of stress. Once children have learned some English and have adapted to life in the United States, they begin to drift away from their parents and grandparents. Quite often, to the dismay of their parents, children lose touch with their home cultures, become strangers in their own families, and are embarrassed by their elders' ethnic customs or clothing.[61]

The cultural rift between the children and their parents or grandparents may be particularly deep if children suffer from *first language attrition* or loss of their home language.[62] First language attrition may be total or partial. There are immigrant families where adults speak to children in a home language and children respond in English. In other families, children retain their home language speaking ability but speak the first language that is rudimentary and impoverished. Loss of first language inevitably affects the quality of adult—child interaction. When their command of a home language deteriorates, children cannot interact fully with their family members. Nuances of meaning are lost in a conversation, jokes are not understood. In the families where children cannot properly communicate with their non-English proficient family members, important emotional and cultural ties become severed. As a result, children may feel estranged from their family members and become unable to turn to them for help with homework or personal matters. In a poem filled with the sense of remorse and regret LeAna Gloor, describes alienation from her Filipino grandfather:

> I don't try to talk to him because I don't speak his language and never did. Even when he stuffed wadded up dollar bills into my fingers, muttering half English words about food and haircuts, I never understood him.[63]

The range of immigrant parents' attitude about the prospect of their children becoming "Americanized" is extremely broad. Some will encourage their children to speak only English and will feel proud that children have abandoned the cultural attributes of their home countries that they perceive as "backward." Many immigrant parents fear "Americanization." Not only do these parents aspire to share a common cultural heritage with their children, they also see the American culture as being overly permissive and granting unnecessary freedom to children. A study of adaptation of Filipino families reports that Filipino mothers are happier ("had higher levels of family satisfaction") when their children behave in a more traditional manner.[64]

While reading this section of the book, the reader may feel overwhelmed by the descriptions of the negative experiences in the lives of immigrant children. Immigrant children's journey to America, their initial adaptation, learning English and their schooling experiences are fraught with difficulty. While challenges faced by immigrant children are great, there is also extensive evidence of immigrant children's success in the United States. Studies conducted by sociologists, ethnographers, and educators suggest that most immigrant children and their parents are optimistic about their immigration and its power to transform their lives. These studies report that immigrant children do master English and adapt to the American culture.[65] The next chapter deals with the U.S. policies that impact immigrant children's language learning experiences.

Main Points

- Throughout U.S. history, young immigrants have experienced a warm welcome and have also dealt with various manifestations of nativism. Past immigrations from Asian and European countries were stopped short by virulent nativist campaigns.

- Parent downward mobility, parent—child role reversal, cultural disorientation, mismatch between school and home culture, first language and culture attrition affect immigrant children's schooling and language learning experiences.

Notes

1. K. Miller (1985), *Emigrants and exiles: Ireland and the Irish exodus to North America*. New York: Oxford University Press, p. 562.

2. Ibid., p. 487.

3. J. Higham (1963), *Strangers in the land: Patterns of American nativism*. New York: Atheneum, p. 26.

4. H. S. Canby (1947), *American Memoir*. Boston. Cited in Higham (1963), *Strangers in the land*, p. 26.

5. Miller, *Emigrants and exiles*, p. xiii.

6. Chang (2003), *The Chinese in America*. New York: Penguin Books, p. 19.

7. Ibid., p. 120.

8. R. Daniels (1990), *Coming to America: A history of immigration and ethnicity in American life*. New York: Harper Perennial.

9. Chang, *The Chinese in America*.

10. Ibid., p. 127.

11. Ibid., p. 130.

12. Daniels, *Coming to America*, p. 213.

13. Ibid.

14. S. Berrol (1995), *Growing up American: Immigrant children in America then and now*. New York: Twayne Publishers.

15. Higham, *Strangers in the land*, p. 151.

16. L. M. Terman (1916), *The measurement of intelligence*. Boston, MA: Houghton Mifflin. Cited in S. J. Gould (1996), *The mismeasure of man*. New York: W.W. Norton and Company, p. 209.

17. Gould, *The mismeasure of man*, p. 260.

18. M. S. Meier, and F. Ribera (1993), *Mexican Americans/American Mexicans: From conquistadors to Chicanos*. New York: Hill & Wang, a division of Farrar, Straus and Giroux.

19. Arnoldo De Leon (1983), *They called them Greasers: Anglo attitudes toward Mexicans in Texas, 1821–1900*, Austin: University of Texas Press.

20. T. Carter (1970), *Mexican Americans in school: A history of educational neglect*. New York: The College Entrance Examination Board, p. 57.

21. T. Jacoby (Ed.) (2004), *Reinventing the melting pot: The new immigrants and what it means to be American*, New York: Basic Books. A member of the Perseus Books Group.

22. C. Suarez-Orozco and M. Suarez-Orozco (2001), *Children of immigration*. Cambridge, MA: Harvard University Press.

23. Chang (2003), *The Chinese in America*. New York: Penguin Books.

24. D. Ranard and M. Pfleger (Eds.) (1995), *From the classroom to the community: A fifteen-year experiment in refugee education.* McHenry, IL: Center for Applied Linguistics and Delta Systems.

25. Read a detailed account of illegal immigrants passage to and lives in the U.S. in R. Martinez (2001), *Crossing over: a Mexican family on the migrant trail.* New York: Henry Holt and Company.

26. Anjanie Persaud, personal conversation 2005.

27. R. Hernandez-Leon and V. Zuniga (2005), *Appalachia meets Aztlan: Mexican immigration and intergroup relations. Dalton, Georgia,* pp. 244–273. In V. Zuniga and R. Hernandez-Leon (Eds.), *New destinations: Mexican immigration in the United States.* New York: Russell Sage Foundation, p. 267.

28. Suarez-Orozco, *Children of immigration,* pp. 96–97.

29. M. Tuan (1998), *Forever foreigners or honorary whites? The Asian ethnic experience today.* Rutgers, NJ: Rutgers University Press, pp. 138–139.

30. S. Mydans, "New Unease for Japanese Americans," *New York Times,* March 4, 1992. Quoted in T. Fong. (1998), *The contemporary Asian American experience.* Upper Saddle River, NJ: Prentice Hall, p. 151.

31. V. Viswanathan, "Seeing the Person, Not Color," *San Francisco Chronicle,* May 17, 1995.

32. M. Asworth (1982), "The Cultural Adjustment of Immigrant Children in English Canada." In R. Nann (Ed.), *Uprooting and surviving: adaptation and resettlement of migrant families and children.* London, England: D. Reidel Publishing Company, pp. 77–83.

33. Suarez–Orozco, *Children of immigration,* p. 68.

34. M. Waters (1999), *Black Identities: West Indian dreams and American realities.* New York: Russel Sage Foundation.

35. Suarez-Orozco, *Children of immigration,* p. 69.

36. C. Suarez-Orozco and M. Suarez-Orozco (2001), *Children of immigration.* Cambridge, MA: Harvard University Press, p. 69.

37. Suarez-Orozco, *Children of immigration.*

38. M. Suarez-Orozco (1993), "'Becoming Somebody': Central American Immigrants in U.S. Inner-City Schools." In E. Jacob and C. Jordan (Eds.), *Minority education: Anthropological perspectives.* Norwood, NJ: Ablex Publishing Corporation, p. 135.

39. Ibid., pp. 129–143.

40. Read about the lives of immigrant domestic workers in P. Hondagneu-Sotelo (2001), *Domestica: immigrant workers cleaning and caring in the shadows of affluence.* Berkeley: University of California Press.

41. X. Bao and R. Daniels (2001), *Holding up more than half the sky: Chinese women garment workers in New York City, 1948–92.* Urbana: University of Illinois Press.

42. K. Park (1989), "Impact of New Productive Activities on the Organization of Domestic Life: A Case Study of the Korean American Community." In G. Nomura, R. Endo, S. Sumida, and R. Leong (Eds.), *Frontiers of Asian American studies.* Pullman, WA: Washinton State University Press, pp. 140–150.

43. C. Suarez-Orozco and M. Suarez-Orozco, p. 73.

44. F. Dumas (2003), *Funny in Farsi: A Memoir of growing up Iranian in America*: New York: Villard Books, p. 10.

45. L. Olsen (1988), *Crossing the schoolhouse border: Immigrant students and the California public schools*. San Francisco, CA: California Tomorrow, p. 71.

46. M. Tuan (1998), *Forever foreigners or honorary whites? The Asian ethnic experience today*. Rutgers, NJ: Rutgers University Press, pp. 81–82.

47. G. Shteyngart (2004), "The New Two-Way Street." In T. Jacoby (Ed.), *Reinventing the melting pot: the new immigrants and what it means to be American*. New York: Basic Books. A member of the Perseus Books Group, pp. 285–292.

48. Suarez-Orozco and Suarez-Orozco, *Children of immigration*.

49. N. Dresser (1996), *Multicultural manners: New rules of etiquette for a changing society*. New York: John Wiley and Sons.

50. H. Mehan (1981), "Ethnography of Bilingual Education." In H. T. Trueba et al. (Eds.), *Culture and the bilingual classroom: Studies in classroom ethnography*. Rowley, MA: Newbury House, p. 173. Cited in B. McLaughlin (1985). *Second-language acquisition in childhood, Volume 2: School-age children*, 2nd ed. Hillside, NJ: Lawrence Erlbaum, p. 149.

51. C. Sato (1981), "Ethnic Style in Classroom Discourse." In M. Hines and W. Rutherford (Eds.), *ON TESOL'81*. Washington, DC: TESOL, pp. 11–24.

52. S. Chan (1998), "Families with Asian Roots." In E. Lynch and M. Hanson (Eds.), *Developing cross-cultural competence. A guide for working with children and their families*, 2nd ed. Baltimore, MD: Paul Brookes, pp. 251–354.

53. Ibid., p. 321.

54. May Paomay Tung (2000), *Chinese Americans and their immigrant parents: Conflict, identity, and values*. Binghamton, NY: The Haworth Clinical Practice Press. p. 64.

55. S. Chan, *Developing cross-cultural competence*, pp. 301–302.

56. V.-S. Sharifzadeh (1998), "Families with Middle Eastern Roots." In E. Lynch and M Hanson (Eds.), *Developing cross-cultural competence. A guide for working with children and their families*, 2nd ed. Baltimore, MD: Paul Brookes. pp. 441–478.

57. T. Gordon, *Speech Act Behavior in the ESL Classroom*. Unpublished paper.

58. W. Hurh (1998), *The Korean Americans*. Westport, CT: Greenwood Press.

59. M. Waters (1999), *Black Identities: West Indian dreams and American realities*. New York: Russel Sage Foundation, p. 220.

60. M. Kalita (2003), *Suburban Sahibs: Three Indian Families and their passage from India to America*. New Brunswick, NJ: Rutgers University Press, p. 2.

61. K. Leonard (1997), *The South Asian Americans*, Westport, CT: Greenwood Press.

62. For example, L. Wong-Fillmore (1991), When learning a second language means losing the first. *Early Childhood Research Quarterly*, 6(3), 323–347.

63. LeAna Gloor (2000), "Reincarnate." In S. Geok-lin Lim and Cheng, L.C. (Eds.), *Tilting the continent: Southeast Asian American writing*. Minneapolis, MN: New Rivers Press, p. 38.

64. P. Agbayani-Siewert and L. Revilla (1995), "Filipino Americans." In P. G. Min (Ed.), *Asian Americans: Contemporary trends and issues*. Thousand Oaks, CA: Sage, p. 163.

65. A. Portes and R. Schauffler (1996), "Language and the Second Generation: Bilingualism Yesterday and Today." In A. Portes (Ed.), *The new second generation*. New York: Russell Sage Foundation, pp. 8–29.

CHAPTER 2

Second Language Policies and the Language Rights of Language Minority Children

Because using language is second nature to us, and because speaking comes to people as naturally as breathing, we seldom stop to think that the way we learn and use languages at home and in school are deeply rooted in the histories and the policies of individual countries. Is a certain language venerated as a symbol of a nation? In what language are children schooled? Is children's home language dismissed or embraced by the society? These issues related to *language policies* and *language rights* vary form country to country and from culture to culture.

This chapter discusses policies that affect language minority children in the United States and also describes the language rights that these children have. Before talking about U.S. language policies, however, the chapter says a few brief words about language policies across the world. These international samplings of language policies are meant to help the reader appreciate how much is at stake as far as young children's language rights are concerned.

Cultural Uniqueness of Language Policies

Take the example of France. Every time French school children put a pen to paper, spell a word, or form a sentence, they are expected to comply with the requirements spelled out by the "immortals," the members of the French Academy of Science. The immortals prescribe spelling and grammar rules and make sure not too many foreign words—for instance English ones—pollute French. This *purist*, stringent language policy is largely embraced by French citizens. When French teachers proposed a spelling simplification reform to the Academy in 1991, the public vehemently objected arguing that teachers' "first duty is to teach rigour."[1]

Children in the Middle Eastern countries do their schoolwork in Modern Standard Arabic language, also known as *fusha* (pronounced *foos-huh*). Fusha is the language of the Quran, a revered part of the Arabic cultural heritage. In their homes or on the street, however, children converse in local dialects, such as Egyptian Arabic, Moroccan Arabic, and many others. In effect, almost all Arabic children take advantage of *diglossia*, that is proficiency in two dialects, and speak both a high-status dialect of schooling and a low-status colloquial dialect of day-to-day life. However, it is not easy for little children to learn to read and write in a language that they do not speak at home. Some reform-minded Middle Eastern policy makers and educators have, therefore, called for the simplification of fusha. Traditionalists, in turn, have insisted that fusha be kept as a means of staying in touch with the rich Islamic culture.[2]

There are countries where repressive government policies have made it impossible for children to be schooled in their mother tongue. Take the example of Kurdish children, members of a 25 million people strong minority group, who live in the oil rich regions of Iran, Iraq, Turkey, and Syria. Fearing a Kurdish struggle for independence, the governments of these four countries have discriminated against the Kurdish language. In Turkey, for example, it is against the law to school children in Kurdish. In Iran, it is illegal to speak Kurdish in school or to own publications in Kurdish. A Kurdish Iranian recalls that her mother "fearing prison and torture of her children" had burned four times during her lifetime "the few Kurdish books and records we [the family] had acquired clandestinely."[3] In Iraq, when Kurds started an armed fight for their independence and language rights, Saddam Hussein used chemical weapons to quench their struggle.

These three samplings of language policies taken from international contexts demonstrate that language policies have enormous significance in the lives of children. Language policies can be popular and unpopular, traditional and innovative, liberal and repressive, and—ultimately— effective and ineffective.

The Rights of Language Learners in the United States

What are language policies in the United States? The answer is that there are none. The United States does not have an official national language policy. Nor does the United States have a specially designated government body (such as the Academy of Science in France) that rules about matters of language. The federal government traditionally has assumed a hands-off attitude about language matters. Residents of the United States use and teach their children language in the way they see fit. However, when individuals have felt that their language rights are being encroached upon, they have taken their grievances to court. As a result, there has emerged a United States body of laws and court rulings about language. Some pieces of legislation pertain to immigrant children and protect their access to public education as well as their language rights.

Role of Home Language and Home Culture in the Curriculum

One of the first legal battles in the United States focused on the place of language minority children's home language and home culture in their education. In the pre-Civil Rights years, policy makers and the public generally assumed that the best way to educate language minority children was to teach them English and discourage them to use their mother tongue. Children's home languages were seen as an impediment to assimilation and academic achievement. Many educators believed that speaking two languages was only likely to confuse and overwhelm a child. In a southwestern school attended by Mexican American children, the teacher's manual said, "Encourage the use of English. All teachers are expected to correct students using Spanish on school property." Many schools practiced "*Spanish detention.*" For instance, in a school in Texas, students who were caught speaking Spanish were usually held after school for an hour, an hour and a half; and if they persisted, they could ultimately be expelled.[4]

Reforming education became one of the major causes of the Chicano movement (the Civil Right movement of Mexican Americans). Chicano leaders demanded that school curricula be reformed to account for a Mexican American cultural heritage and that the Spanish language become part of the classroom. One of the manifestos of the movement proclaimed in the characteristically impassioned style:

> We're going to teach them [children] about this system, the economic problems. We're going to teach them about the legislation that is rotten and corrupt. We're going to teach them about the politicians that are using our people. We're going to teach them about the welfare system that perpetuates itself in order to keep people in bondage.[5]

George Sanchez, an educational psychologist at the University of Texas who was one of the most influential voices behind the movement for reform, stressed that ignoring the child's background experience and culture was bound to result in educational failure:

> Imagine the Spanish-speaking child's introduction to American [sic] education! He comes to school, not only without a word of English but without the environmental experience upon which school life is based. He cannot speak to the teacher and is unable to understand what goes on about him in the classroom. He finally submits to rote learning, parroting words and processes in self-defense. To him, school life is artificial. He submits to it during class hours, only partially digesting the information which the teacher has tried to impart. Of course he learns English and the school subjects imperfectly![6]

Mexican American students were the first to hear the pleas made by the Chicano leaders. Curiously enough, Chicano students, not their parents, became the driving force behind the movement. Inspired by charismatic revolutionary figures such as Che Guevarra; and Chicano leaders, such as Reies Lopes Tijerina and Cesar Chavez; and angry about the quality of their schooling, students decided to take upon the educational system. Their weapon of choice was a school boycott. The first boycott happened on March 1, 1968, when 300 students of Wilson High School in east Los Angeles walked out of their Friday morning classes. Later in the spring, *school walkouts* (or "blowouts" as students called them) extended to other schools in Los Angeles. By the end of March 1968, 10,000 students left their classes throughout the Los Angeles area.[7] They carried placards emblazoned with the words "Chicano Power!" and "Viva la Revolucion."

Even though young Chicanos were organized poorly and often suspicious of leadership as elitist; even though many Mexican American parents frowned upon the extremism of young Chicanismo, fearing that it would hurt the Mexican American community, even though protesters were occasionally violent, destroying and vandalizing school property, even though the movement was perceived by its critics as "unsophisticated, naïve, unprofessional, and ultimately counterproductive,"[8] the blowouts had a significant impact on the educational system. The demands made by young Chicano activists were recognized as legitimate.

The United States Congress responded to the movement's solicitations by passing the *Bilingual Education Act of 1968*, also known as the Title VII of the Elementary and Secondary Education Act. Title VII, provided additional resources to schools that had critically large numbers of language minority students. The moneys were earmarked to train teachers, create materials, and reach out to parent communities.

As a result of the Bilingual Education Act, the education of language minority children gradually started to reform. The act resulted in creation and proliferation of bilingual programs. Students enrolled in bilingual programs receive instruction in two languages: their home language and English. In some programs, students study their subject areas in their home language until their English language competence is developed enough for them to do all their school work in English. In other programs, English-speaking and Spanish-speaking students study side by side with both groups developing full proficiency both in their home language and English. There exist other models of bilingual programs.

While some bilingual programs have been recognized as effective, others have been subjected to criticism. Detractors of bilingual programs have complained about the lack of certified bilingual teachers, the dearth of quality materials in two languages or bilingual programs participants' alleged lack of English language skills. In 2004, Bilingual Education Act was repealed.

To date some states (e.g., California, Massachusetts) have phased out bilingual instruction while others (e.g., New York) continue its implementation. While the legacy of bilingual programs remains controversial, the principal of validation of students' home languages and cultures is embraced by most second language educators. (You can read more about the place of students' home language and culture in the curriculum in Chapter 8 of this book.)

Unique Rights of Language Learners. The 1970s brought about legal efforts to specify what kinds of language programs would guarantee immigrant children's access to public education. Until the early 1970s, generations of immigrant children were integrated in classrooms with English-speaking children. This practice was based on the belief that children have no difficulty picking up English and do not need special help overcoming the language barrier. Proponents of this *"sink or swim"* approach—immigrants and native-born citizens alike—liked to tell stories of family members who had picked up English without having received any English language instruction.

This practice was ultimately brought into question. It happened when Edward Steinman, a California lawyer, found out that Kinney Lau, the son of his client, was failing at school because his English language skills were limited. On behalf of Lau and other 1,789 Chinese-speaking students who spoke limited English, and were not getting any language services whatsoever in the San Francisco Unified School District, Steinman filed a *Lau v. Nichols* class action suit. The plaintiffs lost their case in the lower courts and in the Court of Appeals, which ruled that San Francisco schools were under no obligation to provide any special help to non-English-speaking children. The lower courts reasoned that every student comes to school with some unique strengths and weaknesses, and that schools cannot be expected to create the level educational playing field for every one of their students. The Supreme Court disagreed, however. In the landmark *Lau decision of 1974*, the Supreme Court justices ruled that English language learners have unique instructional needs which schools must meet by providing special educational programs. The justices ruled unanimously that the sink-or-swim approach to the education of language minority students is unconstitutional. They also pointed out that to treat English language learners in the same way as their English-speaking peers meant to deny these children equal educational opportunities:

> There is no equality of treatment merely by providing students with the same facilities, textbooks, teachers, and curriculum [*sic*]; for students who do not understand English are effectively foreclosed from any meaningful education.[9]

The Lau decision does not specify what type of additional instructional support schools should provide to English language learners. The decision about whether to implement transitional bilingual educational or ESL instruction was left up to the schools. But the justices did rule unequivocally that some additional help needs to be provided.

Quality of Programs for English Language Learners. The court decisions of the 1980s are concerned with the quality of the programs available to immigrant children. *Castaneda v. Pickard* 1981, a ruling of the Fifth Circuit Court of Appeals, maintained the standards of an effective language program. The Court of Appeals made its decision in response to a class action suit filed by Mexican American parents in the Raymondville Independent School District (RISD) in Texas. The plaintiffs argued that instructional programs were inadequate and failed to help children take full advantage of the educational opportunities available in the school district. Plaintiffs charged that Mexican-American children were subjected to unfair testing practices, discriminatory tracking, and were denied the opportunity to participate fully in the schooling experiences that the RISD provided to non-Mexican students.

The Appeals Court reversed the original decision of the District Court and ruled in favor of the plaintiff. It also established criteria that helped determine whether a second language program is in compliance with the rulings. The three criteria (also known as the *Pickard standard* or *Castaneda test* established by the Appeals Court) are as follows:

1. *Theory.* An instructional program intended for children who are English language learners has to be based on a sound foundation of recent research.

2. *Practice.* School districts must take the steps to apply theoretical principles in practice. Specially trained personnel must be hired, resources provided, and language lessons taught so that the theoretical instructional principles become a classroom reality.

3. *Results.* Schools are required to demonstrate that their programs for English language learners provide instructional benefits. If the results are not there, schools are under obligation to revise their curricula.

Illegal Immigrant Children's Right to Education. The 1980s became the scene of another legal battle. This time the dispute revolved around the question of whether illegal immigrant children have the right to public education. Some policy makers, school officials, and parents argued that public schools should be off-limits to illegal immigrant children. They pointed out that letting these children attend public schools was going to make illegal immigration more attractive and would increase the influx of undocumented aliens. Those who shared this view also pointed out that illegal immigrant students put huge demands on the already strained resources of the country's public school system. Some argued that it was all right to admit illegal immigrants to public schools as long as the federal government (that had allegedly failed to protect the national borders) paid for educating the young folks.[10] The attitude was captured by Raul A. Besteiro, superintendent of schools in Brownsville, Texas, when he asked, "Why should people be able to come across the border with no papers, totally illegal, and register for school?"[11]

In the midst of this turmoil, illegal immigrant families often chose not to send their children to school for fear that they might be deported. In some families, a child born in the United States went to school and a sibling who had been brought to the United States illegally was kept home.[12] Finally, when the Texas Tyler Independent School District 2 school officials attempted to prevent Mexican children from attending school in 1982, the debate over the educational rights of undocumented immigrant children reached the Supreme Court.

In the *Plyler v. Doe* ruling of 1982, the justices ruled 5 to 4 that it was unconstitutional to bar illegal immigrant children from public education. An opinion by an Associate Justice William Brennan refuted the common arguments against public education of illegal immigrant children. Associate

Justice Brennan argued that it was unfair to penalize children for their parents' illegal status, that preventing children from getting education would exact a heavy toll on society in the future, and that the short-term savings on children's schooling were incomparable to the long-range losses to the children and society.

> "By denying these children a basic education," said Justice Brennan, "we deny them the ability to live within the structure of our civic institutions, and foreclose any realistic possibility that they will contribute in even the smallest way to the progress of our nation. It is difficult to understand," argued Justice Brennan, "precisely what the state hopes to achieve by promoting the perpetuation of a subclass of illiterates within our boundaries, surely adding to the problems and costs of unemployment, welfare and crime."[13]

Under *Plyler*, school officials may not bar illegal immigrant children from attending schools. Justices ruled that undocumented immigrant children have the same right to a free public education that is enjoyed by other children and that they are obliged to attend school as long as they are of school age. According to the *Plyler* decision, schools are prohibited from investigating children's immigration status. For instance, school officials are not permitted to require that children and their parents produce citizenship papers, a green card, or other documents that proves the immigration status of the family. The only paperwork the schools may request to see is documentation that a child lives within the attendance zone of a given school district.

Official Status of English. Another policy issue that concerns immigrant children is that of the status of the English language. Unlike many other countries that have official or national languages, no special legal status is granted to English in the United States. It is the fact of which most Americans do not seem to be aware. When in a 1987 survey, Americans were asked what they knew about the place of English in the United States, respondents said that English is the official language of this country. Survey respondents were in error though. English does not have a special legal status enjoyed by the languages of many other countries.

When some scholars analyze this state of affairs they point out that framers of Constitution saw no need to infringe upon the language rights and liberties of individual citizens. In the words of James Crawford, a prominent opponent of institutionalizing English as the U.S. official language, "This country has a kind of libertarian tradition where language is concerned—a democracy is not supposed to tell its citizens how to talk—which may explain the Founders' "oversight" when it came to mandating an official tongue."[14] Other researchers point out that language legislation did not become part of the Constitution because of the de facto dominant status of English. When the dominance of English was threatened by the purchase of French-speaking Louisiana, Benjamin Franklin insisted that more English-speaking colonists settle in Louisiana in order to assure that French would not become the dominant language of the newly purchased territory. However one interprets the reasons why English does not enjoy official status in this country, it is a fact that concern about the status of English had not featured prominently on the political agenda of the United States until the early 1980s.

In 1981, California Senator Samuel Hayakawa, a Canadian immigrant of Japanese ancestry, sponsored a bill to make English the official language of the United States. "English has long been the main unifying force of the American [sic] people," contended Hayakawa, "But now prolonged bilingual education in public schools and multilingual ballots threaten to divide us along language lines."[15] The bill died in the lower houses but Hayakawa did not give up. In 1983 he created a Washington lobby group called U.S. English and started the *English Only* movement, a multimillion dollar campaign to make English the official language of this country. Among the supporters of the movement have been renowned public figures, such as writers Saul Bellow and Gore Vidal, journalist Walter Cronkite, and countless citizens who embraced the movement's cause.

The first consequence of the English Only movement was the mobilization of the politically inactive and fragmented Hispanic community of the 1980s. Hispanic Americans believed that English Only had a strong anti-Hispanic bias, that the true motive behind the movement was the Anglo sense of demographic and political insecurity, that the movement's hidden agenda was to stop the economic and political advancement of Hispanic Americans. "U.S. English is to Hispanics as the Ku Klux Klan is to blacks," charged Raul Yzaguirre, president of the National Council of La Raza.[16] Proponents of English Only vehemently denied the racism charges, arguing that their sole intent was to maintain the unifying role played by English. Angry, emotionally charged accusations were met with no less angry and emotionally charged rebuttals.

Then, in 1988 a publication came out which suggested that speculations regarding the anti-Hispanic bias of English Only were not altogether unfounded. The *Arizona Republic* published a memorandum written by John Tanton, a Michigan ophthalmologist and a cofounder of U.S. English. In the memo intended for internal use, Tanton warned that the birth rate in Hispanic families was higher than that of Anglo families and that

Hispanic children in the United States were going to outnumber Anglo children, and eventually take over this country:

> Gobernar es poblar translates "to govern is to populate." In this society where the majority rules, does this hold? Will the present majority peaceably hand over its political power to a group that is simply more fertile? Can homo contraceptivus compete with homo progenitiva if borders aren't controlled? Perhaps this is the first instance in which those with their pants up are going to get caught by those with their pants down! As Whites see their power and control over their lives declining, will they simply go quietly into the night?[17]

The scandal erupted, as the result of which Tanton stepped down from U.S. English, and some of the movement's high-profile supporters were quick to resign and dissociate themselves from the movement.

English Only was damaged but not stopped. As the wave of immigration rolled into the 1990s and beyond, proponents of the English Only movement have continued to argue in favor of English Only legislation. They contend that current immigrants fail to learn English, express concerns that immigrants remain loyal to their home countries and home languages, warn of the danger of balkanization and fragmentation, and point to Belgium and Canada as examples of countries where citizens became divided over language issues. They also argue that bilingual education fails to give immigrant children English language proficiency.

To counter these alleged social ills, the English Only movement advocates various types of policy changes. Some proponents demand that English be given an emblematic status and recognized as a symbol of the United States. Others propose that English should be the only language used in the political domain and that election materials (e.g., ballots) should only be printed in English. Still others require that the English language proficiency test be instituted for immigrants who apply for licenses to run their businesses in the United States. As far as the educational sphere is concerned, demands range from the ban on bilingual education to suggestions that school documentation (e.g., notices and letter to parents) should be printed only in English.

To date, in response to the English Only movement, more than 20 states have adopted laws that make English their official language. In other states, court rulings have curbed immigrants' right to use their home language. Some court decisions forbid immigrant adults to use their home language at work,[18] others have prevented bilingual adults from doing jury duty.[19]

There are court decisions which involve very young children. For instance, in a Texas child custody court case the State District Judge Samuel C. Kiser accused Marta Laureano, the mother of a five-year-old girl of child abuse for speaking Spanish to her daughter. The judge ordered Ms. Laureano to teach her child English and threatened to remove the little girl from her mother's care unless she obeyed. The judge put his statement in no uncertain terms:

> If she [the little girl] starts first grade with the other children and cannot even speak the language that the teachers and the other children speak and she's a full-blood American citizen, you're abusing that child and you're relegating her to the position of housemaid.
>
> Now, get this straight. You start speaking English to this child because if she doesn't do good in school, then I can remove her because it's not in her best interest to be ignorant. The child will only hear English.[20]

The English Only proponents say that national unity is their biggest concern. Even though they may be well-meaning in their intentions, the English Only movement has often created a divisive and acrimonious atmosphere. Children, as well as adults, have been affected by the climate of the English Only movement. For instance, in Colorado, which had adopted an official-English language law, a bus driver ordered Hispanic children to stop speaking English on the way to school.

The debate around the status of English in the United States is still continuing. Proponents of English Only say that English is the glue that holds the fabric of this nation together and that loss of the *lingua franca* (the common language) will result in balkanization and fragmentation of society. In contrast, opponents of English Only contend that United States residents are brought together by their commitment to liberal and democratic ideas, not the common attributes of nations, such as religion, race, or language. They also point out that the English Only legislation is divisive and goes against the tradition of welcoming newcomers to the United States.

English Only advocates charge that unlike former generations of newcomers, modern immigrants are unpatriotic, come to the United States with the intention of returning to their home countries, and often fail to learn English. Their opponents point to various studies that have demonstrated that these assumptions are erroneous and that modern immigrant children take less time to master English than their turn of the century predecessors.[21] They evoke studies that show that full English language proficiency in the past was only achieved by third immigrant generation, while most children of immigrants today do master English.

There are those who point out that language loyalties cannot be legally mandated and that children of immigrants are more likely to embrace the United States if they are given access to quality education, effective English language instruction and—as a consequence—a chance to participate in the economy, and take advantage of upward economic mobility.

Main Points

- Validation of English language learners' home languages and cultures is a legacy of *Bilingual Education Act* (1968).

- The *Lau decision* (1974) did away with the sink-or-swim approach to educating English language learners and mandated educational services that help English language learners overcome their language barrier.

- *Castaneda test* (1981) establishes standards of quality second language programs.

- Under the *Plyler decision* (1982), undocumented immigrant children are entitled to public education.

Notes

1. D. Ager (1996), *Language policy in Britain and France*. London: Cassel, p. 122.

2. M. Maamouri. *Language education and human development: Arab diglossia and its impact on the quality of education in the Arab region. Proceedings of Mediterranean Development Forum* (Marrakech, Morocco), September 1998, International Literacy Institute, University of Pennsylvania. http://www.worldbank.org/wbi/mdf/mdf2/papers/humandev/education/maamouri.pdf, accessed January 17, 2006.

3. A. Hassanpour (2000), "The Politics of a Political Linguistics: Linguists and Linguicide." In Phillipson, R. (Ed.), *Rights to language equity, power, and education. Celebrating the 60th birthday of Tove Skutnabb-Kangas*. Mahwah, NJ: Lawrence Erlbaum Associates, p. 36.

4. T. Carter (1970), *Mexican Americans in school: A history of educational neglect*. New York: College Entrance Examination Board, p. 98.

5. R. Gonzales, "Social Revolution in the Southwest," pp 14–15. Cited in J. Hammerback, R. Jensen and J. Gutierrez (1985), *A war of words: Chicano protest in the 1960s and 1970s*. Westport, CT: Greenwood Press, p. 70.

6. J. Crawford (1992), *Hold your tongue: Bilingualism and the politics of English Only*. Reading, MA: Addison-Wesley Publishing Company, p. 75.

7. M. Meier and F. Ribera (1972), *Mexican Americans/American Mexicans: From conquistadors to Chicanos*. New York: Farrar, Strauss and Giroux.

8. Ibid., p. 222.

9. L. L. Wang (1976), "Lau v. Nichols: History of a Struggle for Equal and Quality Education." In E. Gee et al. (Eds.), *Counterpoint: Perspectives on Asian America*. Los Angeles, CA: Asian American Studies Center at UCLA, p. 240.

10. W. King, "Texas Governor Says Compliance with Court Ruling Is No Problem." *The New York Times*, June 16, 1982. Wednesday, Late City Final Edition. Section D; p. 22, Column 1; National Desk.

11. S. Taylor, Jr., "Conflict over Rights of Aliens Lies at Supreme Court's Door." *The New York Times*, September 28, 1981. Monday, Late City Final Edition. Section A; Page 1, Column 5; National Desk.

12. Ibid.

13. L. Greenhouse, Justices Rule States Must Pay to Educate Illegal Alien Pupils. *The New York Times*, June 16, 1982. Wednesday, Late City, Final Edition. Section A; Page 1, Column 6; National Desk.

14. Crawford, *Hold your tongue*, p. X.

15. Ibid., p. 4.

16. Ibid., p. 148.

17. Ibid., p. 151.

18. J. Perea (2001), The New American Spanish War: How the Courts and the Legislatures Are Aiding the Suppression of Languages Other Than English. In R. Gonzalez (ed). Language Ideologies: Critical Perspectives on the Official English Movement, Volume 2. History, Theory, and Policy. Mahwah, NJ: Lawrence Erlbaum Associates, pp. 121–39.

19. G. Valdes. "Bilingual Individuals and Language-Based Discrimination: Advancing the State of the Law on Language Rights." In R. Gonzalez (Ed.), *Language ideologies: Critical perspectives on the official English movement, Vol. 2: History, theory, and policy*. Mahwah, NJ: Lawrence Erlbaum Associates, pp. 140–170.

20. S. Verhovek, "Mother Scolded by Judge for Speaking in Spanish." *The New York Times*, August 30, 1995. Wednesday, Late Edition–Final. Section A; p. 12; Column 1; National Desk.

21. A. Portes, R. G. Rumbaut (1997), *Immigrant America*, 2nd ed. Berkeley, CA: University of California Press.

CHAPTER 3

Children as Language Learners

This book continues with an overview of research in the area of psycholinguistics. Psycholinguistics is a field of science concerned with language learning. How do children learn their mother tongue and what happens when they study a second language? What kind of neurological processes are involved in children's language learning? What happens when children learn new words? How do they master grammar? This chapter will address these pycholinguistic questions which are not merely of theoretical interest but of great practical importance. Insights provided by psycholinguistics have a huge impact on language instruction. They help teachers to be more effective in the classroom.

Over the last fifty years or so, psycholinguists have learned much about children's language learning. While more is known about how children learn their mother tongue, researchers are just beginning to understand the processes of children's second language learning. Some researchers argue that the processes of first and second language learning in children share some important similarities; others even say that the processes are fundamentally similar. That's why it seems impossible to speak about children's second language learning without first saying a few words about how they learn their mother tongue. The parallels between the two processes are too significant to leave out the former when discussing the latter. Throughout this book, the description of the parallel first language learning processes will precede the discussion of various aspects of second language learning in young children.

Children's Language Learning Facility

We seldom stop to marvel at the speed and ease with which children learn their first language. We do tend to take first language learning for granted, and yet the phenomenon is nothing short of a miracle. Perhaps only occasionally, when we travel abroad and see a toddler jabbering away in a foreign language (which we have studied for years in high school and college and have failed to master), do we have a moment's realization of the magnitude of a task that children accomplish when they learn their mother tongue.

All normally developing children master the complexity of pronunciation, grammar, and vocabulary of their first language within the first four or five years of their lives. Not only do children learn to use highly sophisticated grammatical forms of their first language, they also develop an impressive vocabulary. During particularly intense periods of language learning, such as toddlerhood, young children learn a new word every waking hour of their day.

While children's first language facility surprises nobody, we often marvel at how quickly children learn a second language. Most of us have heard or told stories of immigrant parents who struggle with learning ESL while their children effortlessly "pick up" the language. Or you may have met adult immigrants who speak accented English after years of living in an English-speaking country while their children speak English without a trace of an accent after having been in an English-speaking environment for a relatively short time.

Why is that so? Why are young children facile second language learners? Conversely, why do so many adults tend to find second language learning challenging? What kinds of language learning faculties do children have that adults lack?

The Language Instinct

One of the first answers to these questions was provided in the mid 1960s by an American linguist of German extraction, Eric Lenneberg. Lenneberg studied certain behaviors shared by a number of species. In particular, he was interested in behaviors that are

1. shared by an entire species;
2. learned at around the same time by all the members of the species;
3. learned following a rigid and predictable schedule when no amount of instruction would make any difference;

4. learned instinctively, because members of the species *cannot help* developing this particular trait.

Lenneberg came to the conclusion that if a behavior found in a species meets all these criteria, that behavior is congenital or innate. An interesting example of congenital behavior is found in baby ducks. When newly hatched ducks see a moving object (whether it be their mom, the leg of a farmer or the broom), they start walking behind that object. We say that ducks "learn" to follow the moving objects. However, it is important to realize that ducks cannot help this behavior, because it is genetically predetermined. All baby ducks follow a moving object, provided they see it shortly after they are hatched.

Lenneberg argued that just as a duckling cannot help following its mother, a child cannot help learning a mother tongue. Pointing out that human speech develops in all members of the human species, that humans begin to speak at roughly around the same age, and that human language learning follows a predictable sequence of developmental steps, Lenneberg hypothesized that human language ability is innate. Modern linguists who share Lenneberg's position use the term *language instinct* to refer to the innateness of language.

Since Lenneberg's contention about the instinctive nature of language is somewhat counterintuitive and not easy to grasp, it might be a good idea to use an analogy to help the reader appreciate its major thrust. Consider the following example. In the course of their lives, human beings master various skills. We can't help developing some skills, such as walking, because walking is part of our natural endowment. Dancing, on the other hand, is something we only learn if we make up our minds to do so. (To think that babies can be "taught" how to walk is misleading. In fact, there are cultures where babies are not assisted by adults when they make their first steps. However—just like all other babies—babies born into these cultures learn to stand upright and walk when they are about twelve months old.) The premise behind Lenneberg's theory is that learning to speak is akin to learning to walk. You can no more teach a child to speak than you can teach a child about taking its first baby steps. *Provided the child is exposed to language*, a normally developing child will start to speak her mother tongue.

This chapter poses the question: Why are children facile language learners? Examined in the light of Lenneberg's theory, children's facility with language can be explained as stemming from children's genetic predisposition for language learning. In other words, children learn language quickly and easily, simply because they cannot help it.

Universal Grammar

But which aspect of language system may be innate? Surely we are not born with the knowledge that a domestic animal with a tail and whiskers is called *"a cat"* or that the plural of nouns is formed with the help of the ending -*s*.

An attempt to answer the question as to which aspects of the language system are congenital was made by an MIT scholar, Noam Chomsky. The theory developed by Chomsky had an enormous impact on the language science community. In the late 1950s and early 1960s when Chomsky's first studies of language acquisition came out, they unleashed violent debates which came to be known as the "linguistic wars." Generations of linguists have been busy testing Chomskys's hypothesis. He is one of the most frequently cited scholars of all time. What are the ideas that stirred this intellectual commotion?

While Lenneberg argued that language learning is innate (based on the fact that we all learn it at roughly the same age and in roughly the same way), Chomsky corroborated this theory working from a different set of data. Chomsky wondered about the ease with which children acquire grammar. He was particularly intrigued by children's creativity with language and the fact that children have no difficulty in producing grammatically correct sentences they have not heard. Chomsky pointed out that children who are as young as three or four years old learn basic rules of sentence formation and effortlessly produce structurally complex sentences. (Even when children make errors and produce patterns such as *helded or *Did you did it? They only produce language patterns that are potentially consistent with the grammatical patterns to be found in the language.)

According to Chomsky, children's ease at mastering grammar is all the more surprising given the fact that children's exposure to language is limited. The language children hear is hard to use as a material for inducing grammar rules—it is messy, full of false starts, and interruptions. (The argument that children don't have enough exposure to language to be able to induce all the rules that they apply when they speak is known as a *poverty of stimulus* or *dearth of input* argument.)

Chomsky hypothesized that children are quick to master the grammars of their languages, because their capacity to generate grammatically structured speech is innate and because a special grammatical blueprint is prewired into children's brains. Having dubbed this grammatical blueprint *Universal Grammar*, Chomsky argued that because of the universality of this congenital grammatical blueprint, all the world's languages share some universal properties: for instance, a sentence is composed of a noun phrase and a verb phrase.

Using a rather technological, 1960s-style metaphor (inspired perhaps by the budding computer science field), Chomsky further argued that children are endowed with a language organ or *Language Acquisition Device* (LAD). The LAD, according to Chomsky, becomes activated or turns itself on when children are exposed to language that is produced by other people. According to Chomsky, LAD operation enables children to produce sentences consistent with the rules of Universal Grammar.

Not all linguists are in agreement with Chomsky's position. Whereas some argue that we do have Universal Grammar as part of our genetic endowment, others contend that some facts of language learning do not bear out the Chomsky's theory. For instance, Harvard psychologist Catherine Snow, who studies adult—child interaction, points out language to which children are exposed is not impoverished and ungrammatical. Snow and some other linguists who observe mothers interacting with their babies report that mothers use a special kind of language for these interactions. This language, referred to as *motherese*, is slow, repetitive and grammatically correct—not unlike a traditional grammar lesson.

Evidence of Universal Grammar. On the other hand, evidence in support of Chomsky's theory was provided by two fascinating studies. One was conducted in Nicaragua. During the Somosa dictatorship, a small school for the deaf was founded by Hope Somosa, the dictator's wife. In 1979, after the Sandinista revolution had toppled Somosa's regime, the school was expanded; special efforts were made to teach the children how to lip read. Since lip reading lessons are seldom met with success, not surprisingly children were not making much progress. Before long, however, teachers noticed that, once they were no longer isolated from each other, the deaf children began to use some sort of signs. Nicaraguan teachers invited an MIT linguist, Judy Kegl, to study this sign language. Kegl realized that the children had created a language that was not just a random collection of signs but followed a set of structural, grammatical rules.

Nowadays, the language which had been created from scratch by Nicaraguan deaf children is an officially recognized language called Nicaraguan Sign Language (NLS). Interestingly, Kegl reports that 200 deaf adults who took NSL lessons were unable to master the grammar of the language—even though they had little difficulty in learning its vocabulary.

Evidence in support of existence of Universal Grammar is also provided by a groundbreaking study performed by a linguist, Derek Bickerton, who studies *pidgins* or contact languages. Pidgins, the languages that are spoken when people don't have a lingua franca or a common language, tend to arise in colonized areas or areas of heavy trade. For instance, numerous pidgins were used by slave traders and slaves in the Caribbean, Hawaii, or Papua New Guinea. Pidgins are made of a small number of nouns, verbs and adjectives borrowed from different languages spoken in the area of contact. Pidgin vocabularies are limited, just big enough to meet people's basic communication needs; their grammars tend to be highly rudimentary. For example, verbs in pidgins don't have tense markers, nouns lack plural forms. Functional words, such as pronouns, prepositions, or conjunctions are practically nonexistent. The most distinguishing feature of pidgins is that they don't have native speakers. These languages are learned by adults.

However, something quite remarkable happens when children are spoken to in pidgin. When Bickerton compared language patterns used by adults and children, he realized that the children do not merely reproduce language patterns used by their parents. Rather, children begin to introduce grammatical structures into the grammatically less complex language patterns used by adults. The grammatically evolved languages learned by children of pidgin-speaking parents are called *Creoles*. Unlike pidgins, Creoles are children's native languages. Each new generation of Creole-speaking children expands the repertoire of the grammatical forms of a given language until it becomes a fully developed linguistic system. Haitian Creole, an official language of Haiti, is an example of a Creole language that developed from pidgin.

Since Creole grammars are created by children and since Creole languages spoken throughout the world display striking grammatical similarity, *creolization of pidgin* (the process whereby pidgins evolve into Creoles) is viewed as proof of validity of the Universal Grammar theory.

Language Instinct and Second Language Learning

Do theories propounded by Lenneberg and Chomsky have any relevance to second language learning? Is there any evidence that people use the language instinct when learning a second language?

Some scholars say it depends on the age of the learner. When observing immigrant children learning English in the United States or English-speaking children learning French in Quebec (the francophone province of Canada), that is, in situations where children are surrounded by native speakers of a second language, scholars have noticed how similar second language learning may be to first language learning. According to researchers who observed second language learning in the context of naturalistic input, young children acquire a second language naturally, the way they learn their mother tongue. In contrast, adult second language learning is believed by some researchers to be an altogether different process, primarily because adults are not aided by their language instinct when they try to learn another language.

Fundamental Difference Hypothesis

Robert Bley-Vroman, one of the major proponents of this position, explains that children acquire language naturally because they still have access to their Universal Grammars. Adult second language learning is a fundamentally different process according to Bley-Vroman. Since adults are unable to access their Language Acquisition Device, they need to rely on common reasoning skills in order to make sense of a target language grammar. According to this model, children learn a second language instinctively or naturally, and adults' second language learning is similar to learning of any other mental skill. The theory that language learning in children is profoundly different from language learning in adults is known as the *Fundamental Difference Hypothesis*. Some recent studies that compare adult and children language learning seem to corroborate this insight. For instance, a study reports that when speaking a second language, adults do more repairs (i.e., corrections of own errors) than do children.[1]

It is helpful to reflect on one's own language learning to appreciate the thrust of Bley-Vroman's argument. If you have had the experience of learning a second language in post-adolescent years, and if you recall trying to make up your mind which tense form or which idiom would be appropriate in a given situation, you were using the common reasoning skills referred to by Bley-Vroman. Arguably, we are much less likely to engage in ruminations of this kind when learning our first language or when learning a second language at a young age.

Ultimate Attainment

Does the fact that children seem to learn a second language more naturally mean that they become more proficient? Does access to Universal Grammar enable children to achieve greater mastery of second language? Answers to these questions are not straightforward. Studies report that contrary to popular assumptions, during the initial stages of second language learning, little children advance more slowly than do older children and adults.[2] There is evidence that older children start out as more successful grammar learners and pronunciation learners.[3] Additionally, adults and older children have an easier time than young children when it comes to reading and writing a second language.[4]

As time goes on, however, young children make increasingly greater strides in their language learning, eventually outpacing the grown-ups. There is an aspect of second language learning where children inevitably outdo adults. While people who learned a second language at a young age may not necessarily enjoy the advantage of sophisticated second language literacy skills or the advantage of knowing abstract second language vocabulary, all young second language learners achieve native-like fluency—that is they sound indistinguishable from native speakers. As linguists put it, children's *ultimate attainment* of second language mastery is superior to that of adults.[5]

The advantage of early second language learning is particularly noticeable in the area of phonology. A number of studies report that children do better than adults in picking up the English pronunciation. The study that compared immigrants who came to the United States at a young age and as adults demonstrated that age was the most important factor in predicting whether language learners would speak English with or without a foreign accent. Researchers demonstrated that it did not matter how long immigrants stayed in the United States. If they came to this country as young children, they sounded like native-born Americans.[6]

Another kind of fascinating evidence is provided by the *grammaticality judgment* studies, that is, the studies that demonstrate that early language learners have intuitive understanding of whether or not a second language sentence is well-formed grammatically.[7] Researchers worked with 46 native speakers of Chinese and Korean who had arrived in the United States between the ages of 3 and 36. The researchers asked their subjects to perform grammaticality judgment tasks, that is, to pick a well-formed sentence from pairs such as *The little boy is speaking to a policeman* and **The little boy is speak to a policeman* or *Tom is reading a book in the bathtub* and **Tom is reading book in the bathtub*. It was found out that early arrivals consistently did better on the test than did late arrivals. The cutoff age was puberty. If language learners started learning English after puberty, their performance of grammaticality judgment tasks was erratic and inconsistent. The study demonstrates that those individuals who had started learning a second language early have intuitive knowledge of whether a sentence is well formed grammatically. This intuitive knowledge of sentence correctness is missing in learners who studied a second language at a later age.

Fossilization

So what is an adult's limitation when it comes to second language learning? Studies demonstrate that adult learners—even those who are highly competent and successful language users—display a feature in their language attainment which has not been observed in children. This feature is known as *fossilization*. The term fossilization was coined by an American linguist, Larry Selinker, and refers to persistence of a non-native feature in the speech of an adult language learner.[8]

Fossilization may follow two patterns. In some instances, adult learners make initial progress and then reach a plateau, getting stuck at an early proficiency level. Another type of fossilization occurs when learners continue to make progress in all areas of language learning but fail to grasp more challenging language patterns. For instance, a researcher reports that a group of adults who had been learning English for eleven years kept using the Past Present Tense instead of the Past Simple in spite of the efforts of their teacher to correct this error.

If your immigrant friend, a fluent speaker of English, says "Thanks God" or "commit a suicide" or "I live here for ten years" even though you have gently suggested a number of times that the correct forms are actually "Thank God," "commit suicide," and "I have lived here for ten years," you are probably dealing with fossilized lexical and grammatical errors. Notably, errors of this kind have not been observed in the speech of early second language learners. While grammatical, lexical, and pragmatic errors may all be fossilized, phonological errors, that is, speaking with a foreign accent, are particularly common among adult second language learners.[9]

Optimal Period for First and Second Language Learning

Now you know that our facility with language may have to do with the fact that we are endowed with a language instinct or an innate ability to learn languages. You also know that scientists hypothesize that children rely on this instinctive natural ability when they learn a second language. (Learning a foreign language in absence of naturalistic input is a different story.) Is anything known about the cutoff age when we stop using our language instinct?

Critical Period Hypothesis. Lenneberg, who propounded the innateness hypothesis, identified another important characteristic of innate behavior; he pointed out that innate behavior could develop only at a certain developmental stage known as the *window of opportunity* or the *critical period*.[10] If, for some reason, the innate trait does not develop during the designated period of time, it will fail to develop at a later point. For instance, if certain bird species do not hear other birds singing at an early age, they will never learn to sing even if sometime later they hear other birds singing. Applying the window of opportunity rule to human language learning ability, Lenneberg hypothesized that if a human baby is not exposed to language early on in life, the child will never master its mother tongue. Lenneberg believed that if the environment failed to trigger child's language instinct in due time, the window of opportunity would close and the child would miss out on the chance to learn how to speak. This hypothesis came to be known as the *Critical Period Hypothesis*.

You probably wonder if the Critical Period Hypothesis has ever been proven. Obviously, nobody has ever attempted to test this theory by depriving children of exposure to language. However, there have been some tragic circumstances when children who had been lost, isolated, or confined did not grow up surrounded by human speech. Those situations are inadvertent experiments which have enabled scientists to observe what happens if a human child is deprived of language learning. Children who become victims of these situations are called *feral children* from the Latin word "ferus" meaning "wild." The two Indian girls Amala and Kamala who had been found in the wolf's den; Genie, a little girl who had been kept in total isolation by her abusive parents; and some other children who had been deprived of exposure to language during the first crucial years of their lives did not develop language mastery in spite of caregivers' efforts at remediation. It is noteworthy that feral children had *most* difficulty with mastering grammar. Even though they developed vocabulary to a reasonable extent, they never developed full control of morphology (word endings) and syntax (sentence structure) of their mother tongue.

Most scientists today support the Critical Period Hypothesis and believe that mother tongue can be learned only if children are exposed to language during early years. It is generally believed that the window for the language learning opportunity closes and that the language instinct is dramatically decreased around the age of puberty.

Sensitive Period Hypothesis. Does the critical period hypothesis apply to second language learning? Is there a cutoff age after which we will never be able to achieve native like mastery of a second language? While evidence is inconclusive,[11] many linguists believe that the cutoff age is puberty. Language learners who start to learn a second language after puberty, may develop an extensive word power, impressive reading and writing skills—in short, may become highly successful, confident and competent language users. However, only early language learners (those learners who learned a second language during childhood years) seem to be capable of ultimate attainment which makes them indistinguishable from first language learners. The pre-puberty period which is conducive to native second language attainment is known as the *sensitive period for second language learning*.

Over the last years, the hypothesis that second language learning in young children is fundamentally different from second language learning in adults found support from studies of the human brain. Some recent studies that compare neurological processes in children and adults second language learners are discussed below.

A Second Language in the Brain of Young Children

Lateralization and Modularity

Neurolinguists are researchers who examine brain circuitry to determine which neurological processes are involved in language learning, language production, and language comprehension. Until recently neuroscientists did not have direct access to the brains of language learners. They collected data by dissecting the brain of deceased patients who suffered from speech impairment, such as *aphasia*: total or partial loss of language due to brain injury or a congenital lesion. Neurolinguists would dissect the brains of aphasics to determine whether there is a connection between a certain type of language impairment and a congenital brain lesion or a brain injury. More recently, due to technologically advanced research methods such as PET (Positron Emission Tomography) and MRI (Magnetic Resonance Imaging), neurolinguists have been able to study the brain directly and observe "in real time" the processes engaged in language production and comprehension.

Some of the earlier neurolinguistic studies established that the left hemisphere plays a very important role in language use; as neurolinguists put it, *language is lateralized to the left hemisphere*. Interestingly enough, various parts of the left hemisphere are in charge of various language skills. Thus, the so-called *Broca's area* located in the frontal part of the left hemisphere controls fluency and grammatical proficiency. *Broca's aphasics* (individuals whose Broca's area has been injured) suffer from *agrammatism*, an inability to produce well-formed sentences. Broca's aphasia sufferers lose the use of function words, such as auxiliaries, conjunctions, or relative pronouns. An individual who suffers from agrammatism recognizes the noun *oar*, but cannot recognize the conjunction *or*, can use and recognize the noun *eye* but is unable to use the pronoun *I*. Individuals afflicted by agrammatism also lose the use of grammatical endings, such as markers of the past tense of the verb or the plural form of the noun. As a result of agrammatism, aphasics lose the ability to speak fluently. The speech of a Broca's aphasic comes out with a great effort; it is belabored and slow. Another problem experienced by Broca's aphasics is the inability to come up with a list of thematically related words. If somebody asked you to think of words that you associate with a meal, you would have no trouble producing a list of words, such as *food, drink, eat, plate, knife, fork*, etc. Broca's aphasics have difficulty coming up with such thematically framed lists of words. Apparently our ability to speak fluently has something to do both with our control of grammar and our ease with retrieving thematically related words.

Another language center known as Wernicke's area, located in the left back part of the brain (close to the ear), controls language comprehension. A patient whose Wernicke's area has been injured speaks fluently but without making any sense. People afflicted by Wernicke's aphasia are also unable to comprehend language.

Language Centers in Young Language Learners

Does the brain of a young child learning a second language work differently from the brain of a language-learning adult? Studies conducted by Cornell University in New York provide some data that may help us in answering this question.[12] The researchers wondered whether there was any difference in the brain circuitry of the people who learned their second language in childhood or in adulthood. By functional Magnetic Resonance Imaging, the researchers obtained brain scans that illustrate the flow of blood to the brain of late and early language learners. Of the twelve subjects who participated in the study, half had learned their second language at a young age, and the other half during adolescence. The subjects were asked to describe what they had done the day before, using their mother tongue first and their second language next.

When analyzing brain scans, researchers discovered that the brains of their subjects operated differently, depending on whether they had learned their second language early or late. Those of the subjects who became bilingual at a young age used the same part of Broca's area for both languages. In contrast, the learners who had studied their second language in adolescence used one part of Broca's area when pronouncing their first language sentences and a different, adjacent part of Broca's area when speaking in a second language. Researchers did not observe any difference in the functioning of Wernicke's area; both late and early language learners used the same part of the brain to understand language.

Memory and Language Learning in Children and Adults

Recent studies conducted at Georgetown University contribute to our understanding of the mnemonic mechanism of first and second language learning. The researcher who performed one of the studies was particularly interested in figuring out whether we use declarative or procedural memory when learning languages. *Declarative memory* is the memory used to learn new facts and new information. *Procedural memory* is in charge of learning actions, such as riding a bike or swimming. The two memories work quite differently. While procedural memory can be durable, declarative memory often fails us. If you remember how to ride a bike or how to figure skate even though you haven't done it for years and if you have trouble remembering a name of a new acquaintance, you have firsthand experiences with the durability of procedural memory and unreliability of declarative memory.

The researcher wondered about the memorization processes involved in learning first language and also second language by early and late language learners.[13] Examining various psycholinguistic and neurolinguistic data, he came to an interesting conclusion. According to the Georgetown University study, young children use procedural memory to learn grammar. In contrast, children use declarative memory when learning new words. Grammar learning in children seems to be like learning to ride a bike, and word learning is like learning the capital of Delaware (it's Dover). The picture seems to be different when it comes to adult language learning. Whether adults learn new words or grammar of another language, they do so by relying on declarative memory. According to the study, the age at which learners attempted to learn another language had a direct impact on how likely they were to rely on the declarative memory. The older learners tended to rely increasingly on their declarative memory both for grammar and vocabulary learning.[14]

Neurologically Optimal Second Language Learning Age

Is there neurolinguistic evidence that at a certain age our brain is particularly well-equipped to master a second language? So far, there is no conclusive neurolinguistic answer to this question. However, a piece of evidence yielded by a recent study provides some initial insight. The study conducted by a team of scientists from McGill University in Canada and UCLA in the United States used an innovative brain mapping MRI technique that enabled scientists to obtain three dimensional scans of the brain. The aim of the experiment was to determine the age at which spurts of growth happen in different brain areas. The scientists reasoned that if at a certain age an area of the brain goes through a period of intense growth, it is the age of aptitude for learning a skill controlled by this particular area. In the course of the experiment, the brains of six boys and girls aged from 3 to 15 were scanned at intervals ranging from several weeks to four years. The team was unable to work with the children who were younger than three, because of the limitations of current MRI technology, which requires that a subject sit still for 8 minutes, something that very young children obviously cannot do. It was observed that furious growth of the area responsible for language learning started when children were around 6 years old and went on until the onset of puberty. After puberty, the growth rate of the language area declined dramatically.

The brain mapping study confirms some commonly held beliefs and challenges others. On the other hand, it suggests that the commonly held "the earlier, the better" belief may after all be a fallacy. According to this particular brain mapping study, the optimal age to learn a second language is from 6 years to pre-puberty.

Language Beginnings

Up to now this discussion has focused on general issues in language acquisition, such as children's facility with language or the neurological processes of language learning. At this point, a few words are in order about specific aspects of children's language development. What happens at the initial stages of children's language learning when children just begin to speak their native or their second language? How do children learn their first words? What kind of sentences do they produce?

Babies Beginning to Speak in Their Mother Tongue

Babies begin to use their mother tongue almost immediately after birth. At the age of one month they begin to coo, moving on to babbling. Around the age of 20–26 months when babies begin to speak, they start with *one-word utterances,* and then move on to *telegraphic speech*—phrases that consist of verbs and nouns but lack grammatical elements, such as verb endings or prepositions. Significantly enough, all babies move through these stages of language learning. Some babies move fast through these developmental sequences; others take longer. But the stages of language emergence are universal.

Young Children Beginning to Speak in a Second Language

Home Language Use by Second Language Learners. In one important way, second language learning is different from first language learning. Unlike first language learners, young children who start learning a second language have already acquired some mastery of their mother tongue. This accounts for a communicative strategy used by some young language learners when they are immersed in a second language environment. Researchers report that when some children first find themselves surrounded by speakers of a language they don't understand, they make an attempt to go on using the language they already know. Some young children have been reported to go on speaking their first language to care givers and their playmates hoping that this strategy will enable them to communicate. The strategy known as *home language use* has been described in a study of preschool children from various language backgrounds in an American nursery school:

> At lunch: Joaquim tried some yogurt from his lunch, then pushed it away telling me something in Portuguese (which must have involved an explanation for why he wasn't going to eat it). After lunch he asked Johanna [one of the teachers] a definite question in Portuguese. She shook her head and said she didn't understand. Later he tried it on me. I also said I didn't understand. He didn't seem distressed but he didn't get an answer either.[15]

The same study describes Yasushi, a Japanese-speaking child who made attempts to speak Japanese to other Asian children in the nursery school. Unfortunately, the children with whom Yasushi attempted to have a conversation were Korean- and Taiwanese-speaking and Yasushi's strategy did not work.[16]

Sometimes if young children and adults are confronted with situations when they don't have a common language, they resort to a communication strategy known as *dilingual discourse*. When dilingual discourse is being used, young children initiate an exchange in their home language and adults or other children respond in theirs. Speaking in two different languages with one another is not always ineffectual. For instance, the strategy may work when children play a game which involves manipulation of an object or when young language learners' intended message is clarified by context.[17] At other times, when the context does not clarify what is being communicated, dilingual discourse does not go far and leaves interlocutors frustrated. Both home language use and dilingual discourse have only been observed during the initial period of young children's exposure to a second language.

Silent Period and Rejection Period. Not all children go through the home language use stage and resort to dilingual discourse. Children fairly quickly come to realize that their interlocutors do not understand them, and at this point many second language learners stop speaking altogether. The stage when children stop communicating verbally in the second language context is known as a *silent period.*

This is how a Korean American reminisces on his silent period:

> I had spent kindergarten in almost complete silence, hearing only the high nasality of my teacher and comprehending little but the cranky wails and cries of my classmates.[18]

The duration of the silent period varies from child to child. Some children will start speaking after just a few weeks of second language immersion; others take up to several months or even a year before they are comfortable enough attempting first words in a second language. A study describes a Japanese girl who informed a Japanese-speaking interviewer that English was too hard, so she was not going to speak to people who spoke English. She actually followed through with this plan and did not speak any English during the course of the yearlong study.[19]

It should be emphasized that the silent period is by no means unproductive. During this stage of language learning, children become sensitized to the sound system of a second language. As the silent period progresses, children develop fairly evolved comprehension skills; they become proficient at following directions or learn to recognize the names of common objects and actions.

In some instances, the silent period is accompanied by the so-called *rejection period,* the stage when children grow socially isolated and reluctant to interact with other children or adults. Contrary to popular perception, some young second language learners may feel dismayed, uncomfortable, or frightened by the need to converse in a new language. For instance, a study describes a Japanese child who during his first months in an American nursery school, spent most of his time on a tricycle as far as possible from other children, especially English-speaking children. Every time the observer spoke to the boy in English, "he ignored her, turned away, or ran out of the room."[20]

Telegraphic Speech and Formulaic Utterances in a Second Language. When children first begin to speak a second language, they produce telegraphic speech which is not unlike telegraphic speech of first language learners. Just as is the case with first language learners, second language learners' telegraphic speech is made of verbs and nouns and lacks grammatical elements, such as endings of auxiliaries.

During the emergent stage of language use, children also produce the so-called *formulaic utterances,* unsegmented chunks of language that children perceive as whole and undivided rather than made out of several words. They use these undivided chunks of language as a single word. For instance, a preschool Japanese-speaking boy learning English in the United States used grammatically unanalyzed unit *"This-is-a"* in phrases such *"This is a my truck,"* or *"This is a Donald,"* or *"This is a not your."*[21] Another child used the phrase *"I-am"* in phrases such as *"I am jacket"* [I brought a jacket today] or *"I am parade"* [I saw a parade in Disneyland].[22] Yet another study tells of a 5-year-old Cantonese-speaking boy using the phrase *"Lookit"* [look at it!] in a similar manner.[23] Apparently, young children use the copula "to be" or a pronoun "it" as part of unanalyzed, grammatically unpacked phrases long before they have learned to extract these target language items from speech and to use them in syntactically well-formed utterances. Eventually, children begin to do the grammatical unpacking of formulaic utterances and come to realize that these chunks of language are really made of several words.[24] A few months or more go by before children start using language creatively—that is, produce phrases and sentences they have not heard.

Young Grammarians

First Language Grammar

Creative Use of Grammar Rules in First language. A distinct feature of children's grammar learning is creativity. Children do not simply copy the sentences produced by adults. Rather, they *unpack* or analyze the language they hear, infer rules of grammar, and then apply those rules. Children's ability to use grammar creatively was demonstrated in the famous *wug test.*[25] Young children were presented with a picture of a pretend creature and were told that the creature was called *"a wug."* Then the researcher presented the subjects with another picture and asked what they saw. Children replied that they saw "two wugs." The test demonstrates that children are able to produce forms that they have never heard.

Because children don't merely copy adults but apply grammar rules creatively, they do not always come up with the correct forms. Rather, their language is an approximation of the mother tongue syntax and morphology. For instance, children produce malformed words, such as *bringed, or malformed sentences, such as *Why did you did it? Using rules in the situations when they don't really apply. This phenomenon is called *overextension*.

Lack of Effect from Corrective Feedback. So what can adults do to help the child move past the stage of the grammatical trial and error into the stage of mastery? Not a whole lot. Researchers found out that often when adults tried to correct errors in little children's speech, they did not have much luck. Often children simply ignore adult corrective feedback. The dialogue below is a case in point:[26]

Child: My teacher holded the baby rabbits and we patted them.

Adult: Did you say your teacher held the baby rabbits?

Child: Yes.

Adult: What did you say she did?

Child: She holded the baby rabbits and we patted them.

Adult: Did you say she held them tightly?

Adult: No, she holded them loosely.

Researchers who observed adults speaking to children report that adults seem to be intuitively aware of this pattern and are more likely to correct factual than grammatical errors in children's speech.[27]

Natural Order of Grammatical Development in First Language. So how do children finally master the morphology and syntax of their mother tongue? The answer is quite striking. An important study demonstrated that children follow the same order when they learn first language morphemes. The preordained order of grammatical development also known as the *natural order* is as follows:[28]

Step 1. *-ing*

Steps 2–3. *in* and *on*

Step 4. *-s* (plural)

Step 5. irregular past of the verb

Step 6. *-'s* (possessive)

Step 7. *is, am, are*

Step 8. *the, a*

Step 9. *-ed* (regular past)

Step 10. *-s* (3rd person regular)

Step 11. Third person irregular

Step 12. *be* (auxiliary)

Step 13. *she's, he's* (contractible copula)

Step 14. *She's reading* (contractible auxiliary)

According to the study, the *order of morpheme acquisition* was the same in all young first language learning subjects. The study also demonstrated that the rate at which children learned to speak did not impact acquisition orders. One of the children in the study mastered morphemes a little faster, another one took a little longer, but all subjects moved through the same steps in the same order.

Second Language Grammar

First Language Skills Getting in the Way of Second Language Learning? For some time, linguists had presumed that the learning of second language grammar was fundamentally different from first language grammar learning, because second language learners have already developed a set of grammatical habits in their own language. It was predicted that when learning the morphology and syntax of a second language, learners would make errors because of *negative transfer* (interference of first language skills with second language learning). For instance, it was hypothesized that because Chinese languages do not have markers for the plural form of nouns, a Chinese-speaking learner of English would have a hard time learning the ending *-s*. Similarly, because speakers of Spanish place the adjective after the noun, Spanish speakers of English would have difficulty using the adjective before the noun the way one does in English. According to this model, second language is "learned through the screen of the first language."[29]

Researchers further argued that for language learning to be successful, it is important for teachers to analyze disparate, contrastive features of the students' mother tongues and the target language and make predictions about grammatical items that learners would most probably find difficult. The movement in linguistics which is committed to this view is known as *Contrastive Analysis*.

However, when linguists started using Contrastive Analysis to predict areas of difficulty and most likely errors made by language learners, they had a surprising discovery. It turned out that while Contrastive Analysis was effective in accounting for some phonological errors or "foreign accent," it was not helpful in predicting grammatical errors.

It seems that initially language learners do make errors due to first language negative transfer.[30] (For instance, as predicted by Contrastive Analysis, speakers of Chinese produce phrases such as *two hand and speakers of Spanish produced phrases, such as *crayon red.) While errors due to Negative Transfer have been observed in beginning level learners, these errors are less common as learners' proficiency levels grow. Scientists had an interesting realization that the significant bulk of morphological and syntactic errors had little to do with the influence of the mother tongue.[31] Moreover, negative transfer errors are particularly uncommon when children learn a second language in the situation of immersion.

Consider a case of young Norwegian children learning to speak English. When speakers of Norwegian ask a question, they invert the order of the verb and the subject. If negative transfer rules worked consistently, Norwegian children learning to speak English would produce questions with inverted word order with a verb preceding a noun (e.g., Where live Tom?). However, a case study of Norwegian-speaking young language learners revealed that these children produce sentences similar to those used by young children learning English as their mother tongue (i.e., *Where Tom live?).[32] Similar results were obtained in a study that focused on syntactic development of a Japanese-speaking boy learning English.[33] In Japanese, the negative particle follows the verb. So one might expect that a Japanese-speaking child learning English would produce forms, such as *I like no. The study revealed, however, that when learning English negation, a seven-year-old Ken went through the stages strikingly similar to those observed in first language development of English-speaking children. Patterns produced by Ken (e.g., *You no can go. *I no like small.) were like the patterns used by first language learners. Another study of Spanish-speaking five to eight year olds arrived at a similar conclusion. While Spanish-speaking children did say "*they have hungry" because of the negative influence of the Spanish ellos tienen hambre, many of the errors they made were similar to those made by English-speaking babies.[34]

Creative Use of Grammar Rules in Second Language. Analyzing patterns of learner errors, an influential study demonstrated that a great number of errors are *intralingual*, that is universal and common to all learners of English, irrespective of their mother tongue.[35] Learners make these errors in the process of *Creative Construction*, that is, the process whereby the learner analyzes the target language and creates a hypothesis as to what its morphological and syntactic rules might be all about. The rules created by learners as the result of Creative Construction are tested and revised while the learner approximates a grammatical form. Consider a case when a little English language learner said to her teacher, "*My mom think that I garbaged my paper but my sister eat it." The girl had not previously heard the phrases *My mom think or *I garbaged—she created these approximations of target structures based on the forms to which she had been exposed. Very much like first language learners do, she overextended the use of certain language structures.

Lack of Effect from Corrective Feedback in Second Language. What can second language teachers do to help young children get rid of errors? Just as with native language learning, the answer seems to be—not much. There are studies that suggest that teachers' efforts to correct students' grammatical errors (*corrective feedback, negative feedback*) have no long-term effect on young learners' morphological and syntactic maturation. Classroom drills and practice do not seem to have an impact on children's ability to use correct forms in spontaneous speech.[36] Even if children use a form correctly initially (right after the teacher has performed an activity meant to eradicate an error), once some time elapses children go back to making the same mistake.[37]

There exists a rather common belief that *recasting* (repeating an incorrect phrase used by a child with a correction) helps eradicate errors. This belief does not seem to be supported by research findings that suggest that even though recasting is popular with teachers, it has little impact on children's second language grammatical development.[38] (You can read more about what the teacher can and cannot do when teaching young children grammar in Chapter 6 of this book.)

Learning Grammar in Fixed Stages. The new discovery about the intralingual nature of many errors nudged linguistic research in a different direction. Instead of studying what learners could not do (Contrastive Analysis, Error Analysis), linguists decided to look into what they did do. The interest shifted from examining errors to the examination of the order in which students learned various patterns of the target language. Scholars of language acquisition tried to figure out whether grammatical elements of language, such as suffixes or endings are learned in a designated way and whether morphological maturation in second language learning follows a predictable order similar to that in first language learning. The studies that focus on this question are referred to as the *order of morpheme acquisition* or *morpheme order* studies.

One of the most influential morpheme order studies focused on young Spanish- and Chinese-speaking learners of English.[39] Researchers obtained evidence that whether their subjects' first language was Chinese or

Spanish had little impact on what happened when they learned English morphemes. Irrespective of the children's first language, their morpheme acquisition conformed to the following a rigid order:

1. plural -*s*
2. progressive –*ing*
3. copula *be* (e.g., *This game is fun.*)
4. auxiliary *be* (e.g., *They are playing.*)
5. *a* and *the* definite and indefinite articles
6. irregular past tense
7. third person singular ending -*s*
8. possessive ending -*s* (e.g., *My mom's picture.*)

In discussing the findings of their study, researchers were particularly impressed by the fact that acquisition orders proved to be the same for the speakers of languages as vastly different as Spanish and Chinese. Consider the fact that Chinese does not and Spanish does have a copula analogous to the English *be*. Yet both Chinese- and English-speaking children acquired the copula at the same stage of the sequence. On the other hand, even though Spanish plural form is identical to the English one, Spanish-speaking children did not learn plurals at an earlier stage than did Chinese-speaking children. Significantly, the data obtained in one of the first morpheme order studies were corroborated by some later studies which also revealed that orders of morpheme acquisition are identical in children and are not influenced by learner age or language background.[40]

It is illuminating to compare some features of first and second language grammatical maturation in young children. In some respect these processes are quite similar. First of all, whether children learn their first or their second language grammar, they do not simply copy the sentences they hear. Rather children induce the rules from the available input and apply those rules creatively. They overextend rule application when they produce patterns, such as *gived. Second, young mother tongue learners and second language learners are not prone to take heed of corrections provided by adults. Rather they go on using certain patterns until they are developmentally ready to master a target structure. Last, there is evidence that children master target structures in a natural order. While these sequences are not identical in first language and second language, they do not seem to be affected by children's first language. Research suggests that even if children's mother tongue contains a morpheme or a syntactic pattern similar to the English one, the order of morpheme acquisition will remain unchanged.

What are we to make of these findings? Some researchers argue that they provide another piece of evidence that our language learning is biologically determined. After all, as you may recall all innate behaviors are learned in a fixed order. Other researchers contend that it is only possible to speak of the natural order of morpheme acquisition if future studies provide evidence that all world's languages are learned in a fixed order. Researchers also say that the true reason for the preordained order of grammatical maturation of ESL learners has to do with the fact that some grammatical patterns are more likely to catch children's attention. For instance, language learners master the ending –*ing* before the ending –*ed*, simply because they are more likely to notice it in adult speech. As linguists put it, some forms are learned first, because they have greater *perceptual saliency*.

Young Children Learning Words

You are now familiar with some processes that transpire when children learn their first and second language grammars. But what about word learning? How do children learn the first words in their mother tongue? What happens when they learn words in a second language? Research in word learning, or the acquisition of the *lexicon*, is fairly recent. It has, however, provided some interesting data.

Word Learning in the Mother Tongue

At around the time when babies turn two, their word development undergoes a dramatic change. Suddenly, their vocabulary starts growing. Scholars who have studied children's early vocabularies report that babies' vocabulary before their second birthday numbers a few dozen words. However, after their second birthday, babies' word power grows immensely. During this vocabulary expansion (referred to as the *vocabulary burst*, or *naming explosion*, or *word spurt*) some babies learn up to ten words a week. The vocabulary burst goes on through the preschool, the early school, and the elementary school years. It has been estimated that during some particularly intense periods of word learning, children memorize up to ten words a day. (Take a foreign language dictionary, jot down on a piece of paper ten words with which you are not familiar, and try to memorize those words. This little exercise, which most adults find extremely challenging, might give you some idea about the magnitude of the task that children perform quite effortlessly.) The vocabulary burst is particularly remarkable given that babies don't get any help with their word learning. Adults very infrequently take the time to explain to a child what this or that word means. Children simply pick up new words from their environment.

What kinds of processes are involved in this high-speed word learning? A study of the acquisition of color terms by young children provides some insight.[41] Researchers conducted an experiment where they asked 3- to 4-year-old children to give them a block. When children gave researchers a green block, adults said, "No. Not the green one, give me the chromium one." Using context alone, children inferred that the word "chromium" referred to the color of the blocks in the other tray and handed the correct block to the researchers. Perhaps most impressively, even one week after hearing the word "chromium" children still remembered the new word. In later experiments, researchers demonstrated that children learn new words after just a single exposure that lasts only 3 seconds. Thus, children who are as young as two years old have the ability to quickly figure out what a word means after hearing it just once and then immediately remember the word. This ability is known as *fast mapping*.

Learning Words in a Second Language

But what about children who are learning their second language? Do they have a similar ability to understand the meaning of new words and to remember these words after just a single brief exposure? Is teaching new words through exposure alone, without providing explanations, a viable option in second language instruction?

To date, not much is known about how young children learn new words in a second language. There are studies which do suggest that young children are capable of learning second language words at a relatively fast rate. For instance, a three-year-old Japanese-speaking child learning English in the United States over the period of seven months developed a passive vocabulary of 260–300 words learning one or two words on average every day.[42]

There is evidence that target language words are learned most effectively when learners pick them up unconsciously, such as when reading an interesting book or having a meaningful conversation, rather than when learners make deliberate efforts to memorize these words. When such unintentional word learning takes place, words are learned as a by-product of another activity whether it be talking to an English-speaking peer or listening to an English language story. The choice between making deliberate efforts toward learning new words and letting language learners pick up new words through exposure is known as the choice between *intentional vocabulary learning* and *incidental vocabulary learning*.

A series of recent studies provides evidence regarding the relative effectiveness of intentional word learning versus incidental word learning. A study compared students who use different strategies when learning the meaning of new words. Some of the subjects in the study learned new words by reading extensively and guessing word meaning from context, while others used dictionaries to figure out what new words meant. Yet another group wrote the words and their translations down and tried to memorize their lists. Researchers found out that the group that used word lists to memorize new words was the least successful.[43] In another study,[44] researchers compared two groups of students. Students in the first group read passages and answered comprehension questions that involved new words. Students in the second group did vocabulary activities focusing on the same words. The study revealed that students in the group that did exercises focusing on meaning remembered more words than did the students who performed vocabulary activities. The studies above focus on adult word learning patterns.

In a report entitled "In Praise of Incidental Learning," Warwick Elley summarized a number of studies that compare incidental and intentional learning in children.[45] The studies overviewed by Elley reach similar conclusions: young language learners learn more words when they read exciting, interesting books than when they perform vocabulary exercises.

It seems paradoxical that it is harder to learn new words by trying to learn them. There is, however, an explanation for this paradox. The explanation has a lot to do with the nature of word meaning.

It may be hard to learn the meaning of new words intentionally, because the meaning of most words is very difficult to describe or explain. Consider the following example. Suppose the teacher is explaining to her students the meaning of a simple word, such as *sneaky*. She says, "The word *sneaky* is used to describe people and animals. It means 'clever,' and 'not honest.'" This explanation has a problem. It does not capture the complexity of meaning of the word *sneaky*. One intuitively knows that there is more to the meaning of the word than just "clever" and "not honest." It is not easy, however, to pinpoint these additional shades of meaning and to put them into words. If on the other hand, children first hear the word *sneaky* when they listen to a well-illustrated fairy-tale about a sneaky fox that tricked every animal in the forest, and if the shenanigans of the sneaky fox are described in great detail, children have little difficulty understanding the entire complexity of the word's meaning.

This is the first problem with trying to explain the word meaning by providing an explanation or a dictionary definition. When we perform these operations, we break the meaning up into smaller kernels of meaning or *semantic features*. However, in picking the word meaning apart, we lose something along the way. The word meaning is more than a simple sum of smaller individual parts. For instance, the word *mom* means more than "a female parent"; *agony* means more than "sharp pain." Explanations and dictionary definitions approximate word meaning, failing to convey its entire emotional and cultural richness. Linguists say that explanations and dictionary definitions cannot capture *emotional connotations* of meaning.

How do we understand the meaning of words which we can only define so loosely and imperfectly? An insight is offered by a branch of linguistics known as *cognitive semantics*. Cognitive semanticists say that we understand what words mean when we form in our minds mental representation of word meaning. More often than not, these mental representations are formed in concrete situations or when we encounter a new word within a rich context.

We form mental representations for the words in our mother tongue when we learn our first language and label the world around us. For instance, when the child hears an adult saying *"bird"* when pointing to a robin perched on a tree branch, she forms the mental representation of the word *bird*. Linguists call these mental representations *semantic prototypes*.

Incidentally, semantic prototypes vary from one language learner to another. A prototype for the word *bird* formed by a child who grew up in the Caribbean will differ from the one developed by another child who was raised in Maine or New Hampshire.

The most significant thing about semantic prototypes is that they tend to arise in concrete situations. Because semantic prototypes are formed in relation to real life objects, events, or phenomena, they are complete and full. This is why we "just know" what the words of our language mean, even though we may have difficulty in communicating the fullness of our knowledge to another person.

In her book *Lost in Translation*, a Polish American writer Eva Hoffman, a keen observer of her own childhood second language learning, describes the frustration of not knowing the meaning of the word in its entire semantic complexity:

The words I learn now don't stand for things in the same unquestionable way they did in my native tongue. "River" in Polish was a vital sound, energized with the essence of riverhood, of my rivers, of being immersed in the river. "River" in English is cold—a word without an aura. It has not accumulated associations for me.[46]

The prototype theory of meaning helps explain why word meaning is so hard to teach. When the teacher writes new words on the blackboard and then proceeds to explain their meaning, language learners have difficulty learning those words, because they form only a tentative idea of what new words signify.

But that is not the whole story. Let's examine some phrases that contain the word *sneaky*. One is likely to hear somebody use the phrase *a sneaky fox*, but it is very improbable for someone to use the phrase *a sneaky example*. We say: "*She is so sneaky!*" but the sentence **She acted sneaky* is incorrect. Subtle nuances of word meaning ultimately determine in what lexical and syntactic context a word can or cannot be used. The teacher would need a lifetime to explain the subtleties of meaning that cause the word to be used in this or that context. However, when a learner hears a word in a lexical or syntactic environment, she learns a lot about word meaning without teacher intervention. The language context illuminates those nuances of meaning that are hard to communicate through explanations.

A short digression is necessary at this point. An old German story tells of a Baron Munchausen, an unstoppable brag, who claimed that he had once fallen into the water and had pulled himself out by his own bootstraps. Baron Munchausen's story is not entirely credible perhaps. Words, however, are a different business. While teachers have a hard time teaching word meaning, words themselves do a marvelous job of teaching what they mean. When words co-occur with other words or take a position in a sentence, they reveal their own meaning. The potential for the word meaning to be elucidated through the lexical and syntactic context is called *semantic* and *syntactic bootstrapping*.

The Natural Approach

The word "natural" used in relation to children's language learning has been featured many times in the overview of psycholinguistic research provided in this chapter. For instance, psycholinguistic studies suggest that children learn their second language grammar in naturally succeeding stages that cannot be changed by instruction. Also, there is evidence that children learn new words most successfully when they encounter those words in naturally occurring contexts and in naturally occurring situations.

The findings described above gave a blow to the traditional *grammar-based approaches* to language teaching. In the traditional grammar-based second language classroom, language is broken up into smaller discrete entities, such as word endings or auxiliary words; and the teacher subsequently engages children in the manipulation of these artificially extracted bits of language. For instance, in the course of a traditional lesson, the teacher may ask children to provide a correct form of a noun or a verb or to use proper word order. In effect, the focus of a language lesson is on language form or structure, not on communicating a message.

The alternative *communicative approaches* to language teaching shift the focus from the form to the meaning of a language message. For instance, according to *The Natural Approach*, an influential approach to language teaching developed in the 1980s, language acquisition takes place when students are provided with *comprehensible input*, a message coached in the language just above the students' proficiency level.

Do the recent findings in psycholinguistics invalidate the more traditional grammar-based learning methods? The answer is not straightforward. For instance, the Natural Approach is simply not viable in all learning contexts. Relying on comprehensible input alone may not be a viable option in such situations as when adult learners study a foreign language from non-native speakers.

However, teaching young students a second language is different. When young children learn their second language in a situation of ample input provided by native speakers, naturalistic approaches to language teaching appear more fitting. (Chapters 4–8 of this book discuss in more detail the implementation of these approaches.)

Main Points

- Children's facility with language may be due to a language instinct (an innate ability for language learning) which fades in adulthood.
- Contrary to popular assumptions, older learners outperform young children during the initial stages of language learning.
- Children's ultimate attainment is superior to that of adults. Early language learners develop native-like fluency and don't fossilize pronunciation and grammatical errors.
- The neurological processes involved in language learning work differently in adults and children.
- There is evidence that children learn grammar in natural stages which cannot be affected by instruction.
- Children learn everyday words best as a result of incidental exposure.

Notes

1. A. Fathman and L. Precup (1983), "Age Differences in Second Language Acquisition: Research Findings and Folk Psychology." In S. Krashen and R. Scarcella (Eds.), *Issues in second language research*. Rowley, MA: pp. 151–161.

2. See for instance S.D Krashen, M.A. Long, and R.C. Scarcella (1979), "Age, Rate and Eventual Attainment in Second Language Acquisition." *TESOL Quarterly*, 13(4), 573–582.

3. For example, C. Snow and M. Hoefnagel-Höhle (1978), "The Critical Age for Language Acquisition: Evidence from Second Language Learning." *Child Development*, 49, 1114–1128.

4. L.H. Ekstrand (1976), "Age and Length of Residence as Variables Related to the Adjustment of Migrant Children with Special Reference to Second Language Learning." In G. Nickel (Ed.), *Proceedings of the Fourth International Congress of Applied Linguistics*. Stuttgart: Hochschul Verlag, pp. 179–197.

5. For example, Krashen, Long, and Scarcella, "Age, Rate, and Eventual Attainment," 573–582.

6. S. Oyama (1976), "A Sensitive Period for the Acquisition of a Nonnative Phonological System." *Journal of Psycholinguistic Research*, 5(3), 261–283.

7. J. Johnson and E. Newport (1989), "Critical Period Effects in Second Language Learning: The Influence of Maturational State on the Acquisition of English as a Second Language." *Cognitive Psychology*, 21, 60–99.

8. L. Selinker (1972), "Interlanguage." *International Review of Applied Linguistics*, 10, 209–231.

9. Oyama, "A Sensitive Period for the Acquisition of a Nonnative Phonological System," 261–283.

10. E. Lenneberg (1967), *Biological foundations of language*. New York: John Wiley & Sons.

11. K. Hyltenstam and N. Abrahamsson (2001), "Age and Second Language Learning: The Hazards of Matching Practical 'Implications' with Theoretical 'Facts.'" *TESOL Quarterly*, 35(1), 151–170.

12. K.H.S. Kim, N.R. Relkin, K.M. Lee, J. Hirsch (July 10, 1997), "Distinct Cortical Areas Associated with Native and Second Languages." *Nature*, 388, 171–174.

13. M. Ullman (2001), "A Neurocognitive Perspective on Language: The Declarative/Procedural Model." *Nature Reviews Neuroscience*, 2, 717–726.

14. M. Ullman (2001), "The Neural Basis of Lexicon and Grammar in First and Second Language: The Declarative/Procedural Model." *Bilingualism: Language and Cognition*, 4(1), 105–122.

15. P. Tabors (1987), "The Development of Communicative Competence by Second Language Learners in a Nursery School Classroom: An Ethnolinguistic Study." Unpublished doctoral dissertation, Harvard University, Boston. Cited in P. Tabors and C. Snow (1994), "English as a Second Language in Preschool Programs." In F. Genesee (Ed.), *Educating second language children: The whole child, the whole curriculum, the whole community*. New York: CUP, pp. 103–125.

16. Ibid., pp. 103–125.

17. M. Saville-Troike (1987), "Dilingual Discourse: The Negotiation of Meaning without a Common Code. *Linguistics*, 25, 81–106.

18. C. Lee, "Mute in an English-Only World." *The New York Times*, April 18, 1996, Thursday, Late Ed.–Final, Section A, p. 21; Column 2.

19. M. Saville-Troike (1988), "Private Speech: Evidence for Second Language Learning Strategies During the 'Silent Period.'" *Journal of Child Language*, 15, 567–590.

20. H. Itoh and E. Hatch (1978), "Second Language Acquisition: A Case Study." In E. Hatch (Ed.), *Second Language Acquisition: A Book of Readings*. Rowley, MA: Newbury House, p. 79.

21. Ibid., pp. 76–88.

22. In E. Hatch (Ed.), *Second language acquisition: A book of readings*. Rowley, MA: Newbury House, pp. 91–100.

23. J. Huang and E. Hatch (1978), "A Chinese Child's Acquisition of English." In E. Hatch (Ed.), *Second language acquisition: A book of readings*. Rowley, MA: Newbury House, pp. 118–131.

24. Leo van Lier (2005), "Case Study." In Eli Hinkel (Ed.), *Handbook of research in second language teaching and learning*. Mahwah, NJ: Lawrence Erlbaum Associates, pp. 195–208.

25. J. Berko (1958), "The Child's Learning of English Morphology." *Word*, 14, 150–177.

26. C. Cazden (1972), *Child language and education*. New York: Holt, Rinehart and Winston, p. 92.

27. For example, K. Hirsh-Pasek, R. Treiman, and M. Schneiderman (1984), "Brown & Hanlon Revisited: Mothers' Sensitivity to Ungrammatical Forms." *Journal of Child Language*, 11, 81–88.

28. Adapted from R. Brown (1973), *A first language: The early stages*. Cambridge, MA: HUP, p. 274.

29. E. Hatch (1978), "Introduction." In E. Hatch (Ed.), *Second language acquisition: A book of readings*. Rowley, MA: Newbury House, p. 2.

30. B. Taylor (1975), "The Use of Overgeneralization and Transfer Learning Strategies by Elementary and Intermediate Students of ESL." *Language Learning*, 25, 73–108.

31. H. Dulay and M. Burt (1975), "Creative Construction in Second Language Learning and Teaching." In M. Burt and H. Dulay (Eds.), *On TESOL'75: New directions in second language learning, teaching and bilingual education*. Washington, DC: TESOL, pp. 21–32.

32. R. Ravem (1974), "The Development of Wh-Questions in First and Second Language Learners." In J.C. Richards (Ed.), *Error analysis: Perspectives on second language acquisition*. London: Longman, pp. 134–155.

33. J. Milon (1974), "The Development of Negation in English by a Second Language Learner. *TESOL Quarterly*, 8(2), 137–143.

34. H. Dulay and M. Burt (1973), "Should We Teach Children Syntax?" *Language Learning*, 23(2), 245–258.

35. J. Richards (1971), "Error Analysis and Second Language Strategies." *Language Sciences*, 17, 12–22.

36. R. Ellis (1984), "Can Syntax Be Taught? A Study of the Effects of Formal Instruction on the Acquisition of WH Questions by Children." *Applied Linguistics*, 5(2), 138–155.

37. L. White (1991), "Adverb Placement in Second Language Acquisition: Some Effects of Positive and Negative Evidence in the Classroom." *Second Language Research*, 7(2), 133–161.

38. R. Lyster and L. Ranta (1997), "Corrective Feedback and Learner Uptake: Negotiation of Form in Communicative Classrooms." *Studies in Second Language Acquisition*, 19(1), 37–61.

39. H.C. Dulay and M.K. Burt (1973), "Should We Teach Children Syntax?" *Language Learning*, 23: 245–58.

40. For example, A. Fathman (1975), "Language Background, Age and the Order of Acquisition of English Structures." In M. Burt and H. Dulay (Eds.), *On TESOL'75: New directions in second language learning, teaching and bilingual education*. Washington, DC: TESOL, pp. 33–43.

41. S. Carey and E. Bartlett (1978), "Acquiring a Single New Word." *Papers and Reports on Child Language Development*, 15, 17–29.

42. M. Yoshida (1978), "The Acquisition of English Vocabulary by a Japanese-Speaking Child." In E. Hatch (Ed.), *Second language acquisition: A Book of readings*. Rowley, MA: Newbury House, pp. 91–100.

43. Y. Gu and R. Johnson (1996), "Vocabulary Learning Strategies and Language Learning Outcomes." *Language Learning*, 46(4), 643–679.

44. T. Paribakht and M. Wesche (1997), "Vocabulary Enhancement Activities and Reading for Meaning in Second Language Vocabulary Acquisition." In J. Coady and T. Huckin (Eds.), *Second language vocabulary acquisition: A rationale for pedagogy*. New York: CUP, pp. 174–200.

45. W. Elley, http://cela.albany.edu/reports/inpraise/inpraise.PDF, retrieved on January 10, 2006.

46. E. Hoffman (1989), *Lost in Translation*. New York: Penguin Books, p. 106.

CHAPTER 4

Teaching Emergent Second Language Speakers

After being enrolled in a school, young language learners embark on the journey of formal language learning. What can the teacher do to help them? This chapter deals with the instructional needs of young beginning level language learners. It discusses such concerns as creating an environment conducive to language learning, teaching young learners during the preproduction stage, and encouraging early speech emergence.

Creating a Friendly Environment to Help Children Learn a Second Language

The first order of business in the beginning level ESL classroom is to create an unthreatening, comfortable and stress-free environment. If you have studied a second language, you may have noticed that you speak more fluently and have less difficulty coming up with the right word in those situations when you feel relaxed and confident. Conversely, you may have observed that negative emotions inhibit language production. Retrieving the right word and maintaining language flow becomes a difficult task when one feels tense, overwhelmed, or self-conscious. Sometimes, negative emotions make speaking a second language virtually impossible. It is then that people say that their mind "went blank," that they "had a mental block," that they "froze," and were unable to utter a single word in another language.[1] In short, the more relaxed and the more uninhibited we feel, the better are we positioned to cope with the task of understanding and producing a second language.

In an influential study, Stephen Krashen hypothesizes that if people are exposed to a second language, they will inevitably pick up the language provided the new language is comprehensible enough and provided an emotional barrier created by fear, tension, boredom, or lack of interest is not present.[2] Krashen refers to that negative emotional barrier under the name of *affective filter*. Although there are no studies to date supporting Krashen's hypothesis, there is consensus among second language educators that a classroom with a low affective filter provides an optimal language-teaching environment.

In working with young children, the need to tear down the negative affective filter is especially great. Whether or not young language learners are immigrants or whether they were born in the United States, their very first language learning steps may require an emotional adjustment. Some young language learners suffer from being uprooted. Others are traumatized by finding themselves among the people who do not speak their language. There also are children who go through a rejection period when they feel acute distress and are reluctant to communicate in a new language.[3] For many other children, learning a second language coincides with their first-time exposure to the public school system and they need to acclimate to a new environment away from home. Given what is known about the role of emotions in second language learning, it is essential to assure that young language learners feel comfortable and secure when taking their first language learning steps.

Researchers known for their work on the role of affect in second language teaching emphasize the importance of creating a welcoming and warm physical environment in the second language classroom and assuring that the classroom be children's home away from home.[4] To create a home-like environment, researchers suggest that the space where children begin to learn a second language should display elements that validate those aspects of children's identities that are closely linked to their homes. For instance, children can paste treasured personal objects, such as photographs of family members or small toys on their desks, thereby making the desk a home.[5] Another way to help language learners feel welcome on the first day of school is to give them a personalized "starter kit" which contains classroom materials, such as writing implements and a picture dictionary.[6]

Validation of a student's name by the teacher helps a child feel welcome in a new environment. Language teachers need to make an effort to pronounce children's given names as accurately as possible. Banners with children's given names—written in oversized letters and colorfully decorated—can be prominently displayed in the classroom; children who have some literacy skills can make these name displays in their home language.[7]

From day one, language teachers try to communicate to their students the sense of appreciation of language learners' cultural heritage. Some teachers decorate their classroom with a welcoming sign that features students' photographs and flags of their home countries. Other teachers encourage children to wear clothes from their home countries. These seemingly small gestures have great significance, for they let children know that their teacher respects and admires their cultural background.

Encouraging Peer Bonding

A question foremost on young children's minds when they start a new school is whether they are going to make new friends. If children find new playmates, their adaptation to the new environment will be infinitely less painful. This is why creating a close-knit community of language learners is absolutely essential for children's well-being in the second language classroom. There is no denying that young children who come from various cultural and linguistic backgrounds may taunt and tease each other.[8] What is truly remarkable, though, is that even very young children also tend to feel protective and compassionate toward their less proficient peers. Children who have learned a little English and feel sufficiently acclimated in the new environment are often eager to take care of newcomers and to "show them the ropes."

Children's impulse to protect the newcomers, their sense of empathy toward their straight-off-the-boat classmates needs to be capitalized upon in the second language classroom. The culture of peer bonding emerges if the teacher encourages more proficient children to assist newcomers with a myriad of little tasks. Children can help their new buddies perform classroom routines, follow directions, or locate and use classroom objects. Something as simple as being able to hold the hand of one's buddy when going down the hall of the school building will help a new student feel more comfortable in the new environment.

Creating a Teacher–Student Bond

The second language teacher is often the first adult outside home with whom immigrant children communicate in the new country. Under these circumstances, it is particularly important that language learners know that their language teacher is someone they can trust.

Nonverbal clues that help to create a bond between the teacher and the student can be as simple as a smile, singling out a child during play, or offering extra help with a classroom activity. Language, however, is a primary means to create a connection between the teacher and student; it is not only the target of instruction but also the tool that helps the teacher and students develop an emotional bond.

The language that helps teacher and students to connect needs to be not only clear, simple, and accessible but also unstilted, rich, and personally meaningful.[9] An essential element of almost any language lesson is a conversation, which the teacher and students have in relation to the focus of the lesson, whether it is about a picture book they have just read together or a natural science phenomenon they have just explored. These conversations grow richer and more meaningful as students' proficiency levels grow. They should, however, be part of language lesson even at the preproduction and beginning levels of proficiency.

First level language lessons often focus on discussion of students' personal preferences, feelings, and experiences. These exchanges can be particularly interesting if the teacher reaches out to students by sharing a bit of personal information. Describing photographs of the teacher's pet, family members, or a recent trip, can serve as a source of input that assures teacher–student bonding.

Delayed Language Production or Expecting Some Silence

Not expecting learners to speak until they are ready and willing to do so is an important principle of working with beginning level language students. TESOL professionals refer to this principle as *allowing for the silent period*. Researchers recommend that ESL teachers wait for as long as may be necessary—several months or even a year—without coercing learners to produce language.

The rationale for allowing the silent period is provided by nativists, scholars who argue that in some fundamental ways second language learning is like first language learning. Nativists believe that second language teaching is likely to be most effective if teachers take into account the processes that take place when children learn their first language. Proponents of the nativist model point out that little children do not begin to speak their mother tongue right away. Rather, a considerable amount of time elapses during which children just listen to speakers of their first language and learn to understand it in relation to the events of daily life. Nativists argue that second language learning should parallel these developmental sequences and that language comprehension, not language production, should be the focus of the early stages of instruction.

Comprehension-Based Activities

During the silent period of language learning, teachers implement comprehension-based activities. At this stage, helping children understand language becomes the focus of instruction. (By placing emphasis on comprehension in the beginning level classroom, second language teachers act very much like caretakers who talk to babies and do not expect first words to start emerging till many months later.) Whether teachers and children play games, read books, or implement hands-on projects during the initial stages of language instruction, teachers are particularly concerned with honing students' ability to understand oral language. ESL educators sometimes refer to talking to students as *providing comprehensible input*. Providing comprehensible input works best if the language used by the teacher is neither too hard nor too easy, just beyond student's proficiency level.[10] The input that is too easy would not work, because it does not promote language development; the one that is too hard is not beneficial for learners. The latter argument makes sense if you consider that we hardly ever pick up pieces of foreign language we hear on television or on the street, simply because the input is too difficult and we do not understand what is being said.

Some of the strategies used by language teachers to make input comprehensible are the following:

- First and foremost, teachers use phrases whose meaning is clear in the immediate context. Thus, first conversations with language learners are embedded in games and activities where language use is accompanied by movement, manipulation of objects, or demonstrations with pictures. In these activities, the context of teacher–student conversations makes the meaning of input clear.

- Speaking slowly (not loudly!), with frequent pauses, repeating, paraphrasing, and restating utterances are helpful communication strategies.

- Coupling language with nonverbal communication strategies, such as gestures and pantomime are also helpful in making the message accessible to learners. Gestures can help convey various shades of meanings, such as speed and size, distance and shape, motion and immobility.

- To enhance comprehensibility of a message, language teachers also employ dramatic intonations and volume adjustments. For instance, using a dramatic intonation to suggest a character trait when reading a picture book or low and high volume to portray the atmosphere or the mood in a book scene serve as helpful meaning clarification strategies.

- Comprehensible input also has its own grammar. Sentences used by language teachers are as short as possible and syntactically simple.[11]

A crucially important characteristic of comprehensible input is repeated use of patterns and *routines*.[12] Routines are formulaic utterances which language teachers use to signal beginning, transition and completion of activities. If children hear the same utterances, such as *let's share our stories* or *clean up time* repeated several times in the same context, they have no difficulty in understanding their overall meaning and gradually are able to segment the utterance into individual words.

The bulk of comprehension-based activities implemented in the beginning level classroom entail some kind of learner response that demonstrates to the teacher that children have understood the language. In these activities, language teachers provide input, and language learners perform actions or make short one- or two-word utterances that let the teacher know that students process what is being said. Some effective comprehension-based activities implemented with young language learners are discussed below.

Total Physical Response Approach

Language teachers who use the *Total Physical Response (TPR)* instructional approach provide directions to students while language learners respond by performing relevant actions. In the TPR activities, students remain silent while following directions, reenacting stories, accompanying songs with actions, and drawing pictures in response to teacher directions.

TPR is similar to first language learning in that it links speaking and action. James Asher, the founder of TPR noticed that when mothers teach their babies how to speak, they give children directions to perform various actions. We have all observed some instances of language teaching that combine language and movement. Phrases such as—*Sooo big! Clap-clap-clap! Say "bye-bye!" Where is daddy?*—are essentially directions used to encourage babies to perform physical actions in response to verbal stimuli. It is these word-action connections that the TPR activities recreate in the second language classroom.

The use of TPR in the second language classroom assures that students start to understand language sooner and use it with greater confidence.[13] Proponents of linking movement and language teaching suggest that the approach is effective because it is *brain compatible*. It seems that the approach accounts more fully for the neurological processes involved in language learning. Thus, TPR involves procedural kinesthetic memory, not factual declarative memory. An earlier section of this book discussed that procedural memory, which is responsible for motion, is more lasting than declarative memory, which is in charge of word memorization. In effect, language activities that pair up language learning with motion work better, because they leave more durable and profound imprints on learner memories. Just as we do not forget how to ride a bicycle, we do not forget words and phrases we learned when doing something.

Moreover, TPR works, because it enables language learners to develop a better grasp of word meaning. It is one thing if the teacher conveys the meaning of a target language items, such as *turn around* or *pick up your pencil* by flashing cards with relevant pictures or by providing translations into a learner's home language. It is an altogether different story if learners actually get to turn around or pick up their pencils when hearing those phrases. By performing actions and manipulating objects when being exposed to target language items, learners do not take on faith clarification of meaning provided by the teacher. Rather, they get to experience the meaning of target language items as facts of their own lives. When children connect word and action, foreign words cease to be sound shells that contain some tentative meaning. Rather they are filled with full-bodied real life meaning.

TPR Songs and Games

Some popular songs and games adopted in the second language classroom are common TPR activities. Classical children's action songs, such as *Head Shoulders Knees and Toes* or *This Is the Way We Wash Our Hands* or *Hokey Pokey* have been used to teach names of body parts. Classical games, such as *Simon Says* work for teaching common motion verbs. Some TPR games designed by language teachers specifically for the use in the second language classroom are discussed below:

- *Clap and Snap.* In this activity which is used for teaching names of body parts, the teacher alternatively claps her hands or snaps her fingers and directs students to point at different body parts while reciting the following chant:

> Clap! Clap! Clap! Nose!! (Players clap and point at their noses.)
> Snap! Snap! Snap! Ears!! (Players snap their fingers and point at their ears.)
> Clap! Clap! Clap! Shoulders!! (Players clap and point at their shoulders.)

After a few turns, the teacher makes an unexpected "mistake" and tries to confuse students by pointing at the wrong body part; children need to pay attention and keep pointing correctly.

- *Don't Let It Drop.* In this activity which focuses on the use of common verbs, the player picked to be "it" follows the teacher's directions balancing a small object, such as an eraser or an index card on his or her head. The teacher starts out with simple directions, such as *Sit down!* or *Stand up!* If "it" succeeds in not letting the pencil drop, directions get progressively harder. For instance, the teacher can ask "it" to bend down or to sit on the floor. In another version of this game, the teacher gives directions to the entire group of students.

- *Preposition Gymnastics.* Sometimes when performing a TPR activity, students manipulate a toy or a ball. For instance, when performing *Preposition Gymnastics* children move a toy, such as a teddy bear, following the teacher's directions. (e.g., *Place the teddy bear on the chair! Place the teddy bear under the chair!*)

- *Edible or Inedible?* In this TPR game, meant to reinforce the names of food items, the ball sometimes represents something that you can eat and at other times represents something that you cannot eat. The teacher throws the ball to players. However, players are not expected to catch the ball each time, because according to the rules of the game, catching the ball means eating something, whereas letting the ball drop means declining to eat. If the teacher names an edible object, players are supposed to catch the ball. If the teacher names an inedible object, the players should let the ball fall. Students find the game all the more enjoyable if the teacher makes comments about their actions, "Good! You ate an apple!" "Oops! You just ate a chair!"

Directed Drawing

Another subset of TPR activities is *Directed Drawing*. In these activities, children create pictures that follow the teacher's directions. Directed drawing is an effective comprehension-based activity, because the meaning of step-by-step drawing directions is immediately clear as the teacher proceeds to draw elements of the picture on the chalkboard and is further reinforced as children go about following directions. Given the instructional benefit of Directed Drawing, it is helpful for language teachers to stock their classroom libraries with quality "how-to" drawing guides for young children (e.g., *Draw Write Now*.)[14] In performing Directed Drawing activities, the teacher may guide children in creating picture dictionaries or illustrations to their own stories. Some Directed Drawing activities that are akin to games are discussed below:

- *Weather Forecast*. This Directed Drawing activity is meant to introduce children to target language items that describe weather conditions. The teacher starts by drawing a picture of a big window, and a child picked to be "it" draws pictures of different weather conditions following teacher provided directions. (e.g., *It is sunny. It is raining. It is cloudy.*)

- *A Chalk Monster*. This TPR drawing activity focuses on vocabulary items related to body parts. To draw a chalk monster, the teacher gives the students picked to be "it" step-by step directions to draw a picture of a scary monster. (e.g., *Draw the face! Draw five eyes! Draw a huge nose!*)

- *A Funny Face*. In another similar activity, the teacher gives directions (e.g., *Draw the face! Draw the right ear! Draw the left ear!*) to a blindfolded student while the student proceeds to draw a face. Drawing blindfolded is not easy. The more hideous the face created by the blindfolded artist, the greater is the enjoyment of the onlookers.

TPR Pantomime and Stories

While the TPR mode is a natural medium for teaching target language items related to body parts or actions, it need not be confined to these topics. Students can participate in TPR pantomimes that represent various events that range from going to the beach or walking around the neighborhood to morning or bedtime activities. TPR pantomimes are enhanced by the use of props. Slide shows of various scenes projected on the wall, evocative music used for creating the mood, and pictures displayed in strategic locations serve as sets for pantomimes.

- *TPR Tour of the City*. For instance, when teaching nouns related to city life, teacher can paste pictures of the elements of cityscape to the backs of classroom chairs and give children directions to jump or walk from one object to another. (e.g., *Run to the bus! Get into the car! Cross the street! Look at the tree!*)

In TPR stories, students engage in role-playing episodes from their favorite books. Usually after several introductory readings of a short and simple story, the teacher tells the story, and students act it out as the story is being told. Students can act out popular stories or fairy tales, such as *Billy Goat Gruff*[15] or *The Three Bears*.[16] Fairy tales and short stories are particularly amenable to the TPR instructional mode if they describe a succession of varied actions. Simple classroom props add to the effectiveness of TPR stories. Pictures of book characters attached to a piece of string and worn around the neck by actors help identify story characters. Similarly, pictures of a forest or a house pasted to the back of the chair or a desk signal locations to pantomime participants.

Guessing Games

Guessing games also can provide comprehensible input to language learners at the preproduction and the low-emergent proficiency levels. These games work, because they have a unique structure. While providing a rich source of input, they put limited demands on learners in terms of expected output. In a language guessing game, the teacher describes an object, person, or phenomenon and children try to identify the item.

- *Mystery Voice.* In this game, which helps children learn each other's names, players need to recognize voices of their peers. A child picked to be "it" faces away from the group while one of the children from the class says, "Hello!" and names "it" by his or her name. The child facing away tries to identify the child who spoke his or her name. If the guess is correct, the caller takes the place of "it."

- *What's Missing?* This popular ESL game attempts to teach the names of classroom objects or any other small things, such as tableware or clothing. The teacher displays a set of objects on the desk and goes over their names (e.g., *a ruler, a pen, a pencil, a notebook, an eraser*). Having named the displayed objects several times, the teacher asks children to close their eyes upon which the teacher or a child removes one of the objects. When children open their eyes, they guess which object is missing.

- *Guess Who It Is!* This classical language game reinforces vocabulary related to clothing and appearance. The teacher picks a child and describes the child's appearance or an outfit, while other children try to guess the identity of the person being described.

- *Guess How Many.* This game is an effective means of reinforcing numbers. The teacher places a few marbles in a little bag and asks children to guess the number of marbles. After the participants have made their guesses, they count the actual number of marbles.

- *Treasure Box.* This game can reinforce the names of animals, food, or classroom objects. The teacher fills the treasure box with objects related to the same activity or theme. Then the teacher describes an item without removing it from the box, while students try to guess what it is.

- *Peek-a-Boo Stories.* Guessing games can be particularly effective if they are accompanied by the use of flap pictures[17] or Peek-a-Boo[18] books. A flap picture is a graphic representation of an object or a scene that comes with a flap, a piece of paper that covers the picture entirely or partially.[19] Flap pictures can be collected into thematically organized Peek-A-Boo books. The teacher describes the pictures hidden under the flap, and students try to guess the riddle. The teacher can make flap picture books by cutting out pictures of animals, food items, instruments, and other objects, pasting them on an oversize piece of paper and attaching a flap on top. Thematically organized flap books can focus on animals, food items, or articles of clothing. The book on food items can describe taste, color, and shape of children's favorite foods; the one about animals will discuss the animals' habitat, size, and food preferences.

Strategies to Encourage Early Speech Emergence

Choral Singing

While second language teachers do not expect children to speak in the beginning level ESL classroom until they are comfortable with language use, there are activities that help elicit output even from beginning level language students. These activities work best if they are not threatening and if they leave students with an option to remain silent. An instructional strategy used to encourage speech emergence in the beginning level ESL classroom is the use of songs and music. Beginning level language learners derive great pleasure from choral signing. Singing along lowers students' affective filter, because when children sing together, they are not afraid of mispronouncing a sound or getting a word wrong. Singing is also effective, because it provides children with an opportunity to form an emotional bond with their peers. The songs that work best in the ESL classroom have a repetitive structure, simple wording, and an easy-to-follow rhythmical pattern and pace.

When implementing signing activities, ESL teachers start by playing a song several times. Then the teacher works on conveying the meaning of the lyrics by acting out individual stanzas or by using puppets or props. The culminating activity is choral singing. After children have sung the song in chorus, the teacher can implement a follow-up literacy activity. Often, ESL teachers will ask their students to compose a piece of writing modeled on a song they have just sung.

- *My Pet Donkey.* For instance after singing a song *My Donkey Eats* by Raffi about a donkey that can eat, walk, talk, and eat with a knife and fork, the teacher can ask children to draw a picture of their donkey and describe the kind of things that their donkeys can do. Chapter 5 of this book discusses in great detail strategies used by second language teachers to assure that song lyrics and other texts written by young beginning level language learners are grammatically correct, lexically rich, and sustained.

Gesture Approach

A particularly effective second language teaching strategy is integration of language and hand gestures. When this strategy is implemented, language teachers accompany words, phrases, or texts by hand motions or "improvisational sign language" that illustrate the meaning of these target language items.[20]

Researchers of language have long suspected that there exists some intimate connection between the movement of one hand or both hands and language production.

Most of us have experienced the helpfulness of gesturing in generating language. When we were young, we recited classical nursery rhymes, such as *Two Little Black Birds* or *The Itsy Bitsy Spider* and accompanied these recitations with finger play. (If English is not your first language, you most probably have heard similar verses in your own mother tongue.) As we grow older, we continue using hand motions when we speak. Some of us gesticulate more, others are less likely to do so. But most speakers make some use of their hands while talking. Many people make little shaking hand motions when they cannot recall a word or accompany the discussion of physical properties of objects with descriptive hand movements. It looks as if hand motions help us tease out the language and make it more meaningful.

The connection between language production and gesturing is being explored in various studies. Scholars who study the roots of language hypothesize that language may have originated from gesturing.[21] There are also those who point out that the neural control of gestures and language production are closely linked.[22] There are scholars who argue that gestures clarify word meaning and make language easier to understand and remember.[23] (This is the case because in contrast to words, gestures are *iconic*. While there is nothing about the oral and written form of the words *big* or *small* that suggests size, hand motions that accompany the use of these words can portray size quite vividly.) While the nature of the link between gesture and language still remains to be explored, there is little doubt that gestures and hand motions have the power to enhance language learning.

To account for the interconnection between language production and hand motions, language teachers come up with hand gestures which illustrate the meaning of various target language items. They also invent hand motions that illustrate the meaning of poems or compose their own pieces accompanied with hand motions. The meaning of words, such as *big* and *small*, *high* and *low*, *walk* and *jump*, *cut* and *paste*, can be illustrated with the help of hand motions.

Gesture Approach activities tend to follow a sequence. During the first step, the teacher reads aloud an illustrated story or a poem. During the second step, the teacher retells same text with the accompaniment of hand motions. During the third step, the teacher leads students in choral recitation of the text. During the fourth and final step, the teacher conducts students through text recitation. At this point, the teacher does not pronounce the words but just uses hand motions to remind children of the next text segment, very much like a conductor who conducts the orchestra through a piece.

Children's favorite poems, such as *Five Little Monkeys Jumping on the Bed*[24] or other repetitive chants help children build their language skills. Consider the use of gestures in the following short good night poem.

Good Night!

Time for children to go to bed. (*Finger points at an imaginary wrist watch.*)
On the pillow put your head (*Head rests on two hands put together.*)
Mommy and Daddy turn off the light (*Gesture of a hand turning off the light.*)

Close your eyes (*hands are placed on the eyes*) and say, "Good Night!"
(*Children lie down on the rug and lie still while the teacher counts one to
five.*)
Good morning! (*Children "wake up".*)

As soon as children begin to produce their first words and sentences
in a second language, they can be engaged in literacy instruction. (Second language reading and writing lessons intended for young language
learners are described in Chapter 5 of this volume.)

Main Points

- A friendly environment is essential for successful second language
  learning.
- Young learners do not start producing language right away. A prolonged period of silence is to be expected.
- First instructional activities should focus on language comprehension, not language production.
- Combining language use with movement helps second language
  learning.
- Accompanying language use with gestures enhances second language production.

Notes

1. E. Horwitz, M. Horwitz, and J. Cope (1986), "Foreign Language Classroom
Anxiety." *The Modern Language Journal*, 70(ii), 125–132.
2. S. Krashen (1985), *The input hypothesis: Issues and implications*. Longman: New
York.
3. H. Itoh and E. Hatch (1978), "Second Language Acquisition: A Case Study."
In E. Hatch (Ed.), *Second language acquisition: A book of readings*. Rowley, MA:
Newbury House, pp. 76–88.
4. C. Igoa (1995), *The inner world of the immigrant child*. Mahwah, NJ: Lawrence
Erlbaum Associates.
5. Ibid.
6. E. Coelho (1994), "Social Integration of Immigrant and Refugee Children."
In F. Genesee (Ed.), *Educating second language children: The whole child, the whole
curriculum, the whole community*, pp. 301–327.
7. Igoa, *The inner world of the immigrant child*.
8. For example, H. Smith and P. Heckman (1995), "Meeting the Challenge
of Linguistic and Cultural Diversity in Early Childhood." In E. Garcia and

B. McLaughlin (Eds.), *Meeting the challenge of linguistic and cultural diversity in early childhood education.* New York: Teachers College, pp. 64–84.

9. L. Wong-Fillmore (1985), "When does Teacher Talk Work as Input?" In S. Gass and C. Madden (Eds.), *Input in second language acquisition.* Cambridge, MA: Newbury House Publishing, pp. 17–50.

10. Krashen (1985), *The input hypothesis.*

11. Wong-Fillmore, *Input in second language acquisition*, pp. 17–50.

12. Ibid.

13. D. Wolfe and G. Jones (1982), "Integrating Total Physical Response Strategy in a Level I Spanish Class." *Foreign Language Annals*, 14(4), 273–280.

14. For example, M. Hablitzel and K. Stitzer (1994), *On the farm, kids & critters, storybook characters (Draw write now, Book 1: A drawing and handwriting course for kids!).* Poulsbo, WA: Barker Creek.

15. P. Galdone (1973), *The three billy goats gruff.* New York: Clarion Books.

16. P. Galdone (1973), *The three bears.* New York: Clarion Books.

17. A. Wright (1989), *Pictures for language learning.* New York: Cambridge University Press.

18. S. Peregoy and O. Boyle (1997), *Reading, writing and learning in ESL: A resource book for K-12 teachers*, 2nd ed. White Plains, NY: Longman.

19. A. Wright (1989), *Pictures for language learning.* New York: Cambridge University Press.

20. Peregoy and Boyle, *Reading, writing and learning in ESL*, p. 208.

21. M. Corballis (2002), *From hands to mouth: The origins of language.* Princeton, NJ: Princeton University Press.

22. D. Kimura (1993), *Neuromotor mechanisms in human communication.* New York: Oxford University Press.

23. D. McNeill (1992), *Hand and mind: What gestures reveal about thought.* Chicago, IL: University of Chicago Press.

24. E. Christelow (1989), *Five little monkeys jumping on the bed.* New York: Clarion Books.

CHAPTER 5

Developing Literacy Skills of Young Language Learners

ESL Teacher: Children, do you remember the fairy tale *The Fisherman and his Wife*? The magic fish granted every wish of the fisherman's wife. But then, because the wife was being greedy, the fish took away all its gifts. What's the lesson behind this story?

ESL Student: Never-ever take anything from a fish!!

This section of the book deals with the theory and practice of teaching reading and writing to young second language learners. Making a connection between theory and practice is particularly important in a conversation about literacy instruction, because some recent research findings have profoundly transformed the field of teaching reading and writing.

The chapter starts with the discussion of some important findings in the field of literacy and proceeds to examine implications of these findings for the classroom. It also discusses such practical concerns as selection of books most suited to the needs of young second language readers or proven strategies of teaching reading and writing in the primary level ESL classroom.

The Interactive Model of Literacy

So what is known today about the processes that take place in the minds of young readers? And, given our knowledge of these processes, what are the optimal ways of developing literacy skills of young English language learners?

On first glance, there seems to be nothing mysterious about reading. Presumably, being literate is being able to figure out which letters stand for which sounds, to put letters into words and words into sentences, and to glean meaning from the resulting text. According to this *bottom-up model of literacy*, to learn to read is to learn to work one's way from parts of the text, that is letters, to the top, that is text meaning.

Some recent findings, however, have called the bottom-up model of literacy into question. Research of reading has demonstrated that readers do not deploy bottom-up strategies only. When observing readers, scientists noticed so-called saccades, little "jerky" movements of the reader's eyes.[1] The analysis of these miniscule eye movements made researchers realize that while the reader is decoding a word on a printed page, his or her eyes are darting to the next segment of the text and the mind is racing ahead of itself in an effort to predict what the next bit of the text is going to say.

This finding throws light on an important strategy involved in the reading process. Today we know that to be able to read, besides decoding, one also needs to learn to guess or predict what the text is going to say. Reading is thus a kind of "psychological guessing game."[2] Good readers are particularly apt at making predictions about what the text is going to say. Conversely, less proficient readers are likely to get stuck on a small chunk of text and have difficulty grasping the bigger picture.

Our conscious understanding of the role of prediction in reading is fairly recent. Luckily for readers, however, writers and publishers of books have long had an intuitive understanding of the importance or prediction for the reading process. Conventions of written text organization, such as tables of contents, names of chapters, topic sentences in paragraphs, introductory statements—such as the one that opens this very section of the book—all make text more comprehensible by helping readers to figure out what the text is going to be about.

The analysis of your own literacy strategies might be an interesting exercise. For instance, you might notice that when you read, you pay special attention to chapter titles or subheadings to know what you can expect to find in the text. If you do use this particular strategy, awareness of the overall theme of a text helps you read more efficiently.

Research has demonstrated that there is another important strategy which is used by readers. To understand the meaning of the written word, readers need to be able to activate their background knowledge and bring this background knowledge to the reading process.[3] When proficient readers read, they bring memories of past experiences or factual knowledge to the process of text comprehension. Good readers tend to link the information contained on the page with what they already know. For instance, if you have had experience observing children learn languages, you are equipped with the background knowledge that will help you read this book with a more critical eye.

Literacy strategies described above are similar in that when using them, the reader starts with the whole (e.g., background knowledge or ability to predict text content) and brings this knowledge to understanding a part of a text (e.g., a word or a sentence). The model of literacy that accounts for these whole-to-part strategies is known as the *top-down model of literacy.*

Modern literacy experts argue that whole-to-part and part-to-whole processes work in concert by complementing each other when people read and write. The model of reading which accounts both for the bottom-up and top-down processes involved in reading is called the *interactive model of literacy.*[4]

Challenges in Second Language Literacy Instruction

The interactive model of literacy has important implications for teaching young language learners because all aspects of the interactive reading processes (i.e., decoding, prediction, background knowledge activation) present young learners with additional challenges. Young language learners need to overcome some barriers when reading and writing in a second language which are not faced by children who speak English as their first language.

Difficulty in Second Language Decoding. Consider the challenge of learning to decode in a second language. Decoding is particularly difficult for language learners, simply because they do not hear the language the same way as native speaking children. At least initially, language learners perceive English words as a jumble of odd sounds. Parsing words into individual sounds with the purpose of assigning letters to these sounds is particularly challenging for a child who is beginning to learn English. No wonder a writer described the English she first heard as a young child upon coming to the United States from another country as an incoherent stream of "cranky wails and cries."[5]

A little experiment may help you know how a young language learner feels. Tune your radio to a station which broadcasts in a language in which you are not proficient. Note that if you listen to a broadcaster speak Chinese, or Arabic, or Urdu (or any other language which you cannot speak at all), the languages come in a continuous stream of noise. It often is impossible to figure out which individual sounds make up the words.

This is the case, not only because we are not used to the sounds of a foreign language but also because we do not know what foreign words mean. Our ability to divide words into sounds and to identify individual sounds has everything to do with our knowledge of word meaning. We know that the words *pan* and *pen* are made of three sounds and that they have different vowels in the middle, because we know that the two words mean two different things. Similarly, we know that *right* and *light*, *chair* and *share* are made of different sounds, because when we hear these words pronounced, we know that they stand for different things.

Language learners take a while before learning to make these distinctions in a second language; initially at least they "lack the ability to discriminate some American [sic] sounds from others."[6] But even after a prolonged initial period of language learning when children begin the process of parsing chunks of language into separate sounds, a Spanish-speaking child may be unable to hear that *chair* and *share* sound different, the Japanese-speaking child may have a hard time distinguishing between *right* and *light*, and distinguishing between *sheep* and *ship* may give a hard time to a child from Russia. Because sound analysis presents a challenge to young language learners, engaging this group of students in phonics-based activities is not feasible at least initially and needs to be delayed until the time when children have built a basic stock of oral language and a sight reading vocabulary.

Difficulty in Second Language Word Reading. A young beginning level language learner is confronted with another challenge, not experienced by native language speakers. It is difficult (and sometimes impossible) for language learners to figure out where one word ends and another one begins. You may recall that young language learners use numerous formulaic utterances that are grammatically unanalyzed chunks of language made of a few words fused into one unit. These prefabricated chunks of language in the output of language learners such as *thisiseh* [this is a], or *idonna* [I don't know], or *lookit* [look at it] indicate that children studying a second language will most probably have a hard time reading and writing decontextualized isolated forms of words such as *it*, or *in*, or *is*. As far as a young child beginning to learn English is concerned these words are odd, meaningless, strange noises; young language learners may not be aware of having encountered these words in real-life communication. Because of this perception of language by young students, it is hardly possible to engage them in reading phonetically organized texts of the "It is his stick" variety, let alone reading phonetically organized lists of words such as "at, am, has." A young child who is unable to bring the meanings of the words to the reading process is unlikely to be able to deal with reading or writing these words.

Difficulty in Predicting Meaning When Reading in a Second Language. Making predictions or guesses about the text is another strategy that language learners will find difficult. Not knowing colocational properties of language (which words are likely to come together) or syntax (how the sentence tends to be pieced together)—to name just two examples—presents language learners with challenges when they are engaged in the psycholinguistic guessing game of reading. Upon encountering the word *bedtime*, an English-speaking child is able to predict that it will probably be followed by the word *story*. Similarly, she will most probably be able to predict that the word *tuck* will most probably follow the word *in*. So when reading a story about bedtime activities, a child who speaks English as a first language will have little difficulty completing reading a sentence, such as *Mom read me a bedtime s*_____ or *Mom tucked me*_____. Children who are beginning to learn English may not have the linguistic knowledge at their disposal that would help them read these sentences.

Lack of linguistic knowledge is closely connected with the fact that language learners have background experiences that are quite different from those of their English-speaking peers. Children who were raised in the United States draw on a vast repository of information when reading books in English. They have less difficulty understanding texts, because they are familiar with the scenarios and situations which children's books describe. Whether a story tells of a birthday party, a tooth fairy, or a play date, chances are that children who are native speakers of English have participated in these activities and know how they tend to evolve.

Even though English language learners experience some additional difficulties when learning to read and write in English, there exists a consensus among second language educators that even beginning level young learners need to be engaged in literacy instruction. Instructional approaches and strategies used in the second language classroom facilitate an early start to literacy while helping language learners overcome the challenges of learning to read in a second language. Some strategies help children start reading and writing before they are developmentally able to handle decoding. Other strategies help learners make predictions about the text. Still other strategies are useful for establishing the knowledge base essential for text comprehension.

No matter how innovative instructional strategies are, however, they offer no guarantee that children will become proficient second language readers and writers. The factors of time and enjoyment are equally important. Language learners are likely to experience success in learning to read and write if they spend sufficient time reading and writing[7] and if they derive pleasure out of these activities. The approaches and strategies that account for the interactive model of literacy while sustaining language learners' reading and writing are discussed in the next section of this chapter.

Approaches and Strategies in Second Language Literacy Instruction

Starting Early

Second language literacy experts recommend that literacy instruction should start early in the ESL classroom, before children develop full proficiency in a second language. Because writing is less threatening than speaking in that children need not be afraid of mispronouncing an unfamiliar word, children can have their first experiences of producing written statements in English well before they start speaking in a second language.

Using Whole Language in Authentic Literacy Events

As most beginning level language learners will have a hard time dealing with tasks such as "What is the first sound of the word *at*?" or "Use the word *is* in your own sentence!" using instructional strategies that work from the bottom to the top is not feasible with that group of students. To account for this fact, learning to read and write in a second language should start as a whole, not a part.[8] Second language teachers stay away from practicing the reading of disjointed decontextualized target language lists, nor do they ask students to practice writing word lists made of items such as *the* or *in*. Rather, they encourage language learners to use whole pieces of written language while reading for meaning and writing for communication.[9]

In the second language classroom, teachers encourage children to use oral and written language the way it is used in real life. When reading and writing, language learners need to participate in authentic literacy events; they read and write for real purposes.[10] Language learners benefit most from reading and writing stories and fairy tales, letters, newspapers, recipes, prescriptions, travel pamphlets, advertisements, song lyrics, and poems, as well as other authentic literacy pieces.[11] These literacy pieces can have just a few words; sometimes these words are repeated several times for the sake of both practice and clarity. No matter how short and basic these pieces are, they work best if they are similar to pieces of written text that children might find outside the classroom.

Creating a Literate Classroom Environment

First literacy lessons happen in the second language classroom when language learners find themselves in the environment which sends them a message that reading and writing are important and enjoyable activities. Thematic displays of books, displays of children's works, and lists of students as well as lists of classroom rules all contribute to a print-rich environment.[12]

The classroom environment is conducive to reading and writing if the classroom is converted into a virtual dictionary with the help of labels and poster size pictionaries. Each element of the ESL classroom space, whether it be a chair or a wall, a make-believe paleontological excavation site, a doctor's office, a pretend store, or a reading corner, proclaim their name with the help of a label. As for oversize pictionaries, they are particularly effective if they are thematically organized, that is, if they carry lexical items that belong to the same semantic fields, such as animals, body parts, feelings, seasons, clothing, furnishings, common adjectives and verbs, colors, and so forth. It is essential that pictures illustrating the meaning of target language vocabulary be attractive and easy to interpret.

Poster size pictionaries are helpful resources, not pieces of decoration, and it is important that children understand their role in the classroom. When implementing a writing activity, the teacher asks students to identify a pictionary that might help them work on a given piece of writing.

Language Experience Approach and Dictated Stories

The *Language Experience Approach* (LEA), initially developed for the mainstream literacy classroom, has been embraced by TESOL educators.[13] In the field of TESOL, Language Experience Activities are also commonly referred to under the name of Dictated Stories[14] or Dictated Chart Stories.[15]

As evident from its name, the Language Experience Approach integrates teaching reading and writing with some type of a lived experience. The LEA activity consists of four steps: experience, description, transcription, and reading. During the first experience step, the teacher engages children in a group activity. During the second description step, children describe the activity they just experienced in their own words. During the third transcription step, the teacher transcribes the stories as the children tell them. During the final reading step, children read the texts they have created.

Dictated Stories are somewhat different from LEA stories in that they are not necessarily preceded by an activity. In the second language classroom, it is quite common for children to create Dictated Stories that provide personal information or describe objects. For instance, a Dictated Story might describe students' food preferences or a class pet.

LEA stories that are authored by children and portray children's own experiences make excellent reading materials. These stories which are written in children's own language are not only effective because they facilitate text prediction (It is easy for children to make predictions when reading dictated LEA texts, because the texts contain words that the children themselves supplied.) but also because establishing an experiential background for a literacy activity gives children an opportunity to read and write about something they know rather than a situation that is far removed from their experiences.[16]

A class trip, taking care of a class pet, a hands-on project, such as making applesauce or papier-mâché masks, all can serve as bases for LEA activities. Describing a puppet or a stuffed animal is also effective. Virtually every aspect of classroom life, ranging from first introductions to elaborate projects, can be chronicled in Dictated Stories.

The goal behind early LEA activities is to familiarize language learners with their new environments.

- *A Trip Around School.* For instance, new students will benefit from a trip around the school building which will enable them to get to know school staff and various school spaces. After visiting the gym, the cafeteria, and the offices of the principal and the nurse, and after meeting school personnel and taking Polaroid or digital pictures of different locations, students create a story that describes their itinerary (e.g., *We went to the gym. We met Mr. Slaven. Mr. Slaven is a gym teacher*).

- *Building a Model of our Neighborhood.* In another activity, language learners learn to read names of places when building a model of their neighborhood out of recycled materials. Captions of photographs which portray children fashioning buildings out of recycled juice containers and trees out of recycled toilet paper rolls make for reading materials that appeal to young language learners.[17]

Pattern Texts

Shared reading of *pattern books*, such as short stories, fairy tales, poems, or songs that contain a recurrent pattern of words, phrases, or sentences are also effective in the primary level ESL classroom.[18] Pattern books provide for effective shared reading activities, because their repetitive structure scaffolds text prediction. Additionally, pattern books evoke a strong emotional response in young language learners. Children who are beginning to understand English derive pleasure from anticipating and then chanting familiar words.

Pattern books work particularly well if they are published in the big book format and include oversized illustrations that facilitate text comprehension. The language of the books is most beneficial to language learner needs if it is syntactically simple, natural, and reflective of the kind of language that children are likely to hear in their day-to-day communication.[19] It is also important that books address themes and topics that children find relevant and interesting.[20]

Poems and songs that contain a simple, easy to follow, repetitive language pattern can also work as pattern books. Pattern nursery rhymes such as *Five Little Monkeys Jumping on the Bed* [21] or pattern songs such as *The Wheels on the Bus*[22] work particularly well if they are published in the big book format and include attractive illustrations. If a commercial publication is not available, the teacher can create a pattern song book or a pattern poetry book by recording the words of a song or a poem on an oversized experience chart.

Personal narratives created by the teacher make excellent pattern books.[23] Written in simple repetitive language and illustrated with photographs, stick-figure drawings, clip art, or stickers, these books are children's favorite source of reading, because they model language use while helping create a stronger bond between the teacher and the students.

- *Food I Enjoy.* In a lesson that focuses on food preferences, a teacher took some pictures of herself in front of the kitchen table looking happy or miserable depending on whether the pictures portrayed a dish she enjoyed or disliked. She then proceeds to share the photographs with students, encouraged them to draw pictures of their own most and least favorite foods, and to write pattern stories about their own food preferences.

Some of the children's book favorites, such as *A Very Hungry Caterpillar* by Eric Carle; *Brown Bear, Brown Bear, What Do You See?* by Bill Martin[24];

and *Jump, Frog, Jump!* By Robert Kalan[25] are classical examples of pattern books. There also are more recent creations in this genre, such as *Tall*[26] or *Hug*[27] pattern stories about a baby chimpanzee; *Good Night, Gorilla*,[28] a story about animals who followed the zoo keeper from the zoo all the way to his home; *What We Do*,[29] a story about animals and their special skills; *I Went Walking*,[30] a story about animals and colors; and countless others.

Literacy Scaffolds

To help English language learners write in English, second language teachers use literacy scaffolding, which is arguably the most important instructional strategy deployed to foster literacy skills of second language writers.[31] Literacy Scaffolds are text models and patterns provided by the teacher or by more proficient learners, or designed collaboratively by the teacher and students to enable language learners read and write texts beyond their current proficiency level. Among the various literacy scaffolds used in the second language classroom are the following:

- pre-reading questioning;
- sentence patterns;
- pictionaries;
- graphic organizers.

Each scaffold serves a distinct purpose. For instance, when teachers engage learners in the pre-reading discussion of pictures in a picture book, they assure that students will be able to make more accurate predictions when reading a text. When learners create an illustrated pictionary page during a prewriting activity, they are likely to create a piece of writing that is lexically rich and varied.

Literacy Blocks. The scaffolds which work particularly well with beginning level young students are *Literacy Blocks*. Literacy Blocks consist of two elements: the first one is a sentence scaffold or a sentence starter or a stem that assures that students' writing is syntactically well formed. The second part is a word bank or a pictionary page made of nouns, verbs, or adjectives needed to complete the stem; words on the pictionary page are often thematically related. When writing with the help of Literacy Blocks, students finish off the stem with the words on the pictionary page; often writers reiterate the stem, creating a pattern text.

Writing with the help of Literacy Blocks is a little bit like playing a Lego game or building an object out of toy blocks—in both instances, students assemble their creations out of ready pieces. Just as children enjoy fashioning castles, boats, or cars out of prefabricated parts, language learners enjoy playing with pieces of language.

Literacy Blocks are effective when used during the silent or early speech emergence period with the students who still have no control of English syntax and a limited active vocabulary. If students are still at their silent stage, both the stem and the pictionary are provided by the teacher; emergent speakers can create their own Literacy Blocks as part of a teacher-guided brainstorming activity.

First writing activities that rely on the use of Literacy Blocks generally tend to follow up the reading of pattern texts.

- *Good Morning, Classroom!* For instance, after the shared reading of *Good Night, Moon,*[32] a poetic lullaby story bidding good night to things and people surrounding a child about to fall asleep, the teacher can engage students in writing their own illustrated books entitled *Good Morning, Classroom!* In their books, children bid good morning to the people, classroom objects, places, and pieces of furniture which they see in the morning when they come to school. While the more proficient writers can describe their early morning classroom experiences in more detail, emergent writers use Literacy Blocks made of a sentence scaffold *Good morning* and a word bank that lists names of classroom objects (e.g., *desk, chair, pen*). A teacher-created *Good Morning, Classroom!* story makes this activity particularly effective.[33]

As students' proficiency levels grow, they can use increasingly complex target language items modeled by means of Literacy Blocks.

- *My Robot.* For instance, in writing a story that describes their imaginary robots (this activity follows reading of *Sammy and the Robots,*[34] a story of a boy who made a robot to blast his grandma's cold) language learners may use a stem *My robot can ...* and a thematically framed word list or pictionary which contains verbs and verb phrases, such as *talk, drive a car, cook, speak English,* and so forth. The sentence stem is repeated and completed with a different verb or verb phrase. Below is the description of a robot written by an emergent young second language writer.

  My Robot

  My robots name is 0007.
  My robot is strongest.
  My robot can make dinner for me.

My robot can take me to the park.
My robot can play with me.
My robot is the best.

- *Sick Dinosaur.* In another activity, language learners read *How the Dinosaurs Get Well Soon,*[35] a book about the naughty and sickly dinosaur who refuses to follow the doctor's orders. Then as part of a prewriting activity, students create thematically organized dictionaries that highlight language items related to the healthy lifestyle (e.g., *wash your hands, take your vitamins, eat healthy,* etc.) as well as treating a common cold (e.g., *take medicine, get lots of rest, drink lots of juice,* etc.). Next, young language learners assume the parts of doctors. For the role-play to be more enjoyable, students can put up signs which say "Dr. So-and-So" on their desks, wear arm bands which feature red crosses, etcetera. Finally, using authentic looking "Doctor's Recommendations" forms which carry sentence scaffolds such as *To stay healthy you should*_____ or *When you are sick, you should*_____, "doctors" give medical advice to their unruly patient.[36]

- *Snow on the City.* Pattern writing activities enhanced by the use of Literacy Blocks work well if they give children a chance to play with images as well as words. Consider a *Snow on the City* activity which follows the reading of *Snow,* a beautifully illustrated picture book by Uri Shulevitz.[37] The teacher engages students in the shared reading of the book and then encourages children to make their own snow by spraying white paint on a landscape painted against a blue or gray background. Having created their snow-covered landscapes, language learners work with a stem *Snow on the*_____ and a word bank of location words (e.g., *tree, house, fence*) to write short poems about a snow day.

Pattern songs also can serve as a springboard for early literacy activities that integrate the use of Literacy Blocks. Upon singing a song, children can write their own pattern song lyrics. The teacher can record these pattern songs and put them in a big book format or arrange for students to individually record their own work.

- *ESL Students Wore.* For instance, after singing *Mary Wore a Red Dress,*[38] a song that described clothes of different colors, children can create their own pattern song lyrics describing the clothes they wore on a certain day. Supported with the sentence scaffold (e.g., N_____*wore a*_____) and a thematically organized pictionary that depicts articles of wear of various colors (e.g., *white shirt, black sneakers*), children create and sing along songs about their own outfits. This activity is particularly enjoyable if the song created by children is published in a big book format and illustrated with children's photographs.[39]

- *There Was an Old Lady.* Children enjoy pattern songs which have the element of whimsy. For instance, students can write their own version of a song *There Was an Old Lady Who Swallowed a Fly*,[40] telling about other odd objects which were consumed by the song's unfortunate protagonist. The sentence scaffold *There was an old lady who ate_____* and a word bank that lists all kinds of objects can assist students with their writing.

- *The Bug's Journey.* Singing songs and writing pattern stories are effective if they integrate a language experience activity. For instance, after singing a song, *The Itsy Bitsy Spider*,[41] students can participate in an experiential activity by taking a toy animal, such as a puppet spider, on a walk around their classroom, or the school, or even the neighborhood. After discussing the bug's little voyage, students can create its written account. A set of Literacy Blocks made of a sentence scaffold, *My spider went to_____* and a thematically framed word bank which lists names of places will help children create lexically rich, well-formed, and sustained pieces of writing. A plastic spider ring tied to a piece of thread and attached to illustrations of children's stories can complete the project.[42]

- *All Around School.* Writing scaffolded pattern texts is particularly effective if it puts students in the position of observers and recorders of oral language that they hear on a daily basis.[43] For instance, upon listening to the song *The Driver on the Bus*,[44] about the bus that "goes all over town," language learners can write a song that tells about their school. While the song by Raffi tells about the various kinds of things about the bus driver, the bus wheels, its horn, and its motley passenger crew, the school song can incorporate bits of conversations that transpire in the school building. First children brainstorm to record pieces of language one is likely to hear in the school environment. What do teachers say all the time? (Observers of language in one classroom argued that teachers in their school tended to repeat, *Put on your thinking caps!* on a regular basis.) What does the principal say? (*Boys and girls, because of bad weather lunch will be inside* is a phrase which was apparently used somewhat too often by one principal).

After analyzing and recording pieces of language used "all around school," students write their own song lyrics using the following pattern:

The children in the school say, "_____."

The teachers in the school say, "_____."

The principal in the school says, "_____."

The nurse in the school says, "_____."

Once children's proficiency levels grow, the teacher can render scaffolding a little less massive. At this point, Literacy Blocks give way to Sentence Scaffolds, that is sentence starters which enable children to create well-formed sentences. For examples, a repeatedly used Sentence Scaffold, such as *Spring is_____* or *On a rainy day, I_____* or *Vacation is_____* or *First day of school is_____* or *Birthday is_____* will help children create pattern poems about various experiences in their lives.

Sentence Scaffolds sometimes help children produce texts that have fairly sophisticated grammatical structure.

- *If I Were as Big as a Thumb.* For instance, when writing a story after reading *Thumbelina* by Hans Christian Andersen,[45] children could use the following sentence scaffolds for a follow-up writing activity:

  If I were as big as a thumb, I would live in . . .
  If I were as big as a thumb, I would eat . . .
  If I were as big as a thumb, I would sleep in . . .
  If I were as big as a thumb, my pet would be . . .
  If I were as big as a thumb, I would travel . . .[46]

A literacy activity can hardly be successful in the second language classroom unless the community of learners have first worked together to create a Literacy Scaffold for writing (or reading) a particular text. Scaffolded literacy activity created in response to reading poetry are described in the next section of this chapter.

Fixed Form Poetry. While writing activities scaffolded with the help of Literacy Blocks of sentence scaffolds recall a Lego game or playing with toy blocks, creation of *Fixed Form Poetry* recalls playing mad libs. An important subset of literacy scaffolding Fixed Form Poetry is meant to sustain students' writing and to help students produce writing pieces that follow conventions of various literary genres.

A Fixed Form Poetry activity starts with reading a poem that has a distinct organization. After a few readings, children can try to identify the text's structural characteristics. Then the teacher and students work together to create a scaffold or a model that represents the text structure. A Literacy Scaffold used for a Fixed Form Poetry activity can take the form of a graphic organizer; a text with some of its language deleted; or cloze sentences; or any other model which demonstrates text organization.

- *A Counting Poem.* For instance, the text of a classical finger play nursery rhyme below can be a springboard for a Fixed Form Poetry activity.

    One, Two

    One, two,
    Buckle my shoe
    Three, four,
    Knock at the door
    Five, six,
    Pick up sticks,
    Seven, eight,
    Lay them straight
    Nine, ten
    A good fat hen.

By deleting some of the phrases in the text and replacing some others, the teacher can create a Fixed Form Poem scaffold such as the one below:

One, Two. . .

One, two
_____true.
Three, four,
_____store.
Five, six,
_____bricks.
Seven, eight,
_____late.
Nine, ten
_____pen.

Fixed Form poems can be quite elaborate and incorporate sophisticated stylistic devices, such as parallel constructions, or similes, or metaphors.

- *Fall Poem.* This teacher-written poem below models the use of similes.

  Tale of Fall by Deborah Talve

  Autumn leaves.
  They are like feathers floating from above.
  Bare trees.
  They are like skinny people shivering in the wind.
  Rain drops.
  They are like fingers tapping on the window.
  Pumpkins on porches
  Tell the tale of fall.

Upon reading and discussing the poem, the teacher demonstrates to students the things they see in the fall; these can be bare tree branches, dry leaves, jack-o-lanterns, and even rain drops (made with the help of a water spray). The teacher then proceeds to ask children what these objects are like. What is a tree branch like? Does it look like a hand? Or perhaps a comb? What do dry leaves feel like? Would children describe them as "crunchy"? Or maybe "dry"? Once children have brainstormed for similes and epithets, they set about writing their own pieces. Even beginning level young writers can cope with the task if it is supported with the Literacy Scaffold such as the one below:

Tale of Fall

Autumn Leaves.
They _____.
              describe leaves or say what they are like
Bare trees.
They _____.
              describe trees or say what they are like
Rain drops.
They _____.
              describe raindrpops or say what they are like

It is essential that Fixed Form writing scaffold should provide support without stifling children's creativity. There is no rule of thumb as to how much scaffolding should be provided by the teacher and how much text is supplied by the child. It is important to bear in mind, however, that good scaffolds are neither too open-ended nor too tight, and that writing with the help of a good Fixed Form scaffold should feel like a creative game, not a fill-in-the-blanks exercise.

When selecting reading materials for the language classroom, it is a good idea for the teacher to examine the text from the viewpoint of its potential for a follow-up Fixed Form writing activity. Does the text have a distinct pattern of organization? Does it lend itself well to being distilled to a basic grid that can serve as a Fixed Form writing scaffold? Texts that possess these parameters are particularly effective for initiating Fixed Form writing activities.

Valuable guidelines and models for Fixed Form Poetry writing are contained in *Writing Simple Poems: Pattern Poetry for Language Acquisition*.[48]

Entering the Text Activities

As students' proficiency levels grow, pattern-writing activities can become more open-ended. In the second language classroom, response to literature activities work particularly well if students imagine infusing their ownselves in the book and describe what would happen if they found themselves in the situation described in a story, or met one of the story's characters, or owned an unusual, magical object which the story describes. These so-called *Entering the Text* activities work, because they appeal to young language learners' imagination while enabling them to practice target language items which they have encountered when reading their favorite books. Additionally, Entering the Text tasks are effective in the second language classroom, because they can be easily adapted to meet the needs of language learners with various proficiency and literacy levels. While more proficient and more confident writers can create texts with a complex organization, emergent speakers and writers can create texts that are more patterned and more descriptive.[49]

- *My Run-Away Cookie.* For instance, upon reading the classical fairy tale, The *Gingerbread Man*,[50] about an adventurous cookie which ran away from its home, visited faraway places, and encountered various animals before meeting his untimely end in the jaws of a fox, children can create their own fairy tales about the adventures enjoyed by a cookie that ran away from their homes. To further stimulate children's imaginations, after reading the classical version of the fairy tale, teachers can engage children in the shared reading of Robert Egielsky's *Gingerbread Boy*,[51] a modern version of adventures experienced by the mischievous cookie in a United States city. In writing their stories, children try to imagine what would happen if their cookie escaped from an oven or a cookie jar. What kind of cookie would that be? Where would their cookie go? Who did the cookie talk to? While writing the story, less proficient students will use

Literacy Blocks made of a sentence scaffold *My cookie went to_____* or *My cookie saw_____* and a pictionary which lists locations and animals, while others will be willing to take risks and create stories with more elaborate sentence patterns and text organization.

- *My Magic Pot*. Like any other literacy activity intended for language learners, Entering the Text activities are enhanced if children brainstorm to create Literacy Scaffolds during the prewriting stage. Upon reading *Strega Nona*,[52] a story by Tomie de Paola which tells about a witch in possession of a magic pot that could make any amount of pasta, children can write stories describing their own magic cooking utensils while using the sentence scaffolds below:

  My Magic Pot

  My magic pot cooks_____.
  It also cooks_____.
  To start cooking I say, "_____."
  To stop cooking, I say, "_____."

- *Helping Cinderella*. In some of the best Entering the Text activities, children can use their imagination when trying to help book characters resolve their problems. For instance, in a *Helping Cinderella* activity, children pretend that they use imaginary magic powers to help Cinderella. To perform this activity, children first read a book, *What Was It Like before Electricity?*[53] to get a better idea of what doing the house chores was like in the times before modern labor-saving devices became available. Then language learners describe how they would use magic powers to replace antiquated utensils, such as a carpet beater, a washtub, or a fireplace with modern conveniences in order to help Cinderella do the work assigned by her mean stepmother. A thematically framed pictionary that features labor-saving devices will help learners write lexically rich stories when performing this Entering the Text activity.[54]

- *My Friend, the Little Mermaid*. Entering the Text activities work very well when they are part of interdisciplinary thematic units. For instance, a thematic unit on marine life can culminate in the reading aloud of *The Little Mermaid* by Hans Christian Andersen. In a follow-up Entering the Text activity, children can write fantasy stories about their friendship with a mermaid child.

- *My Trip on the Beanstalk*. In another Entering the Text activity which is part of a unit on growing plants, students read *Jack and the Beanstalk*[55] (a story of a boy who went traveling on an enormous magic beanstalk) and then create stories about their own trip on magic beanstalks. To scaffold students' writing, the teacher presents students with a set of specific guidelines. Students are asked to describe how they planted their magic seeds and how they watched them grow. They also are expected to name the places they visited on their magic beanstalks. Last, student list souvenirs they brought home from the journey. To model students' writing, Ellen Craig, ESL teacher who developed this lesson, wrote her own version of the story in which she described her trip to the rain forest that she made on a magic beanstalk. Students particularly enjoyed listening to their teacher's story, because by way of illustration, Ms. Craig brought a suitcase to class which was filled with the gifts from the rain forest.[56]

You can find detailed lesson plans and graphic materials for activities described in this chapter in the "ESL Portfolio" Web site located at http://people.hofstra.edu/faculty/Tatiana_Gordon/ESL/index.html.

Main Points

- Beginning level young language learners benefit from early literacy instruction.
- Pattern texts and Language Experience Activities are some of the top-down instructional strategies that work with young language learners.
- When young language learners use Literacy Blocks to write their own stories, describe imaginary interactions with the book elements when participating in Entering the Text activities, or engage in Fixed Form Poetry writing, literacy activities recall exciting games.
- Literacy Scaffolds sustain children's reading and writing and enable young language learners to produce texts of which students can be proud.

Notes

1. D. Eskey (2005), "Reading in a Second Language." In E. Hinkel (Ed.), *Handbook of research in second language teaching and writing*. Mahwah, NJ: Lawrence Erlbaum, p. 564.

2. K. Goodman (1967), "Reading as a Psycholinguistic Guessing Game." *Journal of the Reading Specialist*, 5, 126–135.

3. P. Johnson (1982), "Effects on Reading Comprehension of Building Background Knowledge." *TESOL Quarterly*, 16(4), 503–516.

4. For example, K. Stanovich (1980), "Toward an Interactive-Compensatory Model of Individual Differences in the Development of Reading Fluency." *Reading Research Quarterly*, 16, 32–71.

5. C. Lee, "Mute in an English-Only World." *New York Times*, April 1996.

6. C. Dixon and D. Nessel (1983), *Language experience approach to reading (and writing)*. Englewood Cliffs, NJ: Alemany Press.

7. D. Eskey (2005), "Reading in a Second Language."

8. For example, J. Hughes (1986), "Inside-Out, Outside-In: Which Approach Is Best for the Second Language Learner?" *Australian Journal of Reading*, 9(3), 159–166.

9. For example, Y. Freeman & D. Freeman (1992), *Whole language for second language learners*. Portsmouth, NH: Heinemann.

10. S. Hudelson (1989), *Write on*. Englewood Cliffs, NJ: Prentice Hall.

11. V. Cook (1981), "Using Authentic Materials in the Classroom." *Modern English Teacher*, 9(2).

12. S. Hudelson (1994), "Literacy Development of Second Language Children." In F. Geneseee (Ed.), *Educating second language children: The whole child, the whole curriculum, the whole community*. New York: Cambridge University Press, pp. 129–158.

13. P. Rigg (1989), "Language Experience Approach: Reading Naturally." In V. Allen & P. Rigg (Eds.), *When they don't all speak English*. Urbana, IL: National Council of Teachers of English.

14. Dixon and Nessel, *Language experience approach to reading (and writing)*.

15. G. Heald-Taylor (1987), *Whole language strategies for ESL primary students*. Toronto: The Ontario Institute for Studies in Education.

16. C. Edelsky (1981), From "JIMOSALSCO" to "7NARANGA SE CALLERON Y EL ARBOL-EST-TRISTE EN LAGRYMAS": "Writing Development in Bilingual Program." In B. Cornell (Ed.), *The writing needs of linguistically different students. The proceedings of a research/practice conference held at SWRL Educational Research and Development*. Los Angeles, CA, June 25–26, 1981, pp. 63–98.

17. Activity developed by Jeanette Tillman, 2006.

18. Heald-Taylor (1987), *Whole language strategies for ESL primary students*.

19. V. Allen (1989), "Literature as a Support to Language Acquisition." In P. Rigg & V. Allen (Eds.), *When they don't all speak English*. Urbana, IL: National Council of Teachers of English, pp. 55–65.

20. P. Rigg (1986), "Reading in ESL: Learning from Kids." In P. Rigg & D.S. Enright (Eds.), *Children and ESL: Integrating perspectives*. Washington, DC: TESOL, pp. 55–92.

21. E. Christelow (1989), *Five little monkeys jumping on the bed*. New York: Clarion Books.

22. *The wheels on the bus* (Raffi songs to read) (1988). New York: Random House.

23. Head-Taylor (1987), *Whole language strategies for ESL primary students*.

24. B. Martin (1996), *Brown Bear, Brown Bear, What do you see?* New York: Henry Holt and Company.

25. R. Kalan (1981), *Jump, Frog, Jump!* New York: Greenwillow Books.

26. J. Alborough (2005), *Tall.* Cambridge, MA: Candlewick Press.

27. J. Alborough (2000), *Hug.* Cambridge, MA: Candlewick Press.

28. P. Rathman (1994), *Good night, gorilla.* New York: Putnam Sons.

29. R. Cartwright (2005), *What we do.* New York: Henry Holt.

30. J. Williams (1990), *I went walking.* San Diego, CA: Red Wagon Books.

31. O. Boyle and S. Peregoy (November 1990), "Literacy Scaffold: Strategies for First-and Second-Language Readers and Writers." *The Reading Teacher*, 44(3), 113–119.

32. M. W. Brown (1991), *Good night, moon.* Harper Festival.

33. Activity developed by Jamie D'Amore, 2005.

34. I. Whybrow (2000), *Sammy and the robots.* New York: Orchard Books.

35. J. Yollen (2003), *How do dinosaurs get well soon.* New York: The Blue Sky Press.

36. Activity developed by Cynthia Reyes, 2005.

37. U. Shulevitz (1998), *Snow.* Farrar Strauss Giroux.

38. M. Peek (1985), *Mary wore her red dress and Henry wore his green sneakers.* New York: Clarion Books.

39. Lesson created by Mary Bridget O'Keefe 2006.

40. S. Taback (1997), *There was an old lady who swallowed a fly.* New York: Viking.

41. I. Trapani (1998), *The itsy bitsy spider.* Watertown, MA: Charlesbridge.

42. Activity created by Michelle Garland, 2005.

43. S. Heath and L. Mangiola (1991), *Children of promise: Literate activity in the linguistically and culturally diverse classroom.* Washington, DC: National Education Association.

44. *The wheels on the bus* (Raffi songs to read).

45. H. C. Andersen (2003), *Thumbelina.* Retold and illustrated by Brian Pinkney. Greenwillow Press.

46. Lesson developed by Kelly McGann, 2003.

47. Poem and lesson by Deborah Talve 2005.

48. V. Holmes and M. Moulton (2001), *Writing simple poems: Pattern poetry for language acquisition.* New York: CUP.

49. T. Gordon (2003), "Romeo and Juliet Come to New York: Integrating Reading and Writing in the ESL Classroom." *TESOL Journal*, 12(3), 49–50.

50. J. Aylesworth (1998), *Gingerbread man.* New York: Scholastic.

51. R. Egielsky (1997), *The Gingerbread boy.* New York: HarperCollins.

52. T. dePaola (1975), *Strega Nona.* New York: Aladdin Publishers.

53. C. Scrace (1995), *What was it like before electricity?* Austin, TX: Steck Vaughn.

54. Lesson created by Nicole Stocker.

55. S. McKay (1997), *Jack and the beanstalk (we both read).* Redwood Coty, CA: Treasure Bay.

56. Activity developed by Ellen Craig, 2005.

CHAPTER 6

Teaching Grammar in the Primary Level ESL Classroom

ESL Student: My mom think that I garbaged my paper but my sister eat it.

Chapter 3 of this book described how young language learners learn grammar, that is, how they learn to form a word, a sentence, or a text correctly. This chapter looks into the questions related to *pedagogical grammar*, the area of research that investigates what second language teachers do to help children apply rules that describe how English words, sentences, and texts are pieced together. The chapter pays special attention to the question of *teachability*. In other words, it attempts to answer the question "Which aspects of English grammar can be taught successfully to young children and which ones are beyond young children's grasp?"

Pedagogical Grammar Revolution—Critique of Traditional Approaches in Grammar Instruction

Because the research conducted in the second half of the twentieth century has revolutionized our understanding of how people learn their first and second language, approaches to grammar instruction have been subject to revision. The Chomskyan revolution, with its hypothesis about the innateness of a grammatical blueprint for language and the corollary hypothesis that teachers are powerless to affect the schedule of children's grammatical maturation, has caused so-called *paradigmatic shifts*, that is, profound changes in the ways linguists theorize and language teachers go about teaching grammar.

While traditional approaches have been called into question, there is no consensus as to the place of grammar in the primary level ESL classroom. On the one hand, scholars whose research draws on Chomskyan ideas suggest that given the developmentally fixed schedule of children's grammatical development, it is futile to teach grammar to young language learners.[1] On the other hand, there are linguists who argue that some attention to the structural properties of language is always beneficial to learners.[2]

Perhaps it is fair to say that an optimal grammar teaching approach does not exist and that language teachers need to take into account a host of factors in order to teach effective pedagogical grammar lessons. Important factors that determine whether and how grammar needs to be taught include children's age, frequency of language lessons, and whether language learners receive *naturalistic input*, that is, whether they are surrounded by native speaking children and adults.

So what about young children who have plenty of opportunities to interact with native speakers? Are there grammar lessons that work with that group of students? Is it possible to teach young second language learners to say *Where did she go?* and not *Where she go?* Or *I don't like carrots* and not *I no like carrots.* And if these lessons are unlikely to have an impact on young children, then what kind of grammar lessons are effective?

Sometimes, to appreciate which approaches work in the classroom, one needs to see which ones do not. Thus, before discussing grammar-teaching approaches that seem to be helpful in working with young children, it might be a good idea to say a few words about the ones that have been demonstrated to be ineffective.

Lack of Impact of Premature Grammar Instruction. There is a good reason to believe that pedagogical grammar lessons do not have an impact on young children's morphological and syntactic maturation if these lessons are delivered too early, at a developmental stage when students are not ready to master a new form. No matter how much time and effort the teacher might devote to eradicating an error, students who are not developmentally ripe to master auxiliaries will not stop saying *What do you doing?* and the ones who are not ready to master verb endings will go on saying *He give me sticker.*

When reading an earlier section of this book, you became familiar with studies suggesting that young children's grammar learning follows a fixed order. For instance, the ending *-ing* is learned before the ending *-ed*. There is evidence that it is only if learners are on the developmental brink of mastering a form, only if they are about to learn how to use an ending or correct word order on their own, do grammar lessons work.

That grammar lessons can speed up the acquisition process but are powerless to change the sequence in which grammar items are learned has been demonstrated by an interesting study. The study involved seven- to nine-year-old Italian-speaking children who were given lessons in using correct word order in German sentences. The study found that children benefited from grammar lessons only if they had begun to use the form in question correctly. However, children who were at an earlier language learning stage derived no benefit from grammar instruction.[3] Given this evidence, linguists say that the schedule of children's grammatical development is *impervious to instruction*.

Lack of Impact of Bottom-up Approaches to Pedagogical Grammar. Most scholars agree that there is another approach that does not provide instructional benefits in working with young children. It is the so-called *bottom-up* approach. When implementing this approach, educators start with "the bottom," the smallest elements of language, such as endings or auxiliaries. The teacher points out this small bit of language to students, explains the rule that describes its use, and proceeds to engage students in the manipulation of this small bit of language in isolation from context. The hope is that eventually students will be able to move up from the bottom language level and use the grammatical item in question in own sentences and texts. When performing typical bottom-up grammar activities, teachers encourage children to practice the use of a correct form by mimicking, drilling, and repeating the model or by performing grammatical transformations. In a transformational lesson, the teacher provides a language pattern (e.g., *One hand* or *I walk to school every day*) and students respond to a physical or pictorial prompt by performing a necessary transformation (e.g., *Two hands* or *I walked to school yesterday*). In another typical bottom-up lesson, students chant a correct form of the verb or noun (e.g., *He IS reading. They ARE reading*).

There is a problem with these bottom-up lessons. The purpose behind the bottom-up grammar activities is to eradicate grammatical errors. It seems, however, that language learners' ability to formulate a grammatical rule and apply this rule within a controlled activity (*explicit knowledge of grammar*) does not translate into grammatical accuracy when learners speak spontaneously (*implicit knowledge*). Even when children perform grammar exercises correctly or repeat patterns modeled by the teacher, they do not use these forms in spontaneous speech.[4]

A study conducted in New Zealand has demonstrated that bottom-up pedagogical grammar approaches lack instructional impact. The researcher used drills to teach children aged 11 to 15 the use of negation and questions. The study demonstrated that whether children did or did not use grammar drills made no difference in their grammar learning.[5]

Another scholar from New Zealand, Warwick Elley,[6] reviewed the studies that compared those instructional programs using traditional grammar instruction to the ones that avoid grammar lessons and rely on rich exposure to literature (i.e., the so-called *book flood* programs). All the studies reviewed by Elley reached the same conclusion: rich, meaningful reading and speaking experiences are more effective than are traditional, bottom-up isolated grammar lessons.

Lack of Impact from Recasting. Many language teachers practice so-called *recasting* or repeating—with a correction—a malformed word, phrase, or sentence used by a student. Often when doing recasting, teachers model the correct form through questioning. For instance if a child says. *"He tooked my sticker!"* the teacher might model correct use by saying, *"He took your stickers, right?"* Essentially, recasting relies on imitation. When teachers use this form of feedback, children are expected to mechanically reproduce a correct form provided by the teacher.

Of course, recasting is not an isolated grammar drill. In recasting activities, children are asked to use a correct form within the context of meaningful communication. Even so, researchers report that recasting does not seem to work. This commonly used strategy does not tend to effect change in young children's speech.[7] When recasting has been provided, children often simply ignore a correct form and do not make a correction. For instance, after the teacher has said *"He took your sticker, right?"* The child might say, *"Yeah! *He tooked it!"*

Why is it that children do not respond to teachers' corrective feedback? Why is it that proficiency in performing exercises (of the *one hand – two hands* variety) or recasting provided by the teacher does not result in grammatical proficiency? Nativists argue that lack of impact of grammar instruction has to do with the severe developmental constraints, a built-in syllabus that determines what children can or cannot learn.

Other researchers argue that the lack of impact of bottom-up grammar lessons in the early childhood level ESL classroom has to do with more general, cognitive developmental constraints, that is children's tendency to focus on the meaning of an utterance, not its form. While adults may agonize over the fact that they have made an error or have used an improper grammatical pattern, young children are much more likely to give all of their attention to getting the message across and are not prone to monitoring their output for grammatical accuracy. Children's tendency to focus on meaning is evident by the following conversation reported in a study of first language development:

Child: Nobody don't like me.
Mother: No, say "Nobody likes me."
Child: Nobody don't like me.
(eight repetitions of this dialogue)
Mother: No. Now listen carefully; say "Nobody likes me."
Child: Oh! Nobody don't likes me! [8]

Grammaticality judgment in children. Maybe because of a grammar syllabus prewired into their brain or maybe because of some more general developmental constraints, children have a limited ability to make *grammaticality judgments,* that is, determine whether a phrase or a sentence is correct or malformed. Researchers presented English-speaking children with a number of sentences, some of which were grammatically malformed while others described implausible situations. Upon being presented with sentence stimuli, children were given the following instructions: "Tell me if these sentences are good or if they are silly." Researchers found that 5-year-olds made some striking judgments about sentences. Some of them judged plausibility of sentences a little too harshly. For example, *"The men wait for the bus"* was rejected by some 5-year-old suburbanites on grounds that only children wait for busses. *The color green frightens George* was rejected on grounds that "green can't stand up and go 'Boo!'"[9] At the same time when researchers presented 5-year-olds with grammatically malformed sentences, such as *Claire and Eleanor is a sister* or *Morning makes the sun to shine,* violations of syntax went unnoticed. Inability to distinguish between correct and incorrect sentences had everything to do with children's age. In observing older children, researchers discovered that their grammaticality judgments were more consistent and more accurate than those of younger children.[10]

A similar inverse relation between age and accuracy of grammaticality judgments was observed in second language learners. A study analyzed *repairs* (self-corrections) and pauses in adult and children speech; researchers' premise was that repairs and pauses were an indication of the speaker's likelihood to monitor own speech.[11] The study found that "children made fewer corrections to morphology and syntax but made more corrections to the meaning of entire utterances than the adults [*sic*]"[12] For instance, when speaking English in informal settings, adults in the study made a total of 65 errors in morphology and corrected 13 of these, while children made twice as many errors and corrected only 5. Notably, children in the study were 12 years of age or younger. It stands to reason to hypothesize that young children are even less likely to monitor their own speech for accuracy.

There is also anecdotal evidence of the limited impact of recasting. An educator tells a story of a little girl who left her coat in her classroom when leaving for home. The child was quick to realize her mistake and went back to the classroom where she spotted her coat next to the teacher. "*This coat is mines," said the little girl. "It's MINE" said the teacher. "*It is MINES" remonstrated the girl. This interesting and comical example of the ineffective use of recasting by an adult[13] provides evidence that the child's primary focus is on meaning, not the form of a conversational exchange.

And yet, the fact that young language learners are unlikely to benefit from premature grammar lessons or isolated bottom-up grammar lessons or recasting does not mean that grammar teaching should be forever abandoned in the second language classroom intended for young children. Teachers can adapt pedagogical grammar lessons to meet the needs of all language learners, irrespective of their age or the context of instruction.

Top-down (Holistic) Approaches in Pedagogical Grammar

An alternative to the bottom-up mode of teaching grammar is a *top-down* (holistic) approach. The starting point of a top-down grammar lesson is the whole text, not its discrete individual elements. As the lesson unfolds, the teacher and students discuss the ways in which the structural elements of the oral or written text used by learners need to be tweaked or adjusted to get the message across more effectively. In a lesson that moves from the whole text (the top) to text elements (the bottom), grammatical phenomena such as word endings, or word order, or text organization do get analyzed, but only in as much as the analysis helps language users make the message more comprehensible or get the message across. Unlike bottom-up lessons which are often based on an artificial presumption about what grammar rules students need to master, top-down lessons address students' needs and are meant to enhance learners' communicative proficiency. Various types of top-down lessons discussed below are meant to help young language learners use language more effectively.

Task-Based Lessons

Task-based grammar lessons are a subset of top-down lessons that has been given a lot of attention lately. It is helpful to start the discussion of the task-based lessons with an example. Consider the lesson where the teacher and her students role-play shopping for groceries. Some children perform the parts of salespersons, others are customers. For the role-play to be more valuable instructionally, as well as more enjoyable and real life like, it is important that the "customers" make their purchasing request in a courteous, proper manner and that "salespeople" reply accordingly. The role-play repertoire might include phrases such as *Can I have a pound of cheese?* or *Is it cash or charge?* In another role-play, in the course of which children role-play a telephone conversation, children may need to use phrases such as *Could I speak to ...?* or *Would you like to leave a message?*

When implementing role-play activities similar to the ones described above, the teacher may choose to emphasize that proper use of a particular language form is associated with certain language tasks performed in certain situations. Using the verb form *could* renders a request more polite. Inverted word order (e.g., *Could you give me a pound of cheese?*) accounts for more polite utterance than does the direct word order (e.g., *Give me a pound of cheese!*).

When these discussions take place, teaching of grammatical structures (the form) is tightly intertwined with the teaching of the meaning of an utterance (its semantics) and the way in which the utterance is used (the function of an utterance).[14]

Lessons that integrate the structural and semantic properties of language and are placed in real life-like communicative contexts exemplify the task-based approach to teaching grammar recommended by leading experts in pedagogical grammar. Researchers suggest that in implementing task-based grammar lessons, the teacher need not get frustrated when young ESL students are unable to produce target forms immediately. [15] For instance, some "customers" at the "store" will make their request by simply saying *"Gimme cheese!"* while others will be able to produce the complete *"Can I have some cheese?"* utterance. Researchers suggests that students be given a choice as to the form they will use, but also be reminded that using certain grammatical forms is associated with certain meaning. The teacher will explain that there are forms that are more polite, more likely to get people's attention, or more appropriate for certain situations than are some other forms.

Teaching Grammar in Relation to Writing

Another approach to teaching grammar holds that grammar lessons are effective when they are integrated with the teaching of writing. There are a number of reasons why grammar and writing lessons make a good match. First of all, written speech is different from oral speech in that it is not spontaneous. When children write, they can stop and plan their utterances. Second and even more importantly, written speech is unlike oral speech in that it contains inherent provisions for monitoring. Unlike speakers, writers have an option of going back to the text that they just produced; they can slowly review the text and edit it for grammatical accuracy. Last but not least, when implementing writing activities, teachers can utilize scaffolds or models that children can refer to in order to assure greater grammatical accuracy of their written pieces.[16]

For instance, when writing about an imaginary trip to another state or land, students are likely to experience difficulty with the use of the past tense of the verbs *go*, *see*, *like*, and others. The scaffold below will assure young learners' use of target-like forms.

My Trip to Alaska

I went to_____.
I saw_____.
I liked_____.

Notably, the emphasis of the grammar lessons taught in conjunction with teaching writing shifts. These lessons do not only focus on the eradication of morphological and syntactic errors that are commonly found in the output of young language learners. Rather, lessons taught as part of writing activities focus on conventions of writing, such as basic rules of punctuation, capitalization, text organization, or spelling. Literacy Scaffolds used as part of these lessons model the use of written language.

Story-Based Grammar Instruction

A strategy that can be used to combine teaching of writing with grammar instruction is the *story-based grammar instruction*. An interesting innovation in the field of pedagogical grammar, this strategy was developed by foreign language teaching methodologists[17]; it can be easily adapted to the primary level ESL classroom.

The story-based grammar lesson consists of four stages—*Presentation, Attention, Co-construction,* and *Extension.* During the Presentation stage, the teacher foreshadows the grammar lesson—that is, provides students with exposure to a target language grammatical item within a meaningful written context. A target grammatical item may be presented in the context of a story, a poem, a riddle, or a picture caption that highlights a grammatical phenomenon in a particularly striking and prominent way.

- *My Name.* For instance, in the *My Name* lesson, a short, teacher-created, clip art illustrated poem below serves to illustrate the use of capitalization. After reading the poem aloud, students work on deducing the rule which explains why certain words are and some others are not capitalized.

  My Name

  My name is Penny. I have a penny.
  My name is Cat. I have a cat.
  My name is Robin. I have a robin.
  My name is Mike. I have a mike.
  My name is Bridge. I am walking on the bridge.

- *Choosing Between the Words "Her" and "His."* Another teacher-created text focuses on the use of pronouns *her* and *his.* Since language learners often find distinguishing between these two words challenging, a language teacher guides students in creating a story that highlights the use of the confusables while discussing students' color preferences. Each page in the book features a photograph of a student who is holding a sheet of colored paper. The captions in the photo-illustrated pattern book run as follows:

  Our Favorite Colors

  This is Miguel. His favorite color is green.
  This is Cynthia. Her favorite color is purple.
  This is Shirley. Her favorite color is yellow.
  This is Marek. His favorite color is red.

During the *Presentation* stage, the emphasis is on understanding an utterance, not analyzing its form. Presentation activities are effective when the text used by the teacher is engaging and appealing. When identifying texts for story-based lesson intended for young learners, it is helpful to use those that exemplify application of the rules that young children find particularly challenging when they write in English.

The purpose behind the *Attention* stage is to further sensitize learners to a target grammatical item—to give students a better feel for it. During this stage, the teacher provides students with multiple exposures to a target grammar point by encouraging children to read the text in chorus or by engaging children in role-play reading or similar attention-getting activity. Often in the attention-getting activity, the teacher will highlight the focal point of the lessons graphically. For instance, after reading the texts above, students can zero in on grammatical items by creating a colorful pictionary of homonymous words (e.g., *Penny, penny, Robin, robin,* etc). The teacher can also write the patterns that constitute the focal point of the lesson on sentence strips or highlight them with colorful markers.

The *Co-construction* stage is a central, crucially important element of the story-based grammar lesson. During this stage, the teacher encourages students to try to formulate in their own words the rule that accounts for a given grammatical phenomenon. Some of the questions related to word, sentence, and text grammar that young learners can investigate are as follows: *Why do some words begin with the letters that are bigger than other letters? Why are some words separated by dots? Why does the story say "one hand" but "two hand_S_"? What is the difference between "wAnt" and "wEnt"?*

It is essential that during the *Co-construction* activity, the teacher should not provide the answers. The questions above are meant to help children build their own understanding of a grammar rule. Encouraging children to formulate a grammatical rule in their own words is of critical importance. If the teacher does not provide the rule, if children construct their own knowledge of a grammatical element, they are more likely to understand that rule in greater depth. Children's unorthodox formulations of grammar rules can be quite insightful. For instance, when a teacher demonstrated the use of periods by making dramatic pauses when reading the text, students commented as follows: *"You put dots [periods] when you rest and go like that Ah-h-h."* Once children have done their best to formulate a grammar rule that describes a grammatical element, the teacher proceeds to recast children's insights in conventional language and familiarize children with the terminology in common use. For instance, the teacher may say that "big letters" are called "capital letters," that a tiny line before the letter 's is called "the apostrophe," and that a sign that looks like a little coat hanger is called a "question mark."

The final stage of the story-based approach is called *Extension*. During that stage, children write their own stories applying the rules they have just deduced. The purpose behind the Extension stage is to reinforce mastery of a grammatical item. When engaging in an Extension activity, children can write their stories independently or coauthor them with a partner. Just as other literacy activities used with language learners, story-based grammar lessons work the best if they incorporate Literacy Scaffolds which give children a little extra support with their writing. The usual array of Literacy Scaffolds, such as Literacy Blocks, and Sentence Scaffolds of Fixed Form poems are included in grammar activities.

For instance, the scaffold below helps students create a pattern book which describes favorite colors of their family members while using the correct form of the pronouns *his* and *her*:

This is my_____ . _____ favorite color is _____ .

          family member   his/her   color

The affective parameters of story-based lessons are of great importance. Even though story-based lessons focus on language rules, they need not be tedious. Stories selected for story-based lessons should be exciting and engaging. The Co-construction activity is effective if all children are excited about exploring the grammatical element and the rule that describes its use. By referring to the rule as a "puzzle" or a "mystery," the teacher can stir children's enthusiasm about finding out the pattern that describes language use.

To implement the story-based approach, it is essential to develop a collection of nursery rhymes, poems, limericks, and short stories that prominently illustrate various grammatical phenomena. Story-based lessons can be based on texts written by language teachers, excerpts from trade books, or on environmental print.

- *My Pet and I.* For instance, a teacher-created story uses photographs and captions to tell about the teacher's pet while simultaneously highlighting the use of the homonyms *to*, *two*, and *too*.

    Patches and I by Regina Paquette

    This is me. And this is Patches.
    When I go to the park, Patches goes to the park too.
    That makes two of us.
    When I go to the store, Patches goes to the store too.
    That makes two of us.
    When I go to bed, Patches goes to bed too.
    That makes two of us.

The riddle that students try to solve in conjunction with reading this piece is quite challenging. What is the difference between the three homonyms?

Once students have come up with the rule, they write their own pattern stories that tell about their pets, or their stuffed toys, or even their shadows. A thematically framed pictionary that portrays various locations and a sentence scaffold completes this activity.[18]

- *Whose Belongings?* Below is an example of another text that is used for the presentation of a grammatical item. In this case, the traditional folk nursery rhyme is accompanied by finger play and is used to highlight the use of the apostrophe

> These are mother's knives and forks. (*Fingers spread out*)
> This is father's table. (*Fingers touch and bend to show a table*)
> This is sister's looking glass. (*Index fingers and thumbs form a circle*)
> This is baby's cradle. (*Arms put together to show a cradle*)

Once the teacher records the poem and engages students in the analysis of the use of the apostrophe, students write similar stories about their family members and their possessions.

- *Whose Hand?* In another lesson that focuses on the use of the apostrophe, the teacher guides her students in putting together a book illustrated with the outlines of children's hands. During the Presentation stage of the activity, each child traces his or her hand. This collection of pictures is made into an album that children examine with the teacher to try to guess whose hand is featured in the picture. While children are making their guesses, the teacher provides each picture with the caption (e.g., *This is Diego's hand. This is Jasmine's hand*). During the Attention stage, children read their book several times. When children are able to read their book with sufficient confidence, the teacher proceeds to ask the children a battery of Coconstruction questions:

> *Teacher*: Look at the funny way we wrote down your names.

> Did we do something wrong?

> Look! After each name, we placed a little funny sign and a letter -*s*? Do you usually write your name with that little sign and a letter -*s* at the end, Diego?

What about you, Jasmine?

We never write your names this way. Why did we do it differently this time?

Only after the children have formulated the rule for the use of the possessive case in their own words (e.g., *Because it's mines! Because the hand is mines!*), the teacher proceeds to recast their insights into more conventional language and explains that the little sign is called "the apostrophe" and that the letter -*s* use is used to indicate possession. During the final Creative Participation stage of the lesson, children put together their own books that feature hands of their family members.

- *I Spy.* Consider another story-based grammar activity that focuses on the use of prepositions. This time, students learn about the meaning of prepositions by reading and discussing the teacher-created and teacher-illustrated poem below.

  I Spy by Kellie McGann

  I eat ice cream, and you take a drink.
  I spy a frog inside of the sink.

  I draw a house, and you paint it red.
  I spy a kitten next to the bed.

  I brush my teeth, and you brush your hair.
  I spy a puppy on top of the chair.

  I feed your fish, and you feed your bug.
  I spy a lizard under the rug.

  We have fun—of this I am certain.
  I spy a star behind the curtain.

First, children read the poem and study the pictures. During the Attention stage of the activity, the teacher places small toys in various positions in relation to a toy sink, a bed, a chair, a rug, and a curtain, and recites the first two lines of each stanza, while children respond in chorus with rhyming sentences that integrate prepositions.

During the Co-construction stage, the teacher places a list of prepositions on the blackboard and encourages students to determine what these words have in common. In what way are they alike? After students have responded that the words on the board say where things are, the teacher introduces the term "prepositions," and engages learners in writing and illustrating their own preposition poems.

The scaffold below and a pictionary page that features various objects to be found in the room facilitate the Extension writing activity:

I Spy

I eat ice cream, and you take a drink.
I spy a _____ _____ sink.
              object   preposition

I draw a house, and you paint it red.
I spy a _____ _____ sink, etc.[19]
              object   preposition

- *Grammar Hunt.* Another lesson that focuses on the use of the auxiliary verb *don't* is based on the use of environmental print. The lesson starts when the teacher demonstrates to her students a flashcard that features the verb. After sight-reading the word and discussing the contexts in which children may have encountered the auxiliary, the teacher takes her students on a grammar hunt[20] during which students look for the auxiliary verb *don't* in the environment. To facilitate the search, each member of the expedition carries a flashcard emblazoned with the verb *don't*. Students who attend school in the city or in the suburbs are likely to spot the auxiliary as part of the DON'T WALK street signs. This discovery can lead to a discussion of the rules of street crossing. After discussing the meaning and the use of the auxiliary *don't*, children create mini-books that feature WALK and DON'T WALK signs, and portray pedestrians either crossing the street or waiting to cross.

The story-based lessons should not be used as stand-alone activities; rather they need to be integrated with the broader curriculum. Comparing and contrasting natural phenomena could invite a lesson on the use of superlatives; writing memoirs goes hand-in-hand with the use of the past tense; a lesson on body parts provides a context for discussing the difference between the singular and the plural forms of noun.

Mini-Lessons

There is another type of grammar lesson which is integrated with teaching writing. *Mini-lessons* are need-based, that is, they are taught when the teacher observes her students lack a grammatical skill needed for completing a writing task. Often, mini-lessons will be implemented on an individual basis if a teacher observes one of the students is experiencing difficulty with a particular aspect of target-language grammar.[21]

Just as task-based and story-based grammar lessons, mini-lessons are effective because they put a grammar lesson in the context of real-life communication. Moreover, mini-lessons address the immediate communicative needs of language learners.

Mini-lessons can focus on the basic rules of morphology (word structure), syntax (sentence structure), and text grammar (text structure). For instance, a mini-lesson intended for young language learners can focus on common confusables, such as *want* and *went*, or the use of basic punctuation marks, or basic principles of text organization.

Focus on Form

At this point, it is important to make a cautionary note regarding the instructional benefit of task-based, story-based, and grammar mini-lessons. It is worth noting that the impact of these instructional approaches may not be immediately apparent in young learner output. In fact in this respect, top-down lessons are not much different from bottom-up lessons. For quite a long time, the teacher may observe students producing well-formed target structures within controlled oral task-based and written story-based activities and then lapse into the use of malformed patterns when speaking and writing spontaneously. This delay of grammatical maturation need not be discouraging. The thing is that the lessons described above are by no means meant to eradicate errors once and forever. Rather, these lessons give the teacher and students an opportunity to have an interesting, intellectually rich conversation about the fact that language use is a rule-governed activity and about enhancing communication by following the rules of language use. When participating in the discussion of grammatical phenomena, children come to the realization that just as there are rules in the classroom that tell them and the teacher how to act and how not to act, there are rules that prescribe the best way to put together a word, a sentence, a story, or a poem.

This focus on grammar consciousness-raising as the emphasis of pedagogical grammar lessons is consistent with the recommendations of modern theorists. Researchers argue that the purpose of grammar lessons is not to eradicate errors but to provide a *focus on form*, that is, the instructional experiences that help students become more aware of the formal properties of language.[22] As the result of focus on form-learning experiences, children will become more conscious of the structural parameters of their own oral and written output.[23]

In conclusion, it should be noted that teaching grammar does not always need to serve the purely practical purpose of fostering morphological and syntactic maturation of young students. Some linguists[24] argue that grammar may and needs to be taught without expecting any practical gain, for pure intellectual enjoyment. If a pedagogical grammar lesson feels like a game, it will be savored even by very young learners. Engaging story-based grammar activities and accompanying graphic materials can be found in the "ESL Portfolio" Web site located at http://people.hofstra.edu/faculty/Tatiana_Gordon/ESL/index.html.

Main Points

- Maybe because children's morphological and syntactic maturation is developmentally determined and follows a built-in syllabus, teaching grammar prematurel has no instructional value for young second language learners.

- Teaching conventions of writing benefits young language learners, because unlike speaking, writing is not a spontaneous activity.

- Grammar lessons that focus on conventions of writing provide a focus on form and may not yield immediate results.

- Children should be encouraged to formulate rules of written language on their own.

Notes

1. For example, H. Dulay and M. Burt (1973), "Should We Teach Children Syntax?" *Language Learning*, 23(2), 245–258.

2. For example, M. Long (1991), "Focus on Form: A Design Feature in Language Teaching Methodology." In K. de Bot, R. Ginsberg, and C. Kramsch (Eds.), *Foreign language research in cross-cultural perspective*. Amsterdam, the Netherlands: John Benjamins, pp. 39–52.

3. M. Pienemann (1984), "Psychological Constraints on the Teachability of Languages." *Studies in Second Language Acquisition*, 6(2), 186–214.

4. B. Schwartz (1993), "On Explicit and Negative Data Effecting and Affecting Competence and Linguistic Behavior." *Studies in Second Language Acquisition*, 15, 147–163.

5. R. Ellis (1984), "Can Syntax Be Taught? A Study of the Effects of Formal Instruction on the Acquisition of WH Questions by Children." *Applied Linguistics*, 5(2), 138–155.

6. W. Elley (1991), "Acquiring Literacy in a Second Language: The Effect of Book-Based Programs." *Language Learning*, 41(3), 375–411.

7. R. Lyster and L. Ranta (1997), "Corrective Feedback and Learner Uptake: Negotiation of Forms in Communicative Classrooms." *Studies in Second Language Acquisition*, 19, 37–66.

8. C. Cazden (1972), *Child language and education.* New York: Holt, Rinehart and Winston, p. 92.

9. H. Gleitman and L. Gleitman (1979), "Language Use and Language Judgment." In C. Fillmore, D. Kempler, and W. S-Y. Wang (Eds.), *Individual differences in language ability and language behavior.* New York: Academic Press, p. 111.

10. L. R. Gleitman, H. Gleitman, and E. Shipley (1972), "The Emergence of the Child as Grammarian." *Cognition*, 1, 137–164; M. Shatz (1972), Semantic and Syntactic Factors in Children's Judgement of Sentences." Unpublished manuscript, University of Pennsylvania. Cited in Gletiman and Gleitman (1979), "Language Use and Language Judgement," pp. 103–126.

11. A. Fathman and L. Precup (1983), "Influences of Age and Setting on Second Language Oral Proficiency." In D. Krashen and R. Scarcella (Eds.), *Issues in second language research.* Rowley, MA: Newbury House Publishers, pp. 151–161.

12. Ibid., p. 154.

13. Doris Fromberg, personal communication, 2002.

14. M. Celce-Murcia (2002), "Why It Makes Sense to Teach Grammar in Context and Through Discourse." In E. Hinkel and S. Fotos (Eds.), *New perspectives on grammar teaching in second language classrooms.* Mahwah, NJ: Lawrence Erlbaum Associates, pp. 119–133.

15. D. Larsen-Freeman (2002), "The Grammar of Choice." In E. Hinkel and S. Fotos (Eds.), *New perspectives on grammar teaching in second language classrooms.* Mahwah, NJ: Lawrence Erlbaum Associates, pp. 103–118.

16. T. Gordon and S. Harshbarger (2002), "The Questions of Grammar: The Place of Grammar in Second Language Teacher Education." In D. Liu and P. Master (Eds.), *Grammar teaching in teacher education.* Alexandria, VA: TESOL.

17. B. Adair-Hauk and R. Donato (2002), "The PACE Model—Actualizing the Standards Through Storytelling: '*Le bras, la jambe et le ventre.*'" *French Review*, 76(2), 278–296.

18. Story and activity by Regina Paquette, 2003.

19. Poem and activity by Kelly McGann, 2002.

20. R. Wong (2005), "Hunting for Grammar in the Real World." Demonstration presented at the 39th *Annual TESOL Convention.* San Antonio, TX.

21. For example, N. Atwell (1987), *In the middle: Writing, reading, and learning with adolescents.* Portsmouth, NH: Heinemann, and L. Calkins (1994), *The art of teaching writing.* Portsmouth, NH: Heinemann.

22. M. Long (1991), "Focus on Form: A Design Feature in Language Teaching Methodology." In K. de Bot, R. Ginsberg, and C. Kramsch (Eds.), *Foreign language research in cross-cultural perspective.* Amsterdam, the Netherlands: John Benjamins, pp. 39–52.

23. W. Rutherford and M. S. Smith (1988), "Consciousness Raising and Universal Grammar." In W. Rutherford and M.S. Smith (Eds.), *Grammar and second language teaching: A book of readings.* New York: Newbury House Publishers, pp. 107–116.

24. For example, N. Postman and C. Weingartner (1966), *Linguistics: A revolution in teaching.* New York: Dell.

CHAPTER 7

Content-Based Second Language Teaching in Primary Grades

ESL Teacher (after reading a book which describes Abraham Lincoln's oratorial skill): Children, why did people enjoy listening to Abraham Lincoln?
ESL Student: Because they wanted to learn English!!

After sometime (ranging from half a year to approximately a year), young language learners are able to sustain a basic conversation in English. They also begin to read and write in a second language. What can the language teacher do now? What instructional focus is most beneficial for that group of students?

Modern second language education experts suggest that intermediate level language learners benefit most from lessons that combine language teaching with teaching of social and natural sciences. Strategies of teaching sophisticated concepts from these subject areas to young language learners are discussed in the chapter below.

Benefits and Challenges of Teaching Content to Language Learners

Sometimes, second language teachers in their efforts to challenge intermediate level students, choose to focus on teaching less common, unusual words. When this happens, students study extended lists of words for body parts, or articles of wear, or pieces of furniture and participate in some kind of labeling activities. Sure enough intermediate level language learners are probably not familiar with the words, such as *cheekbone* or *knuckle*, *parka* or *slush*. Teaching these and similar target language items, however, is not the optimal course of action and may in fact result in the loss of precious instructional time. While expanding students' word power is important, research suggests that there are alternative instructional models that are infinitely more beneficial to language learners. What are those effective teaching models?

When working with students who are able to sustain a basic conversation and understand everyday language, the teacher is in the position to move instruction into a cognitively stimulating domain. Children who have mastered beginning level English skills are ready for the so-called *content-based* lessons. Content-based ESL instruction (CBI) uses academic content from subject areas, such as social studies, mathematics, or science to teach a second language. The focus of content-based instruction is thus on academic language, not the language of daily communication.

At first glance, teaching sophisticated concepts from natural and social sciences domains to students who have not mastered English may seem counterintuitive. Modern TESOL (Teacher of English to Speakers of Other Language) curriculum experts agree, however, that the CBI approach is highly effective. Studies suggest that this approach yields significant gains *both* in students' content learning and in language development.[1] A linguist and an ESL teacher, David Eskey, who is renowned for his work on linking theory and practice in the field of TESOL went so far as to say that he and his colleagues "are more convinced than ever that this approach to language teaching [CBI] is the best one that has been developed so far."[2]

Why does teaching languages through content work? Why does it benefit children? Consider first language learning. Children do not learn their first language by studying word lists and then practicing using words. Rather, first language development is fostered when young children explore the world and discuss these explorations with adults and older peers. Similar processes of simultaneous world and language discovery take place in the content-based ESL classroom.

There is another reason to combine content teaching and language teaching. It is important to bear in mind that there exists profound difference between the language of daily communication and the language of science. While children learn everyday words incidentally, when interacting with adults and peers, they only master science words when getting help from adults. Research suggests that unlike the words of daily interaction, science or social science concepts are not picked as the result of mere exposure.[3] Thus, whether the child is going to become proficient in the language of natural and social sciences depends almost exclusively on the child's school experience.

Additionally, content-based instruction offers a vitally important benefit to immigrant children by laying a foundation for their academic success in American schools. Research suggests that children take as many as seven years to develop academic language skills in a second language.[4] If academic language teaching starts in the early grades, language learners are more likely to do well when they progress to upper levels of education.

An important rationale for implementing content-based instruction can be found in language development theory espoused by a renowned cognitive psychologist, Lev Vygotsky. Vygotsky's own work and numerous studies by his followers argue that if curricula focus on abstract language, they give a powerful boost to children's language development. Systemic and conscious examination of academic language is central to Vygotskian developmental model.[5] The idea that language teaching is most beneficial if it is based on content teaching is thus congruent with Vygotsky's model of language development.

While content-based language teaching benefits children, it is hard to implement. Dearth of content-based instructional materials intended for young learners, the need to account for children's disparate proficiency levels, and educational background make content-based lessons difficult to teach. The greatest difficulty, however, has to do with the fact that academic language is context reduced and in that regard profoundly different from the language of everyday life.[6] Everyday target language phrases such as *Let's do jumping jacks! I have a paper cut! Not fair! He is bothering me!* are easily understood and learned by students. Children can infer the meaning of these phrases from situational contexts.

In contrast, the context immediately available in the classroom cannot clarify referents of concepts such as *seasons* or *fossil*, *mammal* or *hibernation*. Children need elaborate verbal explanations to grasp the meaning of abstract academic language. Needless to say, these kinds of sophisticated explanations can hardly be used with young language learners who are just beginning to master English.

Given that the use of complex explanatory language is not feasible, language teachers deal with the challenge of teaching academic language by designing and implementing experiential activities. These activities provide children with teacher-created contextual clues rendering the meaning of abstract language clear and input comprehensible.[7] The sections that follow include examples of such activities.

Experiential Content-Based Activities

Role-plays

A powerful means of teaching language through content are role-plays.[8] Role-plays are game-like reenactments by children of various adult roles and functions. Role-plays can also be dramatic reenactments of historical events or pieces of literature.

There are several important reasons why role-plays are effective when used with young language learners. First of all, these activities can be described as virtual visual materials that evolve in real time. Role-plays enable children to envision and experience occurrences and contexts that are removed from their day-to-day lives. Often where a lengthy explanation would be needed to clarify the meaning of a target language item, a dramatic skit captures it instantly. Additionally, role-plays give children an opportunity to use language in interactive situations and to receive language input as well as produce language output. Last but not least, because these activities are akin to games, they stir children's imagination and sustain their interest.

Role-play activities can be effective for investigating and learning the vocabulary of natural and social sciences. Young children can

- work with numbers by measuring distance and time as they participate in *Kid Olympics*;
- learn vocabulary related to health and well-being by reenacting a visit to the doctor;
- learn about legislation by participating in *Kid Congress*,[9] that is creating rules for their classroom;
- engage in a mock election to better understand the actual one; or
- learn about the rain forest by creating a tropical jungle in their classroom.

Role-plays are particularly effective for making forays into history. Reenactments of

- Columbus's journey,
- Neil Armstrong's flight to the Moon,
- Rosa Park's act of civil disobedience,

and other important events help young children develop initial understanding of history of the United States as well as histories of their home countries.

To develop a role-play activity, the teacher needs to analyze content material (whether it be a historical event, a contemporary scenario, or a plot of a book) and identify those kernel episodes that are amenable to dramatic representation. A succession of short mini-skits identified as a result of this analysis portrays the meaning of *content obligatory vocabulary*, that is target language words and phrases that are essential for discussing a given topic.[10]

First role-plays enacted by emergent language learners may incorporate very basic and simple exchanges and rely a lot on the miming, TPR format. When implementing these activities, the teacher reads aloud a scenario that portrays a historical event, and students act it out.

- *Coming to America with the Pilgrims.* For instance in a role-play activity which focuses on Pilgrims' journey to and first year in America, a students wearing a crown and stomping his feet represents King George; a group of boys and girls sitting in a cardboard box and rocking that box portrays a hazardous journey on the Mayflower; children trembling and cluttering their teeth reenact the Pilgrim's first cold winter in Plymouth; and planting as well as picking paper fruit and vegetables portray Pilgrims' gardening and harvesting experiences. After the teacher has helped students identify target language items represented through these mini-skits, students create a thematically organized dictionary of words related to Pilgrims' experience in the New World. The dictionary includes target language items such as *mean and bossy king, sail, freeze, pick the harvest, Native Americans.* When in a culminating activity for this role-play students write letters to their *"Dear Family in England,"* they have no difficulty using relevant target language items to describe their adventures in America.[11]

While the overall structure of any given role-play or a simulation may vary, two steps that these activities often have in common are *fishbowl* and *brainstorming.* Fishbowl is a model skit which may be performed by more proficient students and/or the teacher at the beginning of an activity. Fishbowl models role-play and gives children the overall sense of what is going to happen in the classroom. During brainstorming, participants work together to identify content obligatory vocabulary. The product of brainstorming may be a thematically organized dictionary or a set of phrases needed for performing various conversational functions. As students' proficiency level grows, they can use brainstorming to create extended dialogues or conversations between several historical characters. These exchanges are particularly effective if they center around an issue which becomes resolved in the course of a conversation.

- *When George Washington Talked to Betsy Ross.* For instance, in a *Betsy Ross* simulation activity, children reenact George Washington's conversation with the legendary seamstress. During the simulation activity, language learners act out the historic conversation including the exchange when the President suggests that the American flag should have a six-pointed star, and Betsy Ross remonstrates, making an argument that a five-pointed star is a better choice, because it is easier to make.

The use of props and costumes enhances the success of role-plays. Whether these supplementary materials are commercially made or created in the classroom, they make role-plays more enjoyable. For instance, in the Betsy Ross role-play, models of flags, a long skirt, and a shower cap that seconds as a bonnet for Ms. Ross and a paper tricorner hat for the President help the game come alive.[12]

Props and other paraphernalia not only enliven role-plays but also contextualize language use. Rather abstract content vocabulary items which on first glance may not seem amenable to dramatic representation can in fact be rendered meaningful through the use of props. Thus relevant materials can elucidate the meaning of difficult concepts, such as *ballot* and *election*, *bill* and *law*, and many others.

- *ESL Paleontologists.* Consider the use of props in a role-play activity which focuses on dinosaurs. In this role-play, the teacher has children assume the parts of paleontologists and participate in a make-believe paleontological expedition. Children look for "fossils" (parts of the pictures of dinosaurs cut into several pieces) in a "site" (a box filled with styrophone packaging material). Once the fossils have been "excavated," children put them together and use pictures for reference to determine to which dinosaur the fossils belong. As a culminating activity, "paleontologists" write reports in which they describe their findings. This capstone activity can be scaffolded with Literacy Blocks which include the stem *We found a fossil of a*_____ and a list of target language items which refer to dinosaur's fossilized body parts.

Literacy activities are an important element of role-plays. It is essential that children not only use academic language orally but also read texts in the content areas, and produce their own academic writing pieces.

Whether language learners impersonate doctors, work as pretend meteorologists and reenact historical events, they can participate in engaging literacy activities. Thus, meteorologists can write and read weather forecasts, doctors can fill out prescriptions, motorists can read and write road signs, and politicians can write and read campaign speeches. Guided by the teacher, students can write short skits for historical role-plays, or pen down journal entries from the viewpoint of historical characters. Bound blank books, prescription forms similar to those used by doctors in real life, and blank newspapers and books enhance literacy tasks that are included in role-play activities. The use of these and similar texts is important, because it gives children an opportunity to experience *authentic literacy genres* that is to read and write texts of the kind that are used in real life.[13]

- *Imaginary Trip.* Consider the use of authentic literacy genres in an *Imaginary Trip* role-play. In this activity, students participate in mini role-plays which portray activities associated with traveling to another state or a foreign country. In the course of this activity, students buy "tickets," that is they write information related to the plane's departure and arrival on slips of paper; fill out personal information in their passports and have passports checked by airport authorities; after boarding a plane made out of a row of chairs, students assume the part of a pilot and read announcements made by pilots and stewardesses during the plane's takeoff and landing; when students go sightseeing at the place of their destination, they get to read and write texts which describe places of interest. At the end of this activity, students write letters home describing their imaginary trips.

A highly effective literacy activity which capstones role-play is *representation*. During re-presentation, children assume the parts of various characters and produce writing pieces from the viewpoint of those characters.

- *A Day in the Life of the Algonquin Nation.* Consider the use of a representation activity at the end of an instructional unit which explores the story of Pocahontas. After reading aloud a historically accurate account of Pocahontas's story,[14] students learn some basic facts about the famed Algonquin and her tribe. Then they read richly illustrated, child-friendly books about the Northeastern nation,[15] build a longhouse out of desks and sheets, make wampums or bead belts out of paper, and "travel" in canoes made out of chairs. After participating in these mini-role plays, children pen down journal entries, describing a day in the life of the Algonquin nation. A Literacy Scaffold which includes target language items (e.g., *longhouse, bead belt, canoe*) explored through role-play helps students write elaborate and lexically rich pieces.[16]

Young English Language Learners tend to find re-presentation activities particularly engaging if their pieces are published in a creative and evocative way. Photographs of students wearing period costumes, antiquated looking letterhead, stylized stationary all help render representation activities more enjoyable.

- *Writing Letters from Ellis Island.* For instance, after exploring turn of the century immigration through role-play which recreates the experience of Ellis Island immigrants (the activity includes passport check-up, medical examination, an interview, and a reading test), children can describe these events in letters home to their imaginary families in Europe. A thematically framed dictionary that includes target language items, such as *Ellis Island, passport check up, medical examination,* and *reading test,* assures successful completion of this task. When language learners wearing shawls and postman caps write their letters home on the yellowish, tea-tinted ancient looking stationary, they get their first glimpse into the experiences of their predecessors, the Europeans who came to this country a century earlier.[17]

Hands-on Projects

Another powerful means of content-based instruction is hands-on projects.[18] Children construe the meaning of context-reduced vocabulary when they observe natural phenomena first-hand while participating in inquiry-based learning experiences. Learning by doing which takes place within hands-on projects provides highly specific contextual experiences essential for concept clarification. Moreover, hands-on projects provide rich opportunities for problem solving when they enable children to use sophisticated academic language to analyze their observations and to draw conclusions.

Hands-on projects implemented in the ESL classroom consist of two stages: *Group Activity* and *Teacher-Guided Reporting.* During Group Activity, children participate in a goal-oriented, experiential learning event meant to demonstrate a natural phenomenon.

- *Classroom Volcanoes.* For instance, in the *Classroom Volcano* group activity, students learn names of the parts of a volcano while they observe demonstration of the volcano eruption. To model this natural phenomenon, the teacher takes a lampshade and places a plastic cup inside the top narrow opening of the lampshade. (To make the lampshade-volcano look more real life like, the teacher can cover the lampshade with play dough). Then the teacher places two spoonfuls of baking soda in the cup and pours half a cup of vinegar mixed with red paint into the same cup. The foam that forms as the result of the chemical reaction looks like lava coming out of the erupting volcano. In the course of the Group Activity, students become familiar with the target language items, such as *lava, eruption, vent*, and *crust.*

The Group Activity by itself, however, is only the initial condition for language development. Intense language development work happens during Guided Reporting. At this stage of a hands-on project, children use language to make sense of the science phenomena they have observed. During Guided Reporting, language learners try to describe observations, formulate their hypotheses, and also try to draw conclusions.

- *Making Your Shadow Go Away.* Consider the use of Guided Reporting in an activity which focuses on the exploration of shadows. During the first step of this activity, the teacher shines the beam of an overhead projector on the wall while students take turns performing various actions and examining their shadows. Then guiding students in a Language Experience Activity, the teacher takes pictures of children and their shadows and describes the pictures within a simple pattern story. (e.g., *We made shadows. Carla waved her arms. So did the shadow.*) The teacher then asks students what they would need to do to make the shadow go away or disappear. Students come up with their hypotheses and ultimately reach the conclusion that a removal of the source of light (e.g., the overhead projector beam) makes the shadow go away. In a culminating Guided Reporting activity, students discuss whether they see shadows on a sunny day or when the sky is overcast, when lights in the room are off and on, and so on.

Hands-on projects are important in that they often help children make a leap from the intuitive, unconscious knowledge of a natural phenomenon to conscious knowledge of the phenomenon, and then to practice the newly acquired language of science. It is not uncommon for hands-on projects to demonstrate natural phenomena which children have observed in every day life and whose meaning they know, albeit intuitively and unconsciously. For instance, even young children may know that boiling water turns into steam or that hands feel warmer when we rub them together. It is when children become able to analyze and to express this unconscious knowledge verbally that they make a huge leap in their cognitive and language development.

- *Smelling Hot Chocolate.* Thus students who may have noticed that substance sometimes smell stronger when they are heated will come to develop conscious understanding of this phenomenon when observing a diffusion experiment which involves the use of chocolate. In the course of the experiment, the teacher puts lumps of chocolate in a pot and puts the pot on a hot plate. Then the teacher puts children in different parts of the classroom close to and far away from the pot filled with chocolate. As the teacher switches on the hot plate and the chocolate starts getting hotter and hotter, students raise their hands at the moment when they are able to smell the chocolate. (As the chocolate grows hotter, its smell reaches the farthest sitting children.) When discussing this phenomenon, students reach the conclusion that when chocolate grows hotter, tiny drops of chocolate "jump out" of the pot. If the chocolate is really hot, droplets can jump really far.

Needless to say, describing an event sequentially and explaining cause and effect is a difficult task for all young children, let alone those children who are learning to express their observations and thoughts in a second language. Language teachers need to use carefully structured scaffolds, such as questions, cues and prompts to aid children's verbalization efforts.

During the initial stages of Teacher-Guided Reporting, teachers encourage students to use their own words when discussing the Group Activity. They then engage in prolonged exchanges when every child has had a chance to engage in the discussion of an experiment. Afterward, *recasting* is a culminating step of Guided Reporting. During recasting, teachers reformulate children's insights in regards to the meaning of an experiment in the more conventional language of science. For instance, the teacher can explain to children that a special science word used to refer to the fact that magnets "pull" metal is the word, "attract,"[19] that a science word that means that some materials "swim on the water" is the term, "float," or that tiny drops of water or chocolate that jump fast when they are hot are called "molecules."

- *The Sun's Painting Brush.* The use of recasting can be observed in a lesson on photosynthesis. First, the leaf of a houseplant is wrapped in foilpaper. Once children have discussed and established the fact that the sunlight cannot reach (or "touch") the leaf that has been wrapped in foil, the teacher asks children to predict what is going to happen to the wrapped leaf. After a few days, children unwrap the leaf to test their hypotheses and realize that the color of the leaf has changed and that the leaf is no longer green. During the second Teacher-Guided Reporting stage, language learners and the teacher work together to explain why the discoloration has happened. Following carefully constructed leads provided by the teacher, children reach the conclusion that the leaf lost its color because the sun could not "paint" it. While engaging students in recasting, the teacher tells the students that the process whereby the sun paints the leaves green is called "photosynthesis."

Like role-plays, hands-on experiments need to be combined with literacy activities. Hands-on experiments work the best if they are preceded and followed-up by shared reading of books which describe natural phenomena. Additionally, after hand-on experiments the teacher can guide children in a Language Experience Activity whereby children's accounts of learning experiences are transcribed and used as literacy materials.

Communication in the Content-Based Classroom

Questioning

Teacher Talk used in the CBI classroom is similar to Teacher Talk used with emergent speakers. Just as in the emergent level classroom, the CBI Teacher Talk is syntactically simple and repetitive. Just as any Teacher Talk, CBI Teacher Talk abounds in formulaic routinized patterns. For instance, teachers use the same formulaic utterances to signal the beginning and the end of activities and use repetitive language to assure comprehensibility of input. In addition to these general characteristics, Teacher Talk used in the CBI classroom has two crucially important additional features.

The first important feature of the CBI Teacher Talk is recurrent use of questioning. Lessons that integrate extensive use of questioning (as opposed to lecturing) work for a host of reasons. First of all, questions enable the teacher to make sure that her/his input is comprehensible. By coaching input in question form, the teacher assures that she and her students are "on the same page" and that the input is being understood. By eliciting answers from students, the teacher uses students' background knowledge as a foundation for building comprehension of new concepts. Further, when the language teacher poses questions rather than provides answers, language is broken down into small entities that are easier for language students to take in than are larger stretches of text. Additionally, questions increase student talking time and help the teacher establish a classroom environment where language learners produce output as well as get input. Most importantly, perhaps, questioning works because it creates opportunities for interaction.[20] Some studies have argued that interaction and resulting meaning-negotiation is a necessary condition of language learning. Questioning is a teaching strategy that creates ample interaction opportunities.

In the content-based classroom, questions are used not only as a means to check comprehension but also during Group Activities when the teacher or children present new materials. A carefully prepared battery of so-called *display questions* helps the teacher to make input comprehensible while introducing content obligatory vocabulary.[21]

Consider a transcription of an *Insulation* lesson during which the teacher helps children come to the conclusion that some fabrics work better than others for keeping substances (and people) warm.

> *Teacher* (displaying two paper cups filled with hot water and two
>   swatches of fabric made of wool and cotton):
> Children, how many cups do you see?
> Can you guess what's in the cups?
> Do the cups feel warm or cold?
> Do you know the name of this material? (teacher demonstrates a
>   piece of wool.)
> What about this material? (a piece of cotton is demonstrated.)
> What am I doing now? (teacher wraps the two cups in a piece of
>   wool and a piece of cotton respectively.)
> What is going to happen to the water in the cups?
> Do you think the water is going to stay warm in cup number one?
> Is the water going to stay warm in cup number two?

Teacher questioning continues during the Guided Reporting stage. At this point, some open-ended questions are introduced in the conversation. Open-ended questions put greater cognitive demands on language learners. When using these challenging questions, the teacher encourages language learners to try and account for their observations and to link newly acquired knowledge to students' own experiences.

Consider some open-ended questions which are used during the Guided Reporting stage of the Insulation activity once children have realized that the water stays warmer if the cup is wrapped in wool.

Teacher: You just told us that the water stayed warmer in cup number
   one. It's the cup we wrapped in wool. Wool works better for keep-
ing water warm. Why is that?
Let's compare wool and cotton. Let's compare how wool and cotton
   feel. Who would like to touch the wool? Who wants to touch the
   cotton?
What does the wool feel like?
What does the cotton feel like?
You said that wool feels "fuzzy." Do any of our clothes feel fuzzy?
Let's look at the pair of mittens. Do they feel fuzzy?
Does the t-shirt we wear in the summer feel fuzzy?
Do the mittens keep as warm? Does the t-shirt?
Why do fuzzy materials keep us warm?
Guess what, fuzzy materials keep us warm, because they have air
   in them. In all fuzzy materials there are little pockets of air. These
   pockets of air keep things warm.
Why do we wear clothes made out of fuzzy materials in winter?
Have you ever looked inside the house walls? People put fuzzy
   materials in the wall of their houses. Why is that?

For questioning to be effective in the CBI classroom, several important principles need to be maintained. It is important that the battery of questions used during Group Activity and Guided Reporting contain questions that require a simple "yes" or "no" answer, one word answers, and answers in the form of extended utterances. Diversifying questions asked of language learners is important, since it assures the *tailoring of question form* in accordance with proficiency levels of different students.[22] Less proficient students can respond to more basic questions, such as the ones that require a simple nod or one word or two words for an answer. The more proficient students can handle more sophisticated questions.

In a battery of Guided-Reported questions which are part of a unit on reptiles, the teacher alternates close-ended and open-ended questions to maximize class participation.

Teacher: Do snakes have warm or cold blood?
Do frogs have warm or cold blood?
Do snakes sleep in winter or do they stay awake?

Do frogs sleep in winter or do they stay awake?
How come animals which have cold blood sleep in winter?
Why is it that animals that have cold blood can't help falling asleep
   when the weather is cold?

Wait time, that is allowing each student to consider a possible answer
to the question, is another important principle of effective questioning.
According to the studies of Teacher Talk, to assure that language learners
have a chance to formulate their thoughts and produce output, wait time
in the second language classroom needs to be as long as eight seconds.

Affective and prosodic parameters of questioning are also important.
The following questioning strategies help engage students and excite
them about learning:

- Using dramatic intonations,
- Using variations in pitch,
- Referring to teacher posed questions as "a riddle" or "a mystery," and
- Creating a game-like atmosphere.

Even though language teachers distill their vocabulary to the most basic and simple items, trying whenever possible to replace abstract words
with concrete synonyms, the language they use is by no means bland
and boring. In an important study of comprehensible input, Lily Wong-
Fillmore speaks of the richness and playfulness of Teacher Talk.[23] Change
of pitch, the use of simple yet engaging and striking language, and dramatic pauses contribute to the effectiveness of communication. Consider
the choice of words and pitch that a language teacher used in order to help
children understand the concept of a triangle:

Teacher: Look at this figure in my hands. Look at the top ... The top
is sooo skinny! [high pitch]. Now look at the bottom. The bottom is
soooo fat. [low pitch].

Analogies

Teacher Talk used in the CBI classroom has another important characteristic. It abounds in *analogies*. Analogies are comparisons which are
helpful for the teaching of social studies and scientific concepts.[24] Cognitive linguists have demonstrated that speakers consistently use similes
when they try to wrap their minds around new phenomena. This happens

when a little child overextends the meaning of a word and says "cah" (cat) to refer to a thing or a creature (e.g., a fur hat, a dog) that is in some ways similar to a cat. It also happens when a computer programmer refers to a newly created computer contraption used for printing by the name of a "mouse" or speaks of "cutting and pasting" text on the screen. Language teachers use analogies when talking to their students in order to account for children's need to make a connection between the familiar and the unfamiliar when investigating a new phenomenon or a concept.

In a Parts of Speech mini lesson, a language teacher compares groups of words that belong to a part of speech to family members. When implementing the lesson, the teacher puts a group of common verbs on the blackboard (e.g., *eat, sleep, walk, jump, read, write, go, swim*) and then proceeded to compare the group of words to a family. Below is an excerpt form the classroom discussion:

Teacher: Who can tell us about their family?

Students: I have a cousin. . . I have brother. . . My mom have a baby. . .

Teacher: If you look like your brother, your sister or your cousin, raise your hands. [children raise their hands] Wow! Many of you look like your family members. Now, I am going to show you another family. It is a family of [pause] words. I want you to look at these words. Guess what–these words are a family. It's a family of words. Now let's read the words together.

Students [read aloud]: Eat! Sleep! Walk! Jump! Read! Write! Go! Swim!

Teacher: Well. These words are a family. They are all a little bit alike. Who can tell us how these words are alike? How are they a little bit the same? I want everybody to think about these words. . . How are these words alike?

Highly sophisticated concepts can be explained in the ESL classroom by the use of an apt analogy. In a lesson that deals with the states of matter, the teacher tells students that steam is made of "teeny drops" that "jump out of the pot" when the water gets hot. In a lesson on the government bodies, the teacher explains that while the school principal is "the number one person in the school," the president is "a number one person in the country." When explaining the concept of a state, the teacher tells young students that the United States is like a pizza pie sliced into many pieces and that a state is "a slice of the United States."

You can find suggestions for input modification as well as detailed lesson plans and graphic materials for activities described in this chapter in the "ESL Portfolio" Web site located at http://people.hofstra.edu/faculty/Tatiana_Gordon/ESL/index.html.

Main Points

- Combining language instruction with content instruction benefits intermediate level young language learners.

- Experiential activities, such as role-plays or hands-on experiments, help elucidate the meaning of abstract target language concepts to young language learners.

Notes

1. B. C. Hauptman, M. B. Wesche, and D. Ready (1988), "Second Language Acquisition through Subject-Matter Learning: A Follow-up Study at the University of Ottawa." *Language Learning*, 38(3), 439–482.

2. D. Eskey (1997), "Syllabus Design in Content-Based Instruction." In M. Snow and D. Brinton (Eds.), *The content-based classroom: Perspectives on integrating language and content*. White Plains, NY: Longman, p. 138.

3. J. Carlisle, J. Fleming, and B. Gudbrandsen (April 2000), "Incidental Word Learning in Science Classes." *Contemporary Educational Psychology*, 25(2), 184–211.

4. J. Cummins (1979), "Cognitive/Academic Language Proficiency, Linguistic Interdependence, the Optimum Age Question and Some Other Matters." *Working Papers on Bilingualism*, 19, 121–129.

5. L. Vygotsky (1986), *Thought and language*. Cambridge, MA: MIT Press.

6. J. Cummins (1992), "Language Proficiency, Bilingualism, and Academic Achievement." In P. Richard-Amato and M.A. Snow (Eds.), *The multicultural classroom: Readings for content-area teachers*. New York: Longman, pp. 16–26.

7. G. Canton-Harvey (1987), *Content-area language instruction: Approaches and strategies*. Reading, MA: Addison-Wesley Publishing Company.

8. D. Horner and K. McGinley (1990), "Running Simulation/Games: A Step-By-Step Guide." In D. Crookall and R. Oxford (Eds.), *Simulation, gaming and language learning*. New York: Newbury House Publishers, pp. 33–45.

9. Activity developed by Julie Schondorf Segruchni, 2002.

10. M. Met (1991), "Learning Language through Content: Learning Content Through Language." *Foreign Language Annals*, 24(4), 281–295.

11. Activity developed by Veronica Michelle, 2005.

12. Activity developed by Deborah Talve, 2004.

13. T. Gordon (2003), "Romeo and Juliet Come to New York: Integrating Reading and Writing in the ESL Classroom." *TESOL Journal*, 12(3), 49–50.

14. For example, M. Hudson (2001), *Pocahontas*. Chicago, IL: Heinemann.

15. For example, R. Gaines (2000), *Algonquin*. Edina, MN: ABDO Publishing.

16. Activity developed by Stacy Heller, 2005.

17. Activity developed by Cynthia Butron-Gozalez, 2003.

18. N. G. Rosen and L. Sasser (1997), "Sheltered English: Modifying content delivery for second language learners." In M. A. Snow & D. M. Brinton (Eds.), *The content-based classroom: Perspectives on integrating language and content*. White Plains, NY: Longman, pp. 35–45.

19. P. Gibbons (2002), *Scaffolding Language, scaffolding learning: Teaching second language learners in the ESL classroom*. Portsmouth, NH: Heinemann.

20. R. Ellis, *Teacher–pupil interaction in second language development. Input in second language acquisition*. Rowley, MA: Newbury House Publishers, pp. 69–88.

21. J. Zuengler and D. Brinton (1997), "Linguistic Form, Pragmatic Function: Relevant Research from Content-Based Instruction." In M. Snow and D. Brinton (Eds.), *The content-based classroom: Perspectives on integrating language and content*. White Plains, NY: Longman, pp. 263–273.

22. L. Wong-Fillmore (1985), "When Does Teacher Talk Work as Input?" In S. Gass and C. Gass (Eds.), *Input in second language acquisition*. Rowley, MA: Newbury House Publishers, pp. 17–50.

23. Ibid.

24. D. Moore, S. A. Moore, P. Cunningham, and J. Cunningham (1986), *Developing readers & writers in the content areas K-12*, 2nd ed. New York: Longman.

CHAPTER 8

Multicultural Second Language Curricula

I left my heart in Hong Kong because I miss my friends and I miss my teacher. I didn't go back there for a long time. I ask my mother when can we go back to Hong Kong. She always says five year later. But I know it is not real [*sic*]. And I know I never can go back to Hong Kong again.

—*I Left My Heart in Hong Kong*. Jasmine, 9 years old

Teaching young language learners English of daily communication as well as academic English are not the only goals of second language curricula. Most second language educators agree that the teaching of cultural minority students needs to pursue other quite significant goals. One of these goals is to assist students in preserving a connection with their home cultures as well as fostering minority students' sense of appreciation of this country's cultural diversity. Yet another goal is to aid language minority students in making their first steps toward becoming well-informed and active members of the host culture.

Second language study plans that pursue these goals are known as *multicultural second language curricula*. This chapter describes some parameters of multicultural curricula for young second language learners. It discusses why these curricula are important and how they can be implemented.

Rationale for Multicultural Second Language Curricula

The goals behind multicultural curricula may seem lofty but they are really quite pragmatic. By fostering students' pride in their home cultures, multicultural curricula help language minority students maintain harmonious relationships with their families and ethnic communities and help them develop the self-confidence essential for academic success. By encouraging language learners' civic awareness and activism, these programs prevent potential marginalization of cultural minority students, lay the foundation for immigrant students' integration into the host culture, and ultimately help minority language students become productive members of this country.

Development and implementation of multicultural second language curricula is not a simple matter. These curricula take place in the context of a striking diversity among today's immigrant communities. The teacher who seeks to empower her students and help them stay in touch with their home cultures needs to account for scores of different cultural experiences. Moreover, multicultural second language curricula are intended for young students many of whom have experienced the trauma of cultural disorientation and the sense of being uprooted. These curricula are unique in that they meet the needs of students many of whom have to come to terms with life-changing experiences.

While the challenges related to the implementation of multicultural curricula may be great, the need for the study in cultural diversity is urgent. Over recent years, second language education experts have been developing instructional strategies intended for today's diverse communities of first and second generation immigrant language learners.

Cultural Explorations

Modern ESL multicultural curriculum experts suggest that the basis for multicultural curricula is laid when language teachers learn about their students' cultures.[1] Needless to say, it is unrealistic to expect that ESL teachers will know every single culture represented in their classroom. Cultures are complex entities which shape not only people's food preferences, customs, and holiday celebrations but also their values and beliefs, child-rearing practices and expectations regarding children's schooling, and modes of children's interaction with adults as well as patterns of their socialization into peer groups. People's lives in their entirety are shaped by their cultures.

Immigrant community cultures are all the more difficult to understand, because these are cultures in a state of flux. Immigrants do not recreate their cultures in the Unites States. When they adapt and adjust to life in this country, immigrants experience profound transformations that result from abandoning some old cultural ways and adopting new ones. The task of understanding immigrant cultures is all the more difficult, because of the astounding cultural diversity within immigrant communities.

For all these reasons, investigating students' home cultures is one of the greatest challenges of second language teaching. But it is also one of the greatest intellectual rewards of the profession. Here are some questions worth exploring:

- Why did students leave their home countries?
- What were their lives like back home?
- What is known about the students' ethnic communities in the United States?
- What values shape child-rearing practices in various immigrant enclaves?
- What was the child's life like in his or her home country and what is it like in the United States?
- What kinds of activities do immigrant children enjoy?
- What kinds of family stories shape their maturation?

One cannot begin to understand other cultures without analyzing one's own cultural background. This is why cultural self-analysis is an important job undertaken by teachers engaged in multicultural curriculum development. An educator involved in cultural introspection is more likely to see that instructional choices and expectations are culture-specific and is less likely to take her own instructional practices for granted. Do children sit in neat rows in the teacher's classroom or are they sprawled on a rug in a reading center? Does the teacher lavishly praise her students or does she believe that her main task is to point out to a child where he or she falls short? Does the teacher believe that she must instill ethical values in her students or does she feel that it is the job of the parents? Does the teacher feel personally responsible for her students' progress or does she tend to believe that the responsibility lies with the children and their parents? When language teachers begin to realize that answers to these and a myriad of other questions are not self-evident, when they see classrooms as a product of social, political, and historic circumstances, teachers are more likely to withhold their judgment of other cultures and understand these cultures on their own terms.

Validation of Personal Experiences

Second language teachers have a unique responsibility to meet the emotional needs of children who have experienced the shock of immigration and the trauma of being uprooted. Second language teachers move toward this goal by encouraging children to talk about leaving their home countries and coming to the United States. These discussions are all the more important, because in many instances ESL teachers are the first people in this country who will be willing to hear children's stories about their relocation experiences. Parents and other family members may be too busy to have the time to stop and ask children how they feel about leaving their homeland. Occasionally, caretakers will deny that their children may have sustained any losses as a result of immigration. Adults who may feel that children cannot but benefit from the life in the relatively affluent society of the United States may see no point in conversing with children about their immigration-related thoughts and feelings. Children, however, do want to talk about the great changes that have just transpired in their lives. Once they have developed initial English language proficiency, they are remarkably articulate and expressive in describing these experiences. They are willing to talk and write about their home countries, their sense of nostalgia, their journeys, and their adjustment to life in the United States.[2]

- *I See My Country.* Even beginning-level young students will reminisce about their home countries. The feeling of nostalgia which affects many children can become a source of inspiration for interesting writing and drawing activities. In a lesson entitled "I See My Country," the teacher asks her students to imagine that they are going on a journey across their countries. (It can be an imaginary car ride or a hiking tour.) Children can imagine the things, animals, and people they see in their minds, draw and/or write five- or six-line stories using Literacy Blocks consisting of the sentence scaffold *I see* and a picture dictionary or a word bank that lists names of places and animals (e.g., *mountains, river, field, horses, cows, etc*). In performing this activity, children can look at picture books of their home countries for the source of memories and images. Upon completing the writing component of the lesson, children draw pictures of themselves on a nostalgic journey surrounded by images of their home countries. In a piece below, a young writer reminisces on her home country, China.

  I See My Country

  I see mountains. Some people live in the mountains. They can make
     everything.
  I see the store. People go to the store to buy fabric.

I see people who keep chickens when they grow up they lay eggs [*sic*].
In the mountains sometime people drink the nectar of pink flowers.

- *Stories of Immigration.* Reading books about immigration experiences and children's adjustment to the new culture is an important component of the multicultural curriculum. *How Many Days to America*[3] (a story of a child's hazardous journey from a Caribbean country to the United States), *When This World Was New*[4] (a book which portrays a Spanish-speaking immigrant boy's first days in a new country), *My Name Is Yoon*,[5] *I Hate English*,[6] *Marianthe's Story: Painted Words*[7] (stories of little children coming to grips with the English language), *Yoko*[8] (a book which examines culture shock through the eyes of a young child) can be used to engage young language learners in conversations about similar experiences in their own lives.[9]

- *Heart Idioms.* In a lesson intended for older students and taught around Valentine's Day, the teacher demonstrates to her students several pictures that illustrated the literary meaning of common idioms that contain the word "heart." (For instance, a picture that depicts a heart walking toward an injured puppy is meant to illustrate an idiom *my heart went out to*.) Upon discussing the meaning of heart idioms, children write short stories that illustrate an idiom of their choice. Teachers who have implemented this lesson report that immigrant children often chose to write stories that open with the idiom "I left my heart in." One of these stories is an epigraph to this chapter.

Validation of Students' Cultures

The philosophy of validating and celebrating students' home cultures is the bedrock of multicultural second language curricula. When students' cultural backgrounds are altogether overlooked in classroom materials, immigrant children feel insignificant and invisible.[10] Conversely, encountering familiar cultural artifacts in the second language curriculum fosters language minority students' sense of personal worth. It is essential that students recognize their home cultures in the second language curricula, that the classroom environment and classroom activities send them a message that their home cultures are a valuable part of the cultural fabric of the United States. Experts in young children's learning point out that their subject's journey to understand others begins with self-exploration.[11] That is why children begin to learn about the cultures of their peers by analyzing own cultures.

Ethnic Holidays in the Second Language Classroom

Learning about ethnic holidays is one of the very first steps children can make in their attempt to understand diversity. Holiday celebrations are particularly effective in working with young children, because ethnic festivals tend to be enjoyed by immigrant families,[12] and because it is a cultural attribute that even very young children tend to remember and understand.

Celebration of students' cultural backgrounds can become a virtual festivity when students and the teacher recreate some elements of the holidays from students' home countries in the second language classroom. For instance, Indian children will enjoy discussing Diwali, Hindu festival of lights which families celebrate by cleaning and decorating homes with flowers. Children of Chinese ancestry will enthusiastically describe the celebration of Chinese New Year, and children from Vietnam will share their love of Tet, a Vietnamese New Year. Educators who work with students from diverse backgrounds develop strategies for celebrating ethnic holidays in the classroom.[13] These celebrations are particularly beneficial if they go beyond token tributes to cultures, such as decorating the classroom or tasting ethnic food and involve students in the exploration of new concepts.

- *Learning about the Power of Wind while Celebrating Basant.* For instance, when celebrating Basant, a kite-flying holiday from Pakistan, children can learn about the power of wind and write *Where My Kite Went* stories describing their kites' imaginary or actual journeys.[14]

- *Studying Human Anatomy on the Day of the Dead.* The Day of the Dead, a traditional Mexican holiday observed on November 2, is an occasion to learn about human anatomy. In preparation for the holiday, students make outlines of their bodies on black paper with white chalk, label major bones and the skull, and then decorate their classroom with these life-size skeletons.[15]

- *Discussing Why Children Are Special on Children's Day.* Ethnic holiday celebrations can be a springboard for literacy activities. For instance, Children's Day, a Korean holiday observed on May 5 with giving gifts to children and picnicking, can be celebrated in the classroom by engaging children in a *Children Are Special* literacy activity. The activity starts with the reading of a book *What Teachers Can't Do*,[16] which tells about all kinds of things that teachers are unable to do. (Not being able to ride a scooter to school is one example.) After a read-aloud activity, children can write or dictate their version of the story by answering the question *What are the things that little children can do and adults cannot?*

- *Reading Books about Children's Experiences on Ramadan.* Many ethnic holidays have religious meaning which cannot be addressed in the public school classroom. Even so, to the extent that learning about these holidays will sensitize children to various cultural experiences, minority students can familiarize themselves with some rites and rituals associated with religious holidays. For instance, when reading aloud and discussing books such as *Ramadan*,[17] a picture book about a school day of a Muslim American boy who needs to marshal all his willpower to keep on fasting when other children are enjoying their snacks and drinks, language learners will learn to respect cultural experiences which may be profoundly different from those of their own.

Multicultural Games

Children tend to be really excited when they reexperience games that they once played in their home countries in the second language classroom.[18] Games played by young children all around the world are described in volumes such as *International Playtime*[19] and *The Multicultural Game Book*.[20]

- *A Coordination Game from China.* Multicultural games are particularly effective if they explore a theme of importance in a given culture. For instance, the dragon, a symbol of good fortune, is a feature of many Chinese books and holidays. Language learners can learn about the dragon by participating in the traditional Dragon game, a favorite of Chinese children. To make a dragon, the teacher has players form a line by putting their hands on the shoulders of the players in front. The first person on line is the dragon's *head*; the last one is a *tail*. The *head* starts to run, making twisting and turning motions while trying to catch the *tail*. If the dragon's body breaks, the *head* becomes the *tail* and the game starts all over again.

- *A Language Game from Russia.* Multicultural games from around the world are particularly beneficial for language learners if they address the development of language skills. The adaptation of a game called *Don't say "yes" and don't say "no,"* a favorite of Russian children, is a case in point. The game starts when the teacher recites the following little poem:

You've Been Sent a Chest of Goodies. . .

You've been sent a chest of goodies
What is in it? Let me guess!
I will ask all kinds of questions—
When you answer, don't say "yes"!
Don't say "yes" and don't say "no",
Don't shake or nod your head,
Don't laugh and don't giggle,
Don't say "black" and don't say "red."

As is clear from this rules-of-the-game poem, the teacher poses questions and fellow players answer them. When answering, they cannot say "yes" or "no," nod or shake their heads, laugh or giggle, or name the red and the black colors. To engage fellow players in a conversation, the teacher produces a box filled with objects and pictures that portray activities or scenes. The teacher proceeds to take pictures and objects out of the box and to ask fellow players questions. For instance, when pointing to a picture of a spring day, the teacher can ask questions such as *What kind of day is it? Is the day warm or cold? What are the people wearing?* At some point, when the players have stopped paying attention, the teacher asks a yes- or no-question, such as *Is it raining?* or *Do you like spring?* It is not easy to resist the natural impulse of saying "yes" or "no" when answering these questions. Remember that nodding and shaking one's head are off limits too!

Validation of First Language. Validating students' home cultures is closely intertwined with validating their first language. When teachers convey to their students the respect for their families' first language, they acknowledge the most fundamental cultural attribute of the immigrant family. Moreover, when teachers encourage immigrant parents to maintain their children's first language proficiency, they assure that the connection between the children and their parents and grandparents is not severed, and that the family remains a source of support and education in the lives of immigrant children.

The message that their first language is a valuable and important asset[21] can become apparent to second language minority children when teachers encourage children to:

• use their first language around the school;
• communicate with one another in their first language;

- translate English words into their home languages;
- incorporate greetings and other phrases in children's home languages in the school displays.

A particularly effective strategy is using children's first language as a window into their second language learning. When teaching a unit on volcanoes, a teacher drew her Spanish-speaking students' attention to the fact the adjective *dormant* (as in *dormant volcanoes*) sounds similar to the Spanish word *dormir* meaning "sleep" or that *a vent* (as in *volcano's vent*) was similar to the Spanish *ventana* for "window."[22]

Reaching Out to the Parent Communities

Another important principle of multicultural curriculum has to do with reaching out to immigrant communities. Implementing activities that children could perform in collaboration with their family members is an effective strategy for providing parent involvement in their children's education. There are many things that children and their parents can enjoy doing together.

- *Family Histories.* For instance, a child could work with older family members on chronicling family history. Lessons that focus on family history are particularly important, because researchers have found out that telling children about the family's past is something mainstream United States and immigrant parents do most often to promote their children's ethnic awareness.[23] When teaching a lesson on family history, the ESL teacher can ask children to interview adult members of the family about a family member who resides in the home country. Children can draw a portrait of a family member or bring his or her photograph to class and write a few sentences describing this person.
- *My Journey with the Teddy Bear.* In this activity children are aided by adults in creating a photo-illustrated book that tells about a child playing with a teddy bear (or any other toy of the child's choice.) A family member takes pictures of a child alongside the toy at home, in the park, in the store, and at other locations. Then, either at home in collaboration with their parents or at school with the teacher's guidance, children work on creating captions for these photographs. This activity is particularly effective if, during vacation time, children and parents go on a trip around the United States or back to the home

countries and chronicle their journey with the toy in a series of photographs. The teacher can model the activity by creating her own illustrated travelogue which features a toy or a pet.

- *ESL Wax Museum.* In this activity, language learners celebrate important contributions made by individuals from their home countries by impersonating these individuals in a mock classroom museum. To participate in the *ESL Wax Museum*, children, aided by their parents, identify important individuals from their home countries; these can be children's contemporaries or heroes of times long gone, athletes, writers, politicians, or popular performers. Once students have decided on their exhibits, they work with their parents on putting together short biographies of individuals whom they are going to represent. (Children have a choice of writing biographies in English or in their home languages.) Next, with the help of their parents, children dress up as their heroes. Their costumes can be elaborate or quite basic. A pair of shorts and a tank top with the name can represent a famous athlete, a tie and a name tag make do for a politician. Then, the teacher guides children in creating museum signs, pamphlets, and tickets which all add into making the museum experience more authentic and complete. On the day when the ESL Museum opens, each child sits on his or her seat dressed up in the costume of his or her hero and supplied with the biography sheet. On the desk in front of each live "exhibit" is a paper button. When museum visitors made up of parents, school administrators, and other students press the button, the child proceeds to read the text on the biography sheet. If the child has difficulty reading the text, museum visitors can read the text on their own and ask the child questions about his or her hero.

The ESL Museum is a fascinating study in diversity. The museum organized in one New York City school included King Se-jong, a Korean educator-king, the inventor of Hangul, the Korean alphabet believed by some to be the most efficient writing system in the world; Anna Pavlova, a legendary Russian ballerina; Bruce Lee, a martial arts and movie star legend from Hong Kong; Jay Chow, a popular Taiwanese singer; Jennifer Lopez, a singer of Latin-American descent; and many others.

- *Letter to a Future Tourist.* In this activity, children and parents give the teacher their expert advice regarding a prospective visit to their home country. During the initial stage of the activity, the teacher tells parents of her students that she plans to visit their home countries one day and that she would appreciate their recommendations in planning this trip. In response to this request, language learners aided by their parents write letters in which they answer the following sample questions posed by the would-be visitor:

- When should I go on a trip to your country?
- Why is this season a good time to go?
- What dishes should I taste?
- Which places of interest should I visit?
- Which plants and animals should I see?
- Which souvenirs should I buy?
- Which phrases from your language should I learn?

Letter writers have a choice of putting their letters in a book format, providing their letters with relevant illustrations, and using the language of their choice.[24]

The ESL Wax Museum, My Journey with the Teddy Bear, Letter to My Country's Visitor, and other similar activities are effective for a number of reasons. First, they make children proud about sharing the important facts of their home cultures with others. Second, they give language learners an opportunity to explore the cultural richness of their countries together with their parents. Most importantly, perhaps these activities tap into the expertise of immigrant families. Instead of ignoring the vast repository of knowledge which immigrants have, but do not necessarily get a chance to display in the host culture, these learner-centered activities capitalize on immigrant families' knowledge base and become a source of education for the entire school community.

Transformational Multicultural Curricula

Multicultural curricula do not stop at teaching children about their countries' holidays or important people. Modern multicultural curriculum experts argue that merely adding a lesson that has an ethnic theme to the curriculum is not enough. They recommend a more radical restructuring of the second language curriculum—of the kind that would engage children in an ongoing in-depth discussion of the themes and ideas that shape different cultures.[25] The *transformational multicultural curriculum* (as its name suggests) is meant to transform the participants of the educational process. By sensitizing students to the themes and issues that are central to various cultures, these curricula enable students to look at the world through a cultural lens other than their own. Theorists and practitioners of multicultural education make an argument that these in-depth cultural explorations help students develop new cultural perspectives and see the world in a new light.

Multicultural Literature

A powerful component of the transformational multicultural curricula intended for young language learners is multicultural literature. Students who are engaged in multicultural readings draw from a diverse pool of ideas. While children's books from across the world may celebrate values common to all humanity, these books also explore themes and ideas that are particularly important to certain cultures. Numerous Korean, Japanese, and Chinese folk tales talk about the importance of fulfilling—at any cost—one's duty toward others. Middle Eastern folk tales will portray clever, ingenuous characters who show miracles of resourcefulness and wit. The themes of social justice and the plight of an ordinary person resound in the books by authors from Central and South America.

The themes and ideas explored in the books that have originated in various cultures are not necessarily stated directly. Often, it is the expressive style of the books' text and illustrations that are laden with meaning. The choice of language, the rhythm of a piece of prose or poetry, and the color scheme and the composition of an illustration convey important cultural themes. Aesthetic emotions evoked by encounters with books serve as sources of multicultural learning. Theorists of second language education say that "emotion in the arts is cognitive" and that an emotional response provoked by a literary piece can become a source of knowing.[26] You may have experienced the cognitive impact of the arts if you feel that you have come to understand another culture better after hearing a song, reading a book, or watching a film conceived within that culture. Reading multicultural books provides similar experiences to young children. When reading stories that take place in foreign lands or within diverse cultural communities in the United States, when taking in images of faraway places or neighborhoods other than their own, when enjoying the unique styles of authors and illustrators from different cultures, students get to experience diverse cultures first-hand.

For multicultural literature to offer instructional benefits, its language needs to be comprehended and enjoyed by young language learners. Multicultural books work best if they have appealing, colorful illustrations that provide visual clues needed for vocabulary comprehension; are written in repetitive, simple expressive language; and have an engaging and exciting storyline. An engaging, interesting storyline will obviously work better than one which is monotonous and explicitly didactic. Young readers who empathize with the characters of their favorite stories and get to experience the lives of the book's characters, albeit vicariously, respond more personally to the problems and conflicts explored by artists and writers from different cultures.

- *Multicultural Books.* The last decade has seen a publication of multicultural books which can be used even with very young language learners. *Seven Chinese Sisters,*[27] a story of seven sisters who are apt at skills ranging from the martial arts to cooking, *The Littlest Emperor,*[28] a story of a Chinese baby emperor in search of fun, *Mariana and the Merchild,*[29] a Chilean mermaid story, *The Secret Foot Prints,*[30] a Dominican legend of mysterious and beautiful undersea people, *The Little Red Ant and the Great Big Crumb,*[31] a Mexican fable of a tiny ant that discovered its own power, *Cendrillon: A Caribbean Cinderella*[32] are some samples of tales from around the world that can be used with primary-level students.

Multicultural explorations begin with shared reading and continue when children engage in responding to literature. Entering the Text activities described in Chapter 5 of this book are an important part of the multicultural curriculum, because they enable children to experience imaginary encounters with diverse cultures. Young children make a creative connection with the magical world of Middle Eastern folklore if after reading about Aladdin they imagine what it would be like to undertake a journey on Aladdin's carpet. Similarly, language learners connect with the world of Russian fairy tales if, after reading stories about *Bony-Legs,*[33] a wicked witch of Russian folk tales, they imagine themselves living in a house on chicken legs, which serves as a home for Bony-Legs.

Social Action Curricula

Another innovative principle of multicultural TESOL curricula is the emphasis on education for social action.[34] Second language educators argue that multicultural curricula are effective when they empower language minority students and help them become active and informed citizens. It is essential that even very young language learners begin to understand the meaning of democracy and its institutions and the role of individual citizens in improving their own lives and the lives of others.

- *Make Our School a Better Place.* Social action curricula intended for young learners work best if they help students develop the skills and attitudes needed for resolving the problems in their immediate environment. Improving the conditions in one's school or in one's classroom is an objective behind the project called *Make Our School a Better Place*. When this project is implemented, the teacher guides the class in identifying problems in their school environment. Once children have pinpointed an issue they find particularly problematic, the teacher helps them to write a letter to the school administration, requesting that the problem be rectified. Needless to say, it is important that administrators heed children's solicitations and make suggested improvements. Observing results of one's own activism empowers students and motivates them to engage in similar activity in the future.

- *ESL News.* Children can become publishers of ESL News, their own newspaper that covers international and local events. *ESL News* is a class newspaper that integrates photographs from local or national papers supplied with a short account of an event or a student-dictated comment that the teacher transcribes. The first step in publishing ESL News begins when the teacher identifies a newspaper story which is likely to be of interest to children. (It is essential that the story selected by the teacher be provided by a large, detailed photograph that can contextualize the teacher's explanation of the covered event.) After showing the photograph to students, the teacher engages children in a discussion of the event. Then, children describe the event in their own words, upon which the teacher transcribes their stories. Last, each child pastes a copy of the photograph on his or her own blank "ESL News" sheet, copies the dictated story, and practices reading the text. Young language learners tend to respond particularly well to newspaper stories that describe people saving or protecting home or domestic animals. These stories give young language learners first lessons in activism and compassion, and give children their very first lessons in using the media.

It is also essential to engage young children in the intellectual analysis of diverse political and social ideas and actions that have shaped the modern world. Complex ideas and past events can be made accessible to young learners if explorations are coached in hand-on projects, role-plays, or other authentic activities. Reading a book about Rosa Parks and a role-play of the historic bus ride or impersonating Mexican American migrant farm workers whose use of a short-handled hoe was once challenged by the La Causa movement, led by Cesar Chavez, offers students first glances into the history of social activism and political thought.

- *A Monument in the Classroom.* Consider an activity in which the teacher guides students in creating a paper monument to an individual whose ideas and actions they have explored in class. The monument is made of an oversize paper pedestal that features a description of the individual's life and action. On top of the pedestal, students place an oversize picture of their hero. (It can be a student-created drawing or a maximally possible Xerox enlargement of a drawing or a photograph.) In preparation to monument making, students study books that commemorate the life and work of their hero. Upon putting up the monument, language learners participate in its unveiling. The activity is particularly effective if it has all the accoutrements of its real-life counterpart. Inviting members of the school community to participate in the unveiling (the removal of a piece of cloth that covers the paper monument), opening speeches when monument makers explain the contribution of their hero to the audience, placing (or pasting) paper flowers at the base of the monument, taking photographs of the event, and describing it in a class paper all make this activity particularly rich.

  In a *Monument to Mahatma Gandhi* lesson,[35] students commemorate the life and work of the great Indian leader. The study focuses on one particular episode of Gandhi's life and work: his efforts to lift the ban on producing salt that was imposed on the Indian people by the colonial British government and the subsequent Salt March when—to protest the action of the government—Gandhi led a two-mile long procession of people to the Indian Ocean where he scooped up some sea water and made some salt.

  In February, during the Black History Month, after children have learned about the role of Martin Luther King Jr. in the civil rights movement, the teacher announces to the class that they are going to learn about the man who was Martin Luther King's teacher. The teacher explains that Dr. King's teacher was from India and that he taught the great African-American leader the idea that problems may be solved without resorting to fighting. The unit starts with the examination of some pictures of Gandhi's life in a book by Demi.[36] Next, children discuss how they could resolve—without the use of force—some conflicts that might arise within their midst (e.g., What would you do if somebody hit you? How would you act if somebody took your stickers?). After that, to contextualize an understanding of the ban on producing salt, the teacher has children taste and compare foods (e.g., cheese or popcorn) that have been prepared with or without salt, and explains that in India cruel rulers did not let people make salt. Next, children participate in a mock Salt March, an activity during which children walk toward a bowl filled with salty water and dip their fingers in the liquid. As a culminating activity, children build monuments to Dr. King and Gandhi.

Because of their game-like qualities, these rather sophisticated activities work even in primary grades. The rationale for pushing the envelope and bringing intellectual sophistication into the primary level classroom is discussed in the next chapter of this book. Lesson plans for activities as well as accompanying graphic materials can be found in the "ESL Portfolio" Web site located at http://people.hofstra.edu/faculty/Tatiana_Gordon/ESL/index.html.

Main Points

- Teacher exploration of students' cultures lays the foundation of multicultural curricula.

- Validation of young language learners' immigration experiences, home language, and home culture is essential for culturally responsive teaching.

- Involving parent communities in the schooling process aids to the effectiveness of multicultural second language curricula.

Notes

1. R. Scarcella (1990), *Teaching language minority students in the multicultural classroom*. Englewood Cliffs, NJ: Prentice Hall.

2. C. Igoa (1995), *The Inner World of the Immigrant Child*. Mahwah, NJ: Lawrence Erlbaum Associates.

3. E. Bunting (1988), *How many days to America?: A Thanksgiving story*. New York: Clarion Books.

4. D.H. Figueredo (1999), *When this world was new*. New York: Lee & Low Books.

5. H. Recorvits (2003), *My name is Yoon*. New York: Farrar, Straus and Giroux.

6. E. Levine (1989), *I hate English*. New York: Scholastic.

7. Aliki (1998), *Marianthe's story: Painted words, spoken memories*. New York: Greenwillow Press.

8. R. Wells (1998), *Yoko*. New York: Hyperion Books for Children.

9. G. Heald-Taylor (1986), *Whole language strategies for ESL primary students*. Toronto: The Ontario Institute for Studies in Education.

10. S. Nieto (2004), *Affirming diversity: The sociopolitical context of multicultural education*, 4th ed. New York: Allyn & Bacon.

11. D. Fromberg (1995), *The full-day kindergarten: Planning and practicing a dynamic themes curriculum*, 2nd ed. New York: Teachers College Press.

12. M. Waters (1990), *Ethnic options: Choosing identities in America*. Berkeley, CA: University of California Press.

13. http://teacherlink.ed.usu.edu/tlresources/units/Byrnes-celebrations/intro.html. This Web site contains multicultural celebration activities developed by teacher education students enrolled at Utah State University.

14. Activity developed by Massiel Morris, 2006.

15. P. Rigg (1991), "Whole Language in TESOL." *TESOL Quarterly*, 25(3), Autumn. http://www.escort.org/products/rigg_article.html.

16. D. Wood (2002), *What teachers can't do*. New York: Simon and Schuster.

17. S.H. Ghazi (1996), *Ramadan*. New York: Holiday House.

18. T. Gordon (2000), "Language Games Across Cultures." In R. Clements (Ed.), *Elementary school recess: Selected readings, games, and activities for teachers and parents*. Boston, MA: American Press.

19. W. Nelson and H. "Buzz" Glass (1992), *International playtime: Classroom games and dances from around the world*. Carthage, IL: Fearon Teacher Aids, Simon and Schuster Education Group.

20. L. Orlando (1993), *The multicultural game book: More than 70 traditional games from 30 countries*. New York: Scholastic Professional Books.

21. New Zealand Department of Education (1988), *New voices: Second language learning and teaching: A handbook for primary teachers*. Wellington: Department of Education. Cited in J. Cummins (1989), *Empowering minority students*. Sacramento, CA: California Association for Bilingual Education.

22. Examples developed by Mary Bridget O'Keefe, 2006.

23. R. Alba (1990), *Ethnic identity: The transformation of White America*. New Haven, CT: Yale University Press.

24. Activity developed by Barbara Fody, 2004.

25. J. Banks (2003), *Teaching strategies for ethnic studies*, 7th ed. Boston: Pearson Education Group.

26. J. Shier (1990), "Integrating the Arts in the Foreign/Second Language Curriculum: Fusing the Affective and the Cognitive." *Foreign Language Annals*, 23(4), 303.

27. K. Tucker (2003), *The seven Chinese sisters*. Morton Grove, IL: Albert Whitman & Company.

28. D. Seow (2004), *The littlest emperor*. Boston: Tuttle Publishing.

29. C. Pitcher (2000), *Mariana and the merchild: A folk tale from Chile*. Grand Rapids, MI: Wm. B. Eerdmans Publishing Company.

30. J. Alvarez (2000), *The secret footprints*. New York: Knopf Books for Young Readers.

31. *The little red ant and the great big crumb: A Mexican fable*. Retold by Shirley Climo (1995). New York: Clarion Books.

32. R.D. San Souci (1998*)*, *Cendrillon: A Caribbean cinderella*. New York: Simon and Schuster Books for Young Readers.

33. J. Cole (1983), *Bony-legs*. New York: Scholastic.

34. Banks, *Teaching strategies for ethnic studies*, 7th edition, Boston: Allyn and Bacon.

35. Activity developed by Anjanie Persaud, 2005.

36. Demi (2001), *Gandhi*. New York: Margaret K. McElderry Books.

CHAPTER 9

Issues in ESL Instruction

This chapter discusses the need to stimulate young language learners intellectually when teaching them English as a second language (ESL). This part of the book talks about strategies of rendering second language instruction cognitively enriching while respecting developmental constraints unique to young language learners.

Children's Facility with Second Language Learning—A Myth?

After the extensive discussion of children's propensity for second language learning contained in the first chapter of this book, the word "myth" used in relation to the topic may come as a surprise. But the truth is that the popular assumptions about children's second language are somewhat mythologized.[1] While our sense of wonder about the fact that children begin to sound "like natives" after a fairly brief exposure to language is quite legitimate, it is important to bear in mind that there are some aspects of language learning that children do find challenging.[2] For instance, as you already know from Chapter 3 of this book, older learners often outperform children during the first stages of language learning.

Difficulty with the first stages of language learning, however, is not the only challenge that young language learners need to overcome. It is important to bear in mind that there are some other elements of language which children can find difficult to master. Thus, while they may fairly quickly pick up the language of day-to-day communication or the so-called *playground English* from their peers, learning the abstract language of schooling is a task that young language learners find difficult and which they cannot accomplish on their own, without concerted help from adults.

The first piece of research to draw attention to the fact that language minority children have significant difficulty in mastering academic language was performed by a Canadian, Jim Cummins. In an influential study published in 1979, Cummins first pointed out that there are two types of second language proficiencies: BICS (Basic Interpersonal Communication Skills) and CALP (Cognitive Academic Language Proficiency). BICS have to do with the child's ability to use language to interact informally with peers or adults. The term CALP refers to the student's ability to use the language needed for performing school tasks.[3] In a 1981 study, having analyzed the data provided by the Toronto Board of Education, Cummins reported how long children take to develop BICS and CALP. He established that a child needs the average of two years to develop BICS and a time period as long as 5–7 years to master CALP.

A study by an American researcher Virginia Collier yields similar results. Collier found that children required 4–8 years to reach national grade level norms of academic achievement.[4]

Studies by Cummins and Collier are important for two reasons. Firstly, they alert parents and educators to a rather common misperception, namely, that a child who speaks fluently and confidently has mastered English. In fact, a child who is proficient in playground English usually needs a considerable additional amount of time to master the language of school. The studies by Cummins and Collier are also important, because they identify the task of top priority to language teachers. The task is to help young language learners learn academic language, something they cannot do without their teachers' help.

Insufficient Cognitive Stimulation of Language Learners

While there is consensus among TESOL educators that focusing on academic language development is one of the top priorities in the ESL classroom, teachers and students note that second language lessons that are being taught in schools do not always meet that goal. Immigrant children do tell researchers about the sense of comfort and security that they find in the ESL classroom; they also speak about the frustration of being insufficiently challenged. Even though children do not use sophisticated phrases such as "lack of focus on academic language" when describing the disappointing schooling experiences, their stories reveal that young language learners often feel that they do not get all the stimulation they could use.

In a study of immigrant children, a language learner told the interviewer about feeling bored when being asked "the same question—things you already know." So you don't learn new stuff,"[5] said this informant about the language lessons she experienced. Another child from Mexico said to a researcher, "I am learning again what I already knew in Mexico and I get bored in class."[6] A similar story is told by a girl from El Salvador, "I was two years in ESL and I didn't like it. My English level is not that low, but they treat you like your level is so low and you are stupid."[7] Immigrant parents also complain that their children are not properly challenged. For instance, in a study of immigrant children's experiences in the United States, a Chinese mother told interviewers that her son was not encouraged to learn new material even though he attended one of the highest-ranking schools in the Boston area. This parent noted, "School is mainly a place for kids to interact with other kids. [My son] does not really learn much from his teachers." The sentiment was echoed by a Dominican father who told researchers, "I think classes should be more challenging. Homework should be expected *and* corrected. Teachers should pay more attention to students' achievements. I would think that there are greater expectations for white American [students]."[8] Researchers who observe ESL classrooms describe some of the current ESL curricula as being "cognitively undemanding" and not providing students with the opportunities to develop higher-order thinking skills.[9]

The Challenge of Providing Cognitively Stimulating Instruction

There are various important reasons why it is hard to render ESL instruction cognitively stimulating. To begin with, there is a dearth of academic language materials for ESL students. There are not enough science, social studies, and math books that are written in a language that is accessible, clear, and at the comprehension level of English language learners. ESL teachers deal with the problem of shortage of instructional materials by developing their own materials or by adapting already existing ones. Needless to say, creating instructional materials is not easy and puts a big demand on ESL teachers' time.

There is also the challenge of teaching the abstract language of academic disciplines to children whose command of English is still limited. Academic language items are different from everyday vocabulary items, because their meaning is abstract. When teaching the meaning of a noun such as *a sticker* or *a desk*, the teacher can rely on incidental learning. To teach the word *crayon* or *picture* for example, all the teacher may need to do is encourage the children to use crayons or draw pictures, and then discuss these activities.

You may recall that Chapter 3 of this book discusses evidence that words which refer to concrete objects or actions are very likely to be picked up by a child incidentally, after a brief exposure. Teaching academic language, on the other hand, is an altogether different story. Unlike playground English, academic language is not learned incidentally. The teacher needs somehow to get around the fact that content vocabulary is *context-reduced*; in other words, academic language does not have immediately available referents in the classroom environment.[10] The teacher must display tremendous ingenuity and creativity when teaching the meaning of words such as *city* or *extinction* or *weightlessness* and *mammal* to a child whose command of English is still limited if the child is not familiar with these concepts in their first language.

Arguably the greatest challenge behind teaching academic language is establishing whether a child is ready to master a new abstract concept. It is not easy to evaluate the needs of ESL students accurately. To develop an academic language lesson, ESL teachers need to assess both the level of their students' English language proficiency and the level of their academic preparation,[11] and then set instructional objectives that are linguistically feasible yet cognitively stimulating. It is hard to reach these inherently disparate goals. Often children's limited academic language proficiency obscures the fact that children have a wealth of experiential knowledge and solid academic skills. No wonder ESL students are more often than not exposed to intellectually undemanding lessons.

Too Hard versus Too Easy: Age-Appropriate and Cognitively Stimulating Instruction

How can the teacher establish whether or not a language learner is ready to handle an academic language task? The answer to this question can be found in examination of the work of two renowned psychologists, Jean Piaget and Lev Vygotsky. While Piaget established a general framework for assessing whether or not a child is able to deal with a task, Vygotsky elucidated the extent to which a child can be challenged.

When observing his own son and two daughters, Laurent, Jacqueline, and Lucienne, Piaget came to the realization that children's modes of reasoning were not at all like those of adults. Piaget conducted a series of experiments that confirmed his insights. For instance, Piaget asked young children to compare two rows containing eight blocks each—the blocks were spread out in one row and placed close together in the other. When asked which row had more blocks, children pointed to the first row. In another experiment, children compared the amount of liquid in two cups. One of the two cups was narrow and tall, so the liquid in it reached almost to its brim. The other cup had a little more liquid in it, but was shallow with a broad mouth, and so the liquid covered only its bottom. When children were asked which cup had more water, they picked the first cup. These and similar observations led Piaget to argue that children think differently from the way adults do, and that they have to have reached a certain developmental stage before they are ready to handle abstract concepts, such as the concept of number. Piaget concluded that teachers need to take these stages of children's development into account when setting instructional goals. When modern teachers say that a child is "not ready" to perform a task or understand an idea, they are referring to the need to respect developmental constraints previously identified by Piaget.

Piaget's position was challenged by a Russian psychologist, Lev Vygotsky. Until recently, Vygotsky's work (conducted in the 1930s) was not well known. In fact, even in his home country of Russia, Vygotsky's research had been ignored by mainstream government-supported science and barely acknowledged in colleges. Nor was Vygotsky's work fully appreciated outside Russia, in part because of Russia's isolationist policies under communism. These days, however, Vygotsky is hailed as "Mozart of psychology;" educators all over the world are embracing his views. What were Vygotsky's ideas regarding readiness and academic language?

Vygotsky objected to the notion that teachers and caregivers need to stand back and wait patiently until the child becomes developmentally ready to master a concept. Vygotsky further contended that instruction does not need to trudge timidly behind development—on the contrary, it should proceed ahead of development. According to Vygotsky, in addition to the child's actual, current developmental stage, there exists another one—that is the developmental stage that a child is about to reach. He used the term *Zone of Proximal Development (ZPD)* to refer to this upcoming, potential, about-to-happen developmental stage and argued that teaching is only good if it is positioned at the cutting edge, the furthest reach of the child's ZPD, not at the stage of the child's actual development. Thus, good teaching, according to Vygotsky, needs to be positioned at the child's budding, emerging developmental level. As Vygotsky puts it, "Instruction is good only when it proceeds ahead of development. Then it awakens and rouses to life an entire set of functions which are in the stage of maturing."[12]

The second part of this quotation is particularly important. Why is it necessary to position instruction ahead of development? Why not wait until the child is "ready?" According to Vygotsky, instruction needs to proceed ahead of development, because some developmental processes are not going to take place without instruction. The child cannot reach certain developmental stages on his own, without mediation from the teacher. Rather, development takes place when children interact with adults or more proficient peers; it is these novice–expert interactions that make child development happen. As Vygotsky himself puts it, development "first ... appears on the social plane, and then on the psychological plane."[13] In other words, instruction actualizes development.

According to this model, the role of instruction is particularly great when it comes to the use of academic concepts and the development of academic reasoning skills, which do not happen in young children without mediation from the school. Consider the following instances of language use discussed by Vygotsky. Psychologists have demonstrated that there is a difference between the cases when children use a word correctly (but unconsciously) and use another word not only correctly but also consciously. This difference is striking when young children use everyday language and abstract academic language. For instance, young children may use the word *brother* or *son* correctly but may be unable to explain what they mean or perform a simple intellectual operation of giving an example of a brother or a son. (A little boy in Vygotsky's experiment denied that a man was somebody's son on the grounds that the man had a beard.) In contrast, children have no difficulty in defining concepts that they study at school. The same child who uses the word *brother* and cannot explain its meaning may be able to define the word *revolution* and describe a Russian revolution. (The example used by Vygotsky comes from postrevolutionary Russia of the 1930s.) A modern American child who may have similar difficulty with the word *son* may be able to define an abstract word, such as *neighborhood* (provided the word has been studied in school). A child who has mastered some abstract academic language has also learned to define and categorize abstract language items and perform similar reasoning operations. For Vygotsky, to know academic language is to know how to use language in a conscious way. Vygotsky pointed out that conscious use of language and the cognitive development that it entails do not happen without mediation by the school.

But how can the teacher establish whether a language skill that she is about to teach is within a child's grasp? How can she determine that a child has reached that "budding" developmental stage at which he or she can benefit from instructional stimulation? For followers of Vygotsky, the rule of thumb is the child's ability to imitate an activity or to perform an activity with the help of an adult.

Interestingly enough, according to Vygotsky, imitation is not an intellectually vapid activity; it is never mindless copying. Vygotsky argued that children can imitate only what they are beginning to understand or in Vygotsky's words, "imitation is possible only to the extent and in those forms in which it is accompanied by understanding."[14] It follows that if children are capable of imitating a task, they will soon be able to perform that task on their own. For instance, if children can write stories using a graphic organizer provided by the teacher, they will soon be able to create similar pieces of writing unassisted. Conversely, if the child is unable to mimic or copy a model, he or she is still developmentally removed from mastering a certain skill.

A child's ability to perform an activity with the help of an adult is another litmus test that helps determine the extent to which a child can be challenged. An activity that children are able to perform with adult help is an indication of their budding developmental stage or the ZPD. Children can handle a challenge if they can take advantage of adult assistance when dealing with that challenge.

Characteristics of ZPD-positioned Instruction

At this point, it is a good idea to flip the coin and to look at the problem of language development from another point of view. A few words are in order about the kind of instruction that can be described as cognitively stimulating. What exactly happens in the ZPD-positioned classroom? What kinds of lessons promote children's intellectual growth?

First of all, according to Vygotsky and his followers, ZPD-positioned instruction has an essential characteristic—it examines abstract, theoretical *academic language*. Moreover, in the ZPD-positioned classroom academic language is examined as a system.[15] For instance, in a cognitively stimulating lesson intended for young students, a teacher might encourage language learners to explore concepts such as *dinosaur, reptile, fossil*, and *extinct* and to examine the interrelationships among these words. Similarly, in a lesson that focuses on bats children might examine concepts such as *mammal, nocturnal*, and *echolocation*. Or in a lesson on volcanoes, children would explore the meaning of words *eruption, lava, earth crust*, and *magma*. It is these "big" words which describe the concepts the child is unlikely to encounter outside school and which cannot be incidentally grasped without some degree of conscious understanding that are the bread and butter of intellectually stimulating teaching.

Vygotsky identified another characteristic of developmentally stimulating instruction. He argued that an instructional activity promotes cognitive growth if a child could not possibly handle it on her own, without the guidance provided by a teacher or a more proficient peer. In the ZPD-positioned classroom *instruction is conceptualized as assistance*. According to this teaching scenario, the teacher does not simply assign a task and check how well (or poorly) it has been performed by children. Rather, the teacher becomes her students' collaborator, helping the class with every step of a task. In today's world, young children perform a myriad of complex language tasks without adult assistance. We have all observed little children solving elaborate word puzzles or playing language games at computer stations. According to the Vygotskian model, these seemingly complex activities do little to promote a child's language growth. It is only when children engage in activities for which they need adult help that they reach the next stage of their cognitive development.

Proponents of cognitively stimulating teaching further argue that the activity that the children and their teacher perform together needs to be authentic and have a clear goal. In the ZPD-positioned classroom, children may carry out an experiment, create a model, go on a class trip, participate in role-play, put on a show, publish a book or a class journal, plant a garden, go on an imaginary trip, enact a historic event, carry out pretend jobs, and so forth.[16]

Vygotsky also pointed out that teachers who work in a ZPD-positioned classroom use special instructional psychic tools to help children master abstract language or perform difficult tasks. These tools (to which more recent studies refer under the name of *scaffolds*) can take the form of models, graphic organizers, questions, or word walls and are created jointly by the teacher and language learners. The scaffold is used initially as a support mechanism that helps the child cope with a task; once the student has an initial grasp of a concept or a skill, the scaffold can be removed.

Language Tasks and the Problem of Language Learners' Readiness

The two developmental models developed by Piaget and Vygotsky are both antithetical and complementary to one another. When setting instructional objectives for the classroom and deciding what to teach and when to teach it, teachers need to be mindful of children's developmental limitations, and at the same time, render instruction that is cognitively demanding and stimulating. This seeming contradiction between principles is of particular relevance for language teachers. On the one hand, they need to reckon with the limitations set by their students' language proficiency levels and prior academic experience. On the other hand, within these very tight constraints, they need to create and implement activities that help children grow.

A careful assessment of a language learner's needs is required before the teacher can establish whether or not the young student is ready to handle a task. While this assessment is highly individualized, some general principles of what can and cannot be done in the language classroom need to be borne in mind. There is a skill area where breaking out of developmental constraints is extremely difficult or perhaps impossible in the early childhood second language classroom. That skill area is use of the grammar of oral language. Research suggests that recasting, corrective feedback, imitation exercises, and instructional strategies have no impact on the morphological and syntactic maturity of young students' speech.[17] Imitation in particular has been proven to be powerless to help students master grammar. There is evidence that asking students to repeat the correct form after the teacher or to memorize the form does not translate into the control of grammar.

Can grammar be taught at all? Can teachers help young ESL students use word endings and sentence structure correctly? Research by Manfred Pienemann,[18] Rod Ellis,[19] and others throws some light on these intriguing questions, which are known as questions of *learnability* and *teachability*. A study conducted by Pienemann focused on Italian-speaking students learning German. Pienemann wanted to know whether instruction made any difference in the way students learned German word order. He demonstrated that when students were developmentally ready to master an item, instruction speeded up the process. However, if students were not ready, explanations provided by the teacher made no difference.[20] The study suggests that instruction is powerless to change the order in which students master grammar—the stages of grammar learning are *impervious to instruction*. All the teacher can hope for is to speed up the rate of students' morphological and syntactic maturation. The conclusions are even more dramatic when researchers analyze grammar learnability and teachability in young children, especially those who are learning ESL in an environment when they are hearing a lot of native speakers using English. These children seem to have a very hard time copying corrective grammatical feedback provided by adults. Either they do not hear a correction provided through recasting or some other form of feedback or even if they do repeat a form correctly, they fail to do so in spontaneous speech.

While teaching young second language learners the grammar of oral language seems to be hardly possible, there are numerous studies that discuss ways of positioning instruction at the cutting edge of young language learners' development when teaching academic content or literacy skills. Ways of rendering instruction intellectually challenging when teaching young English language learners are discussed in the previous sections of this book. In that part of the book, you read about various tools that help render second language instruction intellectually stimulating. For instance, Chapter 5 explores the use of various kinds of Literacy Scaffolds to help young language learners create extended and sophisticated literacy pieces. Similarly, Chapter 7 examines the use of role-play for investigating concepts in the areas of social studies.

These instructional strategies have several important features in common. First of all complex role-plays, science experiments, or fixed form writing (to name some instructional strategies) are examples of assisted practice. Children can experience success in these activities only if the teacher scaffolds their action through directions, or questioning, or graphic organizers. Further, these activities are unique, because they rely on children's ability to learn through imitation. When a child uses a Fixed Form writing scaffold to create a written piece of his or her own or when students impersonate adults in a role-play, they begin to develop complex literacy skills and grasp complex concepts by copying a model. The child's skill in and enjoyment of imitation becomes key to the success of these activities. Young language learners can be very good at using models provided by role-play fishbowls or literacy scaffolds. Moreover, they derive great pleasure in imitating sophisticated language use. If one little "radio announcer" says in a role-play "Attention ladies and gentlemen. The speed of the wind is thirty miles per hour. We are expecting a hurricane," others are sure to say "My turn!" Similarly, when children write using Literacy Scaffolds, they experience a sense of satisfaction and accomplishment. In the words of one researcher, "[If] ESL students are adequately supported in tasks to elicit certain knowledge and discourse structures, they are able to produce texts of which they can be proud."[21] That pride that young language learners display when they participate in activities which help them speak, read, and write like grown-ups is an important affective characteristic of a ZPD-positioned lesson. If little language learners look poised and pleased with own language output, they are probably engaged in a cognitively stimulating lesson.

Main Points

- Effective language lessons for young language learners need to be both within learners' linguistic grasp and intellectually challenging, or positioned at the highest reach of children's ZPD.

- Conceptualizing instruction as assistance, focusing on academic language, and massive use of scaffolding are some of the features of ZPD-positioned lessons.

- Language learners benefit from using models. A child's ability to perform an action when imitating a model is an indication of a budding developmental stage.

Notes

1. B. McLaughlin (1984), *Second-language acquisition in childhood: Vol. 1. Preschool children*, 2nd ed. Hillsdale, NJ: Lawrence Erlbaum Associates.

2. Leo van Lier (2005), "Case Study." In Eli Hinkel (Ed.), *Handbook of research in second language teaching and learning*. Mahwah, NJ: Lawrence Erlbaum Associates, pp. 195–208. Van Lier provides an interesting overview of case studies that demonstrate that children do need an extended time period to develop full proficiency.

3. J. Cummins (1979), "Cognitive/Academic Language Proficiency, Linguistic Interdependence, the Optimum Age Question and some Other Matters." *Working Papers on Bilingualism*, 19, 121–129.

4. V. Collier (1987), "Age and Rate of Acquisition of Second Language for Academic Purposes." *TESOL Quarterly*, 21(4), 617–641.

5. C. Suarez-Orozco and M. Suarez-Orozco (2001), *Children of immigration*. Cambridge, MA: Harvard University Press, p. 146.

6. Ibid.

7. L. Olsen (1988), *Crossing the school house border: Immigrant students and the California public schools*. San Francisco, CA: California Tomorrow, p. 63.

8. Suarez-Orozco and Suarez-Orozco, *Children of immigration*, p. 147.

9. M.A. Snow, M. Met, and F. Genesee (1992), "A Conceptual Framework for the Integration of Language and Content Instruction." In P. Richard-Amato and M.A. Snow (Eds.), *The multicultural classroom: Readings for content-area teachers*. White Plains, NY: Longman, pp. 27–38.

10. J. Cummins (1992), "Language Proficiency, Bilingualism, and Academic Achievement." In P. Richard-Amato and M.A. Snow (Eds.), *The multicultural classroom: Readings for content-area teachers*. White Plains, NY: Longman, pp. 16–26.

11. J.D. Bragger and D.B. Rice (1998), "Connections: The National Standards and a New Paradigm for Content-Oriented Materials and Instruction." In J. Harper, M. Lively, and M. Williams (Eds.), *The coming of age of the profession: Issues and*

emerging ideas for the teaching of foreign languages. Boston, MA: Heinle & Heinle, pp. 191–217.

12. L. Vygotsky (1934), "Myshlenie I rech': Psykhologicheskie Issledovaniya [Thinking and Speech: Psychological Investigations]." Moscow: Gosudarstvennoe-Sotsial'no-Ekonomicheskoe Izdatel'stvo. Cited in J. Wertsch (1985), *Vygotsky and the social formation of mind.* Cambridge, MA: Harvard University Press, p. 71.

13. J. Wertsch (1990), "The Voice of Rationality in a Sociocultural Approach to Mind." In L. Moll (Ed.), *Vygotsky and education: Instructional implications and applications of sociohistorical psychology.* New York: Cambridge University Press, p. 113.

14. L. Vygotsky (1997), *The collected works of L.S. Vygotsky, Vol. 4: The history of the devlopment of higher mental functions.* New York: Plenum Press, p. 96.

15. C. Panofsky, V. John-Steiner, and P. Blackwell (1990), "The Development of Scientific Concepts and Discourse." In L. Moll (Ed.), *Vygotsky and education: Instructional implications and applications of sociohistorical psychology.* New York: Cambridge University Press, pp. 251–267.

16. Y. Goodman and K. Goodman (1990), "Vygotsky in a Whole-Language Perspective." In L. Moll (Ed.), *Vygotsky and education: Instructional implications and applications of sociohistorical psychology.* New York: Cambridge University Press, pp. 223–250.

17. L. White (1991), "Adverb Placement in Second Language Acquisition: Some Effects of Positive and Negative Evidence in the Classroom." *Second Language Research,* 7(2), 133–161.

18. M. Pienemann (1989), "Is Language Teachable? Psycholinguistic Experiments and Hypotheses." *Applied linguistics,* 10(1), 52–79.

19. R. Ellis (1984), "Can Syntax Be Taught? A Study of the Effects of Formal Instruction on the Acquisition of WH Questions by Children." *Applied Linguistics,* 5(2), 138–155.

20. M. Pienemann (1984), Psychological constraints on the teachability of languages. *Studies in Second language Acquisition,* 6(2), 186–214.

21. M. Early (October 1990), "Enabling First and Second Language Learners in the Classroom." *Language Arts,* 67, 574.

CHAPTER 10

Using Technology with Young English Language Learners

Ekaterina Nemtchinova, Seattle Pacific University

To say that technology has had an enormous impact on the world of education is to state the obvious. Today, teachers and researchers attempt to conceptualize the potential of technology for language teaching and learning in relation to early English language education. Can technology benefit young English language learners? Does it offer instructional gains that cannot be found in other teaching materials? How should technology be used in language teaching, if at all?

The Benefits of Technology as an Instructional Tool

The use of technology in the primary-level ESL classroom enjoys support from researchers and educators. Thus, "many reports present strong assertions that technology can catalyze various other changes in the content, methods, and overall quality of the teaching and learning process, most frequently, triggering changes away from lecture-driven instruction and toward constructivist, inquiry-oriented classrooms."[1] Specifically, technology benefits young learners by enhancing their physical abilities such as hand–eye coordination and fine motor skills. It can also improve children's understanding of the world around them, develop their flexibility and ingenuity, enrich their worldview, and expand their openness of mind.[2] Finally, if children start to develop appropriate knowledge and skills early in their schooling, they can be better prepared for life outside the classroom where technology is an integral part of many everyday activities.

An important benefit of using technology in the classroom is the medium's potential to motivate children[3] and to produce a positive attitude toward learning. Apart from the excitement of novelty caused by the appearance of a new teaching tool, technology builds substantial interest by adding variety and bringing new experiences to the classroom. Technology allows the teacher to establish a meaningful context for communicative activities and to engage students in authentic and realistic experiences that add excitement to the learning process. Additionally, various combinations of text, pictures, and sounds offered by an assortment of technology can be used to improve receptive language skills, inspire classroom discussions, elicit target language from individual students, and stimulate different learning styles while engaging the learners.

Another advantage technology has to offer the language learner is authenticity, a feature that scholars regard as essential to language learning experience. Scholars generally suggest that authentic materials should be introduced in their original form early in instruction, provided that the tasks are tailored to the students' linguistic abilities.[4,5] Audio, video, and Internet-based materials created for native speakers of English are also a vital means of providing comprehensible input. Novice language learners are often intimidated by unfamiliar words, colloquial expressions, and grammatical structures beyond their proficiency range. While it is almost always possible to modify authentic material to make it accessible to students, another alternative is a clearly focused task design that can diminish the risk of students being overwhelmed.[6] Opting for structured rather than open-ended tasks, asking very specific questions, focusing on familiar words and topics within students' base of knowledge, asking about the understanding of the basic idea instead of every fact and detail are just some of the possible solutions to the problem of complexity of authentic input. Clear step-by-step directions also help to avoid students' confusion.

Challenges in the Use of Educational Technology

While more traditional types of educational technology (e.g., an overhead projector, audio and video players) may be primarily operated by teachers, newer technologies such as word processing software and the Internet often require an active participation on the part of students. It is recommended that teachers assess students' knowledge about computers before asking them to engage in an activity.[7] Students with no previous exposure to computers will need several preparatory sessions to become familiar with word processing software, develop their keyboard and mouse skills, and learn some elementary computer terminology.

In case a computer laboratory is not available for the class session, students in groups of two or three can rotate at the single computer in the classroom while the rest of the class is doing another assignment. More advanced computer users usually can pair with less computer literate students in order to increase interactivity and free the teacher to assist as needed.

Perhaps the greatest challenge to using technology tools effectively is the all-too-familiar constellation of problems with technology. On the one hand, there is a problem of reliability: electrical equipment, hardware, or software can break down in the middle of the lesson, resulting in students' giggles, teachers' frustration, and the loss of the precious teaching time. Having an alternative technology-free activity at hand in case technical problems arise can greatly reduce possible stress while conveying the same point and retaining the format of the lesson. There is a problem of availability: there simply may be no audio, video, computer equipment, and/or Internet access at the teaching site. To the extent that technology is available, however, it needs to be used, because benefits offered by technology by far outweigh the challenges presented by its use.

Technology-Based Resources and Activities

The sections that follow concentrate on how to incorporate technology into the English language classroom and discuss activities specifically aimed at young learners. Staying away from commercial ESL materials, the chapter focuses on resources that are available to the general public.

Overhead Projector

The overhead projector (OHP) is probably the simplest and most accessible technology available in the classroom. Teachers use the OHP to write and draw on transparencies and to project magnified images on the screen or a blank wall while facing the audience. The use of an OHP rather than chalkboard is advantageous in several respects. First, the OHP grabs students' attention and focuses all learners in one direction. Concealing and revealing parts of the text provide even more emphasis on important points. The use of the OHP also increases teaching time by eliminating the need to write and erase the chalkboard because the teacher can prepare in advance the necessary materials, including student writing.[8] Second, unlike chalkboard writing, which is erased after the lesson, transparencies can be reproduced, recycled, and retained for another usage. The content and focus of a basic transparency can be easily changed by overlaying and/or using color markers. Depending on the activity at hand, students can also write and draw on transparencies to exhibit their work. Finally, instead of providing photocopies for each student in the class, the teacher can prepare a single set of slides for the lesson. Using a printer or a photocopier can greatly enhance the input and result in professional-looking material. Overall, an OHP increases flexibility of instruction and increases visual and emotional appeal of materials, thus facilitating the language learning experience.

- *My Special Friend.* For instance, in this activity which focuses on target language items related to personal information, the teacher starts by demonstrating a transparency picture which features his/her special friend (it can be a pet, a stuffed animal, or a person). The teacher invites students to ask questions about the picture, eliciting a list of who-questions (e.g., *Who is your best friend? What does your best friend like to eat? Where does your best friend live? When does your best friend get up in the morning? What does your best friend enjoy doing?*). Then students can draw their special friends on a blank transparency using color markers and create their own questions to ask their classmates. The teacher may choose to display a Literacy Scaffold with question words or a list of complete questions to support student output. Finally, volunteers share their pictures and answer their classmates' questions.

- *Pin the Nose on a Face.* This activity allows students to give and follow directions while reviewing target language items for location and body parts. A blindfolded player (either a teacher or a student volunteer) has to dress up a person drawn on a transparency using cutout clothes (e.g., pants, a shirt, socks, etc.). In order for the player to place pieces of clothing in the right position, the audience must help by telling him/her what piece he/she is holding and where to put it. The player can also ask questions. For example, to find out what piece the player is holding in his hands, he or she can ask, "What is this?" As the player places the piece on the outline of the body, the other students tell him or her to move the piece of clothing to the right or left, up or down. The same format can be used to practice vocabulary related to food (food items can be put on the drawing of a table or in a refrigerator) or town (when students fill an empty pictorial street map with buildings) or home (students "furnish" a drawing of a room).

Audio

Audio has long been popular among English language teachers as a tool that is easy to access and use at a low cost. It is used to practice listening skills, provide context and motivation for speaking, reading, and writing activities, and to access listening and speaking. Audio extends linguistic input of the classroom by affording exposure to a wide range of speakers, voices, accents, situations, and a rich cultural content.[9] Teachers use a variety of media for listening practice. While many teachers turn to newer technologies such as CD, CD-ROM, and the World Wide Web to plan their lessons, more traditional tools including radio broadcasts and audiocassettes are still in use.

Teacher and students can handle an audiocassette or a CD player with little, if any, training. Teachers use commercial listening materials (many ESL/EFL textbooks now come with an audio component) or make their own recordings to suit their teaching objectives. An obvious benefit of recording and playback equipment, in addition to saving teachers' energy and voices, is the degree of control enjoyed by a listener. Unlike a real-life broadcast where the sound is gone once in the air, the child can pause a tape and rewind it as many times as needed to understand the meaning. These simple features can be creatively used in language instruction in several ways. For example, a longer passage can be divided into manageable portions by pausing at natural breaks. A teacher can also pause the listening to ask children to predict what they might hear next, to write or draw an answer, transcribe a sentence, or simply repeat after the speaker in order to practice pronunciation. Or, the teacher can edit an audio segment by recording parts of the passage on different tapes in order to create an information gap activity in which groups of students each listen to a tape and try to collectively reconstruct the whole story.

No matter what medium is used and what type of listening material the activity is based on, educators suggest that listening comprehension exercises are most effective when they are structured within the framework of pre-listening, listening, and post-listening.[10] Each of these stages has a specific purpose that contributes to building listening skills. Thus, pre-listening tasks are designed to help students prepare for listening the text by activating vocabulary and background knowledge on a particular topic. They can also arouse students' curiosity and provide motivation for further listening of the passage. Examples of pre-listening activities include writing the title of the text on the board or playing the first few sentences of the text and asking students what they think the text is going to be about. The class can also brainstorm keywords or create a semantic map associated with the topic of the text. Unfamiliar vocabulary that students will come across while listening to the text is also pre-taught at this stage.

Listening activities are active exercises that make students attend to the text in order to complete the task assigned by the teacher. Many educators recommend listening to the same text several times; a clear, explicit purpose for each listening is important because it increases students' involvement with the text and reinforces listening comprehension. Teachers can ask students to state the main idea of the text or to listen for specific information. Other popular activities include answering comprehension questions based on the text, filling in the blanks with or without a list of missing words, and correcting deliberate mistakes in the transcript while listening. Teachers could also use dictation, scrambled sentences, a completion exercise, or a true/false activity at this stage of the lesson.

Post-listening activities serve as an extension of listening and enable students to apply target language items found in listening texts in a different context. These activities help develop oral and written fluency skills and engage students in an active use of target language. In groups or as a class, students who are emergent language learners can act out role-plays and simulations, create alternative endings to stories, or perform TPR activities connected to the topic of listening. At a more advanced language level, students can analyze the register of the text and the emotions conveyed by the speaker(s). If a listening text contains some kind of problem (e.g., a student is missing classes), a class can discuss how to deal with it and write or discuss possible solutions to the problem.

Songs

Despite the multiplicity of resources that can be used for listening, many teachers favor songs as the most appropriate material for children. There are many reasons for making songs a part of the English language curriculum. On the one hand, songs present a natural opportunity for meaningful repetition in context. Pronouncing target sounds, words, and forms many times increases retention of the language that students can later use as ready-made chunks for communicative purposes.[11] On another hand, songs convey valuable cultural information and deal with topics that are relevant to students. The lyrics focus on theme of interest to children and can initiate more speaking, reading, drawing, and writing activities, and provide additional practice for students. Another benefit of using music activities in the classroom is that they foster relaxation, positive group dynamics, and make learning the language a memorable experience. Students at all levels of proficiency are excited to participate in music-based activities.

- *Wiggle in My Toe.* This song's uncomplicated lyrics, appealing music, and repetitive pattern make it an excellent exercise for practicing body parts vocabulary.[12] After reviewing body parts, the teacher demonstrates the meaning of the verbs *wiggle* and *giggle*. During the first listening the children perform the actions of the words that involve various body parts. To reinforce sound-spelling correspondence of the vocabulary the teacher creates a fill-in-the-blank sheet with the body parts missing from the lyrics. Students fill in the gaps during their second listening to the song. For the third listening, students work in several groups of three or four. Each group receives an envelope with strips of paper containing lines of lyrics. Students have to put the strips in the correct order as they listen to the song.

- *What Do You Do Every Day?* Daily routines are often studied in an ESL/EFL classroom at the beginning level of language proficiency. The song *The Land of Slow Motion*[13] can be an interesting way to review vocabulary on the topic. The teacher starts by distributing cards with pictures or words representing everyday actions (e.g., *get out of bed, brush my teeth, eat with my family*). Children act out these action words without showing them to other students while the class has to guess what action is being performed. The students then listen to the song together while acting out every action mentioned in the song. The alteration of slow and fast tempo in the song provides for a fun-filled pronunciation practice.

- *So Many Shoes!* More advanced students enjoy an activity based on the song *Late Last Night*.[14] Not only does it contribute to expanding children's vocabulary related to different types of footwear, but it also provides an opportunity to practice action verbs in context and to engage in physical activity. The song is fairly long and some of the vocabulary may be unfamiliar to students. The teacher may choose to limit the song to several easier verses or to introduce new words by using pictures and mime. For pre-listening, the class brainstorms to identify different types of shoes and actions that can be performed in these shoes (e.g. *ballet shoes to dance*); nouns and verbs are put on the board in two columns. The teacher asks students to match the shoes with the appropriate verbs and to check their matches while they listen to the song. For the second listening, the sheets of paper with action verbs printed on them in large font are randomly attached to the board and walls of the classroom. The students take turns for pulling the sheet off the board when they hear an appropriate verb. For the third listening, students act out the action while listening to the music after each verse. For a follow-up activity, they choose one type of shoe and draw or write their own sentence about what they can do in it.

Audio Books

Books on an audiocassette, a CD, or online are yet other excellent sources for listening practice. These books can enhance an English language program by building vocabulary and comprehension, expanding background knowledge, and providing good examples of fluent reading in English. Audio books facilitate reading by highlighting the connection of the sounds and the written language, and increasing reading rate, and word attack skills.[15] They are particularly beneficial for emergent readers who can understand much more than they can read. Beginners often struggle with decoding a written text in a target language, whereas listening to a book on tape can alleviate some of this burden and allow children to participate in language learning tasks.

Audio books provide an opportunity for children to experience reading through the voice of others. A captivating plot and colorful characters come alive as professional readers narrate the story. The music and background effects enable children to picture actions and events and create a special mood, stirring the children's creativity and imagination. Listening to stories on tapes assists with fluency, comprehension, and prediction; invites wide-ranging discussions; and motivates reluctant readers to explore literature.

Different kinds of literature are available in audio format. A visit to a local library or a search on the Internet reveals scores of fiction, folk tales, nonfiction, poetry, and even children's magazines; many titles exist in both abridged and unabridged versions. Some teachers also record themselves as they read a story. To select suitable material the teacher has to consider the length and complexity of the text. Ten minutes of listening seems to be the maximum young language learners can handle before their concentration flags. The level of vocabulary is another important consideration: if less than 75–80 percent of the vocabulary is familiar to students, they may feel frustrated and overwhelmed by the story.[16] Finally, the success of the listening activity depends on whether the topic of the book is interesting for young listeners.

Different books on tapes, with or without the support of a printed version, can lead to a variety of activities in a second language classroom. The teacher can play an entire book part by part, making it a regular listening activity, or choose short excerpts that suit the objective of a given lesson. To make sure that students are actively engaged and following along as they listen, it is important to provide a listening purpose by giving specific instructions about what to listen for. "The definition of a purpose enables the listener to listen selectively for significant information which is easier and more natural than trying to understand every word."[17]

- *Hide and Seek.* A simple language, familiar concepts, deliberate pace, and short duration make *The day I had to play with my sister* an exciting playful activity for beginning learners.[18] Prior to listening, to activate students' background knowledge, the teacher asks children if they are familiar with the game of hide-and-seek and elicits their native-language equivalents of the *Ready or not, here I come* phrase. Then, students listen to the tape without reading. After discussion and clarification of any confusion they listen again, repeat after the tape, and read along. As they listen to the story played for the third time, the students put the pictures from the book in the correct order. To follow up on this activity children play the popular game of hide-and-seek, saying the chant in English.

- *Anastasia Krupnik.* More proficient learners can perform a variety of tasks based on a recorded story. For example, the activities based on selective, spaced listening to *Anastasia Krupnik*[19] integrate grammar instruction (e.g., imperative mood, present perfect) as well as focus on such discussion topics as likes and dislikes, the relations in the family, appearance, and the way people dress, to name just a few. Students also ask and answer questions about the content and predict how the chapter will end or what Anastasia is going to write in her green notebook. To expand their vocabulary students fill their own vocabulary journals with words that seldom occur in everyday speech, just like Anastasia.

On the Web

An infinite supply of interesting, authentic, and recent listening materials is available through the Internet. There are many Web sites that offer a variety of recordings ranging from separate sounds, words, and sentences for pronunciation practice to dialogs, texts, and songs that teachers can integrate into a sequence of lessons in order to develop listening and understanding of the target language. Selecting an appropriate Web site for a particular lesson can be a challenging task given the wealth of resources available. First, Web-based audio materials vary in their authenticity: while some are created specifically for ESL/EFL learners, others are intended for a native speaking audience and may contain vocabulary, grammar, and content beyond students' language proficiency. Second, the degree of control over listening may vary as some, but not all, sites come with a time monitor, a start/stop/pause button, and a recording function. An additional consideration concerns the availability of support materials. Does the site offer activities, and/or transcripts of the recording, or will you need to create appropriate support materials to make an audio more accessible to your students? Also, is the content appropriate for young English language learners?

- *A Trip to the Zoo.* Incorporation of authentic texts makes learning more meaningful and helps students gain courage and confidence as well as skills toward successful language use in different situations. In the zoo activity, aimed at developing the skill of listening for the gist, students listen to the text accompanying an *Animal Planet* video clip about pandas (http://animal.discovery.com/convergence/pandas/videogallery). To help students understand the text the teacher hands out questions: *What animal is it? Where does it live? What does it eat?* After listening to the text several times students can watch the video to check their answers.

- *Happy Birthday!* An example of a listening Web site designed specifically for second language learners is *Randall's ESL Cyber Listening Lab* (http://www.esl-lab.com/) that features recorded conversations and listening exercises. To follow up on the multiple-choice activity provided on the Web site, students can describe their dream birthday party and make suggestions for their dream party activities and participants.

- *Breakfast, Lunch, Dinner.* Another excellent online resource is *English Listening Lounge* (http://www.englishlistening.com). Although it is designed for an older audience, many clips in the New Listener section are suitable to adapt for younger students. For example, *A young woman's diet* can be used for practicing food vocabulary and talking about eating habits. Word-level listening tasks include labeling pictures of food items with words, categorizing food items mentioned by the speaker into breakfast, lunch, and dinner categories, and making lists of what the speaker eats for each meal. As a follow-up activity, students compare the speaker's diet with their own and place different types of food on a food pyramid.

Video

Like audio, video is a familiar medium. It is available in a variety of formats, and is designed for the general public as well as specifically for ESL learners. Feature films and cartoons, movie trailers, commercials, educational programs on television, and video have many practical applications in an English language classroom. Video is used to expose students to target language in context, present cultural information including nonverbal cues (gestures and facial expressions), and prompt student discussion.[20]

Research suggests that students enjoy learning language with video.[21] To make video-based activities more effective, educators recommend playing segments rather than a whole video, since students might become distracted after six to ten minutes of watching.[22] It is also important to provide a clear purpose for watching in order to focus students' attention on the content of the video and to supply pre-viewing and post-viewing activities. Similar to listening, pre-viewing activities draw on students' background knowledge in order to facilitate comprehension and clarify language items that are essential for understanding the video. Post-viewing exercises follow up on the content and language of the video clip by answering comprehension questions, interpreting, summarizing, discussing, and acting out.

The choice of a particular video depends on the objectives of the lesson, the level of students' language proficiency, and the video material itself. While some excerpts lend themselves to presenting language to students, others are more suitable for eliciting language about the video from students.[23] Most video fragments are appropriate for more than one activity; a thoroughly utilized piece can generate a lot of active viewing and teaching.[24]

- *What Do You See?* This activity provides practice in listening and speaking skills while emphasizing verb tenses. The most suitable video for this activity is a short segment that has plenty of action and little or no talking, for example, *Red's Dream*.[25] The students are arranged in two rows and seated face to face so that the video can be seen by one row (watchers) but not by the other (listeners and writers). The watchers' task is to describe the action on the screen using the target verb tense. The writers have to listen carefully and jot down as much information as they can. After watching half of the video segment, students exchange seats and watch the other half for a new row of watchers. Then, groups of students from both rows pool their notes and create the complete version of events. A follow-up activity can include showing the clip again for everyone to see, compare, and discuss their original understanding with what actually happened in the video clip.

- *Only at a Toy Store!* In this activity, the teacher shows the class a commercial that advertises an age-appropriate toy without the sound. The students have to answer the following questions: What toy is being advertised? How can you describe it? What can you do with it? Do you like it? After discussing the answers to the questions, the class watches the commercial again, this time with the sound on, to check their answers to the questions. As a follow up, students create their own text by advertising their favorite toy and practicing saying their advertisement with the correct intonation.

- *Molly's Thanksgiving.* Video can prompt a discussion of issues to which students can relate. For example, *Molly's Pilgrim*[26] tells a story of a young Russian-Jewish emigrant who tries to adjust to her new life in the United States. The themes of a culture shock, acceptance by a peer group, and human relations can each lead to an engaging discussion in which students may want to compare their experiences with those of Molly and voice their feelings and/or concerns. A different activity involves people's emotions and moods. The teacher provides a list of five to seven adjectives and asks students to match the words with the moods of the characters in the video.

Word Processing Software

Word processing software has been used extensively both by English language teachers and students. While teachers enjoy the ease and flexibility with which they can manage, modify, and save teaching resources and students' records, students are motivated to articulate their ideas in writing, work on multiple drafts, and actively interact with written text.[27] Several features of word processing programs are particularly popular in second language classrooms. Numerous editing functions (e.g., cut and paste, find, and replace) are creatively used by teachers to teach text organization and revision strategies, encourage self- and peer-editing, and engage students in the writing process. Even low-proficient students benefit from using a keyboard to reinforce such basic literacy skills as comparing lowercase and uppercase letters, and practicing spelling and fine motor coordination.[28] Spelling and grammar checkers as well as thesauruses provide flexibility in making appropriate changes and aid in developing students' spelling, expanding their vocabulary, and refining their writing.

Finally, by varying the size, color, font, and alignment of the text, using attractive borders, and inserting ClipArt images, students can create a visually appealing product that they proudly share with others.

- *A Book about Us.* This activity allows students to write about a particularly memorable episode they experienced together. After a discussion of a recent field trip or a school event children produce individual paragraphs reflecting their impressions of the episode, which are typed and saved on the computer. Scanner or digital pictures inserted into the text add interest to the final product that is compiled into a class book and distributed to students.

- *Look at My Picture!* In this activity, students use a drawing tool to create various shapes and objects and fill them with different colors. The teacher may want to tell children how many and what objects to create for more uniformity in responses, or allow complete freedom in choosing and coloring the shapes. Students make descriptive and comparative sentences based on their pictures, for example, *The red square is bigger than the blue one. There is a green circle and a red arrow on my picture.*

- *Editing.* Word processing software makes error correction enjoyable while making students focus and reflect on errors in their writing. For this activity, the teacher prepares two copies of the same text. One group of students is instructed to populate a copy of the original text with incorrect forms of language use; focus on the conventions of writing errors (e.g., capitalization, punctuation, spelling) is most suitable with young language learners. The "incorrect" copy is saved and passed on to another group of students who have to find all the errors and correct them, using highlighting and different colors of font. The two copies of the text are then compared and all the errors and corrections are discussed. This activity can be extended to different texts, including student-created ones, as well as different aspects of writing: spelling, grammar, paragraph structure, and organization.[29]

- *Describe the Picture.* The ability of word processing software to insert ClipArt images into the text can lead to speech production and grammar practice. After choosing a ClipArt picture and inserting it into a document, students write about what is happening in the picture.

- *Postcards.* In this activity, students use word processing software to compose a birthday or holiday message with words, pictures, and decorations. First, the class brainstorms words and expressions they find on a greeting card with the teacher teaching any necessary additional vocabulary and grammar. Then, students create their greeting cards. To add authenticity to the task, the teacher may want to provide a template that looks like a back of the postcard; it can be easily created on the computer, and students will type their message into it.

Presentation Software

Presentation software (PS) is an authoring computer application that makes it possible to combine text, graphics, images, and sound to create sophisticated multimedia presentations. PS exists in a Macintosh or PC version and usually comes as a part of an office-oriented software package. PS such as PowerPoint[30] or Keynote[31] has become increasingly popular with language teachers because it is flexible, user-friendly, and can be mastered with a minimal amount of training.[32] Teachers can create and manage the content of PS-based activities in terms of vocabulary, grammar, level of difficulty, and themes to address specific student needs and focus the learners on a particular linguistic task.

The greatest appeal of this software lies in its ability to present materials in both visual and auditory formats. By interactively combining text, digital images, sound, and simple animation, teachers can establish a meaningful context for language practice and create stimulating and enjoyable activities that address various learning styles. Teachers also appreciate the efficiency of classroom management offered by PS. Not only does it provide relief from switching between several isolated tools such as OHP, audiocassette player, and a chalkboard, but it also offers a multimedia and Internet capacity available from a single platform. Illustrations, sounds, texts, and Internet links of any activity can be retrieved and presented at the same time with a simple click of the mouse. Projected on a screen, the slides are visible from every corner of a classroom; they capture students' attention and allow for more eye contact during instruction.

- *Rebus*. This activity invites students to read a text where miniature pictures are inserted in place of words. The text should be appropriate to the level of students, written in clear language, and incorporate language items that can be represented with pictures. After students articulate the words in question, each image is replaced by its written representation by clicking a mouse. Students then try to retell the text in their own words without looking at the original. The pictures can optionally be displayed on another slide to help students follow the plot.

- *Matching Game.* An effective way to practice the target vocabulary or grammar is to create a matching activity that asks students to match vocabulary and grammar items to corresponding words, images, or even sounds representing them. As students come to the screen to point at the match, the red arrow connecting the two items shows up. To follow-up on this activity, the teacher can prepare an interactive fill-in-the-blank exercise where the animated fill-ins appear on the slide after students identify them correctly.

- *Jeopardy!* PS makes it possible to design a Jeopardy-style game. The speed and ease with which the game can be played and changed to suit the intended teaching points make it a stimulating practice and review activity. The class is divided into several teams that take turns choosing a category and a question and then collaborate on the answer while the teacher monitors and keeps score.

- *Storytelling.* This popular activity draws on young learners' imagination and stimulates a natural use of the target language by fostering creative writing and speaking. As students create a story based on one or several pictures projected on the screen, the teacher uses the PS to record students' sentences as they speak so that everybody's contribution is displayed on the slide. As an option, computer-literate students can take turns typing their sentences while the teacher monitors. The class then discusses and edits the story; the final account can be printed out or posted on the Web.

The World Wide Web

The World Wide Web is a popular educational tool both with English language teachers and students. Teachers and other adults use its unlimited teaching resources to gain access to a wide range of interesting, current materials that they can use for content and cultural instruction.[33] Young learners profit from Web-based activities by being actively engaged in meaningful interaction, in which they have to process the new information, think critically, and articulate what they have learned. Because computer and Internet are associated with fun, children devote their full attention to Web-based activities, which makes learning the language even more effective. The use of the Web is seen as a desirable component of the learning experience as it can lend itself to student-centered and individualized teaching in a foreign language classroom as well as offer authentic language input and valuable cultural information.[34] Web materials can enhance students' confidence and increase their self-esteem as they engage in real-life tasks designed around a target language Web site. As young learners successfully unscramble a sentence or send a postcard online they get a sense of accomplishment. Thus authentic experiences and realistic practice with the language and the opportunity to independently explore and carry out tasks empowers children. They also enjoy a certain degree of control over their learning, because of the opportunity to repeat the activity as many times as they want and move on to a new one at their own pace.

An important benefit of Web-based activities is their flexibility. Depending on the content of the site, the activities can be structured so that students can practice isolated language skills such as reading, writing, and communicating, as well as larger projects in an authentic, interesting, and meaningful context. Activities can involve collaboration or promote individual work; they can be done in or outside the class, and adapted to various levels of language proficiency.

One common problem associated with the Internet is that of fluidity. Web pages and even whole sites that are fully functioning one day may temporarily or permanently disappear the next. The best prevention strategy is to test the activity and visit the Web sites as close to the class time as possible. If the target Web site is not available, it is easy to find an alternative one by typing in a few keywords in the search engine.

- *Picture Dictionary.* This interactive user-friendly Web site provides clear and accurate illustrations of common English words that teachers can use in order to introduce and help children practice basic vocabulary categories. For example, to practice clothing vocabulary, the teacher starts by modeling personal preferences, using grammatical forms and clothing items, for example, *I like to wear jeans. Sometimes I wear a skirt and a blouse.* The students then use vocabulary handouts containing pictures of clothing items and directions for accessing online Picture Dictionary, or the teacher can locate the Web site for the children, as needed (http://www.pdictionary.com). Students look up words individually or with partners and write the correct labels on the lines by each picture. Additional practice can take place with online activities such as flash cards, fill-in-the-blanks, word scrambles, spelling activities, and a recall exercise to assess learning.

- *What Is the Weather Like?* A thematic unit on weather and climate can be augmented by using an authentic weather forecast Web site (e.g., www.intellicast.com; www.weather.com). Assuming the roles of weather reporters, students describe weather conditions based on the national forecast map. They can produce simple sentences (e.g.,

It is raining in Seattle) in past, present, and future tenses; compare the weather in different cities (e.g., *It's warmer in Miami than in Denver*), or create a weekly forecast using words instead of pictures provided on the Web site. To develop listening for specific information skills, students listen to an authentic weather report available at www.weatheraudio.net and mark familiar words (e.g., weather, rain, wind, snow) that are mentioned in the text. Low-proficiency students circle appropriate pictures instead of words. As a follow-up, groups of students can create a script for a weather report for any city on a national map; volunteers deliver the weather forecast to the class afterward.

- *Now I Know My ABCs.* Designed for native speaking first graders, www.starfall.com is an excellent learn-to-read Web site. Depending on their level of literacy, students can practice symbol–sound correspondence by clicking on individual letters and doing suggested on-line activities; sing along focusing on specific sounds; follow simple instructions on the screen to perform specific actions (e.g., making a snowman); or read more challenging texts. To promote oral practice, students should be reminded to repeat after the speaker.

- *Happy Holidays!* After discussing holidays in the target culture as well as those holidays that represent a variety of cultural traditions and learning traditional expressions associated with a particular holiday, students visit electronic postcard sites (e.g., http://www.bluemountain.com; http://cards.amazon.com; http://www.e-cards.com). They select and read several cards on the site and write down three to five sentences appropriate to the occasion. After that, they choose one card, compose a message using new as well as familiar expressions, and send it to the teacher or other real-life addressee (several e-mail addresses should be prepared in advance).

- *Visit Our Web Site!* Creating a Web site on a topic the class has studied can motivate students to write as well as to learn the basic computer and Internet skills. After agreeing on general content of the Web site, students brainstorm about specific pages that will make up their site. Students compose all entries either on paper or using the computer, discuss the images and the appearance of the Web site, and participate in editing sessions that can help to improve the quality of work. The content is then posted on the Web either by the teacher or by a technical support staff member. Some knowledge of Web editing software, such as FrontPage or Dream Weaver, facilitates the composition, editing, uploading, and management of a site.

In conclusion, technology can enhance second language teaching by providing more resources, increasing motivation, adding interactivity and variety to classroom procedures, and offering students greater opportunities to practice and use the language. It also advances students' technical literacy, by preparing them for the challenges of modern life. However, it is important to remember that no technology can replace the teacher and students in the class together. The technology is simply another device in the teacher's toolbox that can expand and enrich communicative language learning activities. Audio, video, computers, and the World Wide Web are capable of delivering content in a very appealing way, but it is the teacher's responsibility to select the content, provide effective instruction, and guide students through educational experiences. It is worthwhile to consider incorporating technology-based activities into teaching children in the primary grades. While technology does not eliminate the need for other communicative practices, the various formats of media offer teachers creative opportunities to promote active and versatile learning.

Notes

1. K.M. Culp, M. Honey, and E. Mandinach (2003), *A retrospective on twenty years of education technology policy.* U.S. Department of Education, p. 5.

2. M. O'Hara (2004), *ICT in the early years.* London: Continuum.

3. Ibid.

4. J. McDonough and C. Shaw (1993), *Materials and methods in ELT.* Malden, MS: Blackwell.

5. A. Omaggio-Hadley (2001), *Teaching language in context.* Boston: Heinle & Heinle.

6. K. Brandl (2002), "Integrating Internet-Based Reading Materials into the Foreign Language Curriculum: From Teacher- to Student-Centered Approaches." *Language Learning and Technology*, 9(3), 87–107.

7. C. Feyten, M. Macy, J. Ducher, M. Yoshii, E. Park, B. Calandra, and J. Meros (2002), *Teaching ESL/EFL with the Internet.* Upper Saddle River, NJ: Prentice Hall.

8. J. Duncan (1987), *Technology assisted teaching techniques.* Brattleboro, VA: Pro Lingua Associates.

9. S. Gillette, K. Goettsch, J. Rowekamp, N. Salehi, and Tarone, E. (1999), *Connected! Using audio, video, and computer materials in the communicative classroom.* Bloomington, MN: Master Communications Group Inc.

10. A. Omaggio-Hadley (2001), *Teaching language in context.* Boston: Heinle and Heinle.

11. M. Abbott (2002), "Using Music to Promote Second Language Learning Among Adult Learners." *TESOL Journal*, 11(1), 10–17.

12. J. Scruggs (1984), Wiggle in My Toe. On *Late last night* [CD]. Austin, TX: Shadow Play Records.

13. Susan Nipp (2002), "The Land of Slow Motion." On *Wee sing and pretend* [Audio cassette]. New York: Price Stern Sloan.

14. Scruggs. On *Late last night* [CD].

15. L. Brinkerhoff and M. Banerjee (2000), "Do Audio-Taped Books Improve Reading Rates, Decoding and Reading Comprehension Among High School Students?" Poster, LDA 2000 International Conference. Retrieved November 29, 2005, from http://www.ldonline.org/ld_indepth/reading/podhajski_booksontape.html.

16. E. Brown (2004), "Using Children's Literature with Young Learners." *The Internet TESL Journal*, X(2), February 2004. Retrieved November 29, 2005, from http://iteslj.org/.

17. P. Ur (1991), *A course in language teaching*. Cambridge, UK: Cambridge University Press, p. 108.

18. C. Bonsall (2000), *The day I had to play with my sister*. Prince Frederick, MD: Recorded Books.

19. L. Lowry (1993), *Anastasia Krupnik*. Prince Frederick, MD Recorded Books.

20. T. Secules, C. Herron, and M. Tomasello (1992), "The Effect of Video-Context on Foreign Language Learning. *Modern Language Journal*, 76, 480–490.

21. C. Canning-Wilson (2000), "Role of Video in the F/SL Classroom." In S. Riley, S. Troudi and C. Coombe (Eds.), *Teaching, learning and technology*. TESOL Arabia 1999 Conference Proceedings, *TESOL Arabia 1999 Conference*, March 8–10, 1999.

22. I. Balatova (1994), "Impact of Video on the Comprehension Skills of Core French Students." *Canadian Modern Language Review*, 50(3), 506–531.

23. P. Arcario (1992), "Criteria for Selecting Video Materials." In S. Stempleski and P. Arcario (Eds.), *Video in second language teaching: Using, selecting, and producing video for the classroom*. Alexandria, VA: Teachers of English to Speakers of Other Languages.

24. S. Stempleski and B. Tomalin (1999), *Video in action*. New York: Prentice Hall.

25. J. Lasseter (Producer/Director) (1987), *Red's Dream* [VHS]. Pixar Animation Studios.

26. J. Brown and C. Pelzer (Producers/Directors). (1985), *Molly's Pilgrim* [VHS]. Phoenix Films, Inc.

27. R. Ager (2003), *Information and communications technology in Primary Schools*. London: David Fulton Publishers.

28. Arlington County Public Schools, VA. (1999). Technology and the ESL classroom: Equipping students to function in the modern world. Arlington Education and Employment Program: Spring Institute for International Studies, Denver, CO. ERIC Document Reproduction Service No. ED 427561.

29. T. Boswood (1997), *New ways of using computers in language teaching*. Alexandria, VA: Teachers of English to Speakers of Other Languages.

30. Powerpoint [Computer Software] (2003), Redmond, WA: Microsoft Corporation.

31. Keynote (Version 2) [Computer Software] (2005), Cupertino, CA: Apple Computer Inc.

32. E. Nemtchinova (2003), "Creating Original Language Teaching Materials with Presentation Software." In L. Lomicka and J. Cooke-Plagwitz (Eds.), *Teaching with technology*. Boston: Heinle and Heinle.

33. K. Cameron (1999), "CALL: The Virtual Revolution and the Millennium." *Computer-Assisted Language Learning*, 12(5), 401–407.

34. M.M. Osuna and C. Meskill (1998), "Using the World Wide Web to Integrate Spanish Language and Culture." *Language Learning and Technology*, 1(2), 71–92.

CHAPTER 11

Assessment of Young English Language Learners

This chapter deals with some ways to assess young language learners' second language acquisition and academic progress. It opens with a discussion of procedures that are used in order to place young children in ESL programs; then deals with assessment instruments that are used with young English language learners; considers ways to decide whether or not a given assessment instrument is effective; and also discusses some new trends in the assessment of the language and academic attainment of young English language learners.

Language Assessment Tools Guiding the Placement of Young English Language Learners

Standardized Tests Used with Young English Language Learners. When students are newly admitted into schools, their parents or caregivers fill out a *home language survey* or a *home language questionnaire*. These evaluative instruments, used for preliminary screening, contain questions about a language or languages that children and their caregivers speak at home. Overall, this type of preliminary screening works fairly reliably for the identification of English language learners. However, there is evidence that due to immigrant parents' lack of English language proficiency, or concerns about their legal status in the United States, or reluctance to have their children identified as limited English proficient, language surveys and questionnaires are not always filled out correctly.[1] If the survey or questionnaire does reveal that a child speaks a second language at home, the school must administer a federally mandated standardized language test to determine whether or not a child is proficient in English and whether or not she would benefit from placement in a second language program.

Usually, the test is administered again at the end of the school year to measure the child's second language attainment and academic language development. Once standardized test demonstrates that a child has achieved a level of proficiency that enables him or her to function in the mainstream classroom, the student exits a second language program.

Some of the language tests commonly used with young children are the following:

The Language Assessment Scales (LAS);

IDEA Proficiency Test (IPT);

The Language Assessment Battery (LAB);

Basic Inventory of Natural Languages (BINL)

The Maculaitis Assessment Program (MAC);

Woodcock-Munoz Language Survey Test.[2]

Standardized language tests play an important role in the lives of language learners, because they yield information used for the funding of second language programs. These tests are also a subject of controversy, because many second language educators argue that standardized language tests do not provide an adequate measure of language learners' second language proficiency. The debate around the use of standardized testing is contained in the following section of this chapter.

High-Stakes Achievement Tests. Aside from standardized language tests, young English language learners have also been taking the so-called *high-stakes tests* in English Language Arts, mathematics, and other subject areas. High-stakes test are meant to provide parents, community, administrators, and policymakers with information about the effectiveness of instruction in individual schools.

Until 2001, English language learners had been exempted from standardized testing procedures used with their mainstream peers. The situation changed in 2001 when the federal government, in an attempt to make schools more accountable to the public and to assure that all children benefit from quality instruction, signed into law the *No Child Left Behind (NLCB)* act. Under NLCB, all students, whether they are native speakers of English or English language learners, must take standardized tests to demonstrate their progress in English and content area learning. NLCB further mandates that if schools that educate English language learners fail to demonstrate adequate yearly progress (AYP), measured in terms of standardized test scores, these schools may be subject to restructuring; parents may enjoy the option of transferring their students to another school. Some of the high-stakes achievement tests used with language learners are

California Achievement Test (CAT);

Iowa Test of Basic Skills (ITBS);

Metropolitan Achievement Test (MAT);

Stanford Achievement Test (SAT); and

Comprehensive Test of Basic Skills.[3]

Both standardized language tests and high-stakes achievement tests draw criticism on the part of second language researchers and practitioners. The next section of this book contains a theoretical framework that underpins a debate around the use of standardized testing with English language learners.

Characteristics of Assessment Instruments Used with Young Language Learners

The question considered in this section of the chapter is as follows: What features does the language test (or any other test for that matter) need to possess in order to be useful?

Reliability. To answer the question above, let us compare a language test to another measurement device such as a thermometer, a scale, or a speedometer. While the thermometer measures temperature, the scale measures weight, and the speedometer measures speed, the language test is meant to measure a child's command of language or demonstrate to the public the rate of academic progress of English language learners.

Just like any other measurement devices, language tests can be good or poor. What characteristics does a language test need to possess in order to be good? First and foremost, quite obviously, it must provide accurate measurements or, to use the term employed by assessment specialists, be *reliable*. To consider what constitutes test reliability, let us compare a test to a scale. Think of the bathroom scale. If you step on it five times within half an hour (without having snacked in between) and see that the scale shows the exact same figure, you are assured that your scale is in good repair. If, on the other hand, every time you step on the scale, a different figure pops up on the display, you are likely to suspect that there is something wrong with the instrument. This very important principle is observed in all kinds of measurement. Accurate measuring instruments are consistent. If an object being measured has not changed, an accurate measuring instrument should show the same or a very similar result.

The same consistency principle is applied to language tests (and all other tests for that matter). If a language learner takes versions A, B, and C of the same test without having done any additional preparation and without having expanded her English language skills, and if each time she earns a different score on that test, the teacher has every reason to say that the test is no good. Similarly, if two students who read, write, and speak English equally well or equally poorly earn vastly different scores on a standardized language test, the teacher will question reliability of this evaluative instrument. Like any other measuring device, an educational test is reliable when it is consistent. We observe test consistency or test reliability when many children who are equally well or equally poorly prepared earn scores within a very close range of each other.

Reliability of Standardized Language Tests. In order to be reliable, a measuring device needs to be well made, that is, it needs to be well calibrated and well constructed. The same holds true of a language test. What kind of a language test can be described as well made? Some of the criteria that determine reliability of assessment instruments meant for young second language learners are as follows:

- The language test has clear directions. It tells language learners what exactly they need to do in simple, clear, and unambiguous language.
- If the test has an open-ended task, it explicitly tells test takers the extent of the desired response.
- The test is made of tasks that are free of ambiguity and easy to interpret.
- The print and graphic materials are user-friendly; its pages do not look overcrowded; its graphics are lean, simple, and attractive.
- The language test is neither too short nor too long. (If the test contains too few tasks, students might get an inaccurately low score by inadvertently getting just one answer wrong or an inaccurately high score by accidentally getting just one answer right.)
- The well-made assessment instrument also has provisions for reliable scoring. By providing scoring rubrics and unambiguous scoring guidelines, it enables the test reader to interpret test results accurately and to assign correct scores to test takers.

- The test site staff and physical environment provide a supportive atmosphere. Learners' state of mind at the time they take a language test and the physical environment at the test site are all part of test reliability. If the learner is overly nervous or distracted at the time of testing, the test will fail to provide accurate results.

Evaluating Test Reliability. We can find out whether a language test is reliable or not by performing some relatively simple procedures. One of the reliability evaluation procedures is known as a *split half test*. When this procedure is implemented, a group of students complete all even numbered tasks contained in a test and then do all odd numbered tasks. If both times students get the same (or almost the same) score, the test is reliable. Another method used to evaluate reliability of a language test is the so-called *test–retest* procedure. When this method is used, two different versions of the same test are taken by the same group of individuals within a short time period. If subjects of the test–retest procedure get a low score one time and a high score a second time, the test is clearly unreliable. Conversely, when each individual who participates in a test–retest experiment earns the scores that fall within the close range of each other, the test is pretty reliable.[4]

Reliability of a test can be measured or quantified. On a highly reliable test, scores earned by the subjects of a test-retest procedure or a split half procedure should fall within a very close range of each other in 90 percent of cases or more. The figure that expresses reliability of a test is called the *reliability index*. A highly reliable test will have a reliability index of 90 percent or above. Referring to the fact that reliability of a test can be expressed in terms of an objective number, assessment experts say that reliability of a test is *quantifiable*.

Using the scale analogy which is featured in the earlier section of this chapter, we can compare a well-made language test to a well-made scale. Like that scale, a reliable test should measure second language proficiency or language learners' academic attainment both accurately and consistently.

Validity. Reliability is not all there is to a good language test. A good test is also *valid*. To understand the concept of validity, let us again consider a scale analogy. There are all kinds of scales out there. Some scales are used for weighing human bodies, others are for weighing huge containers, and still others are for weighing miniscule amounts of chemicals. It is not enough that these measuring tools should be well made and reliable. It is also important that they be able to provide the kind of information that one needs to collect. You would not get very far if you tried to weigh electronic particles with a bathroom scale no matter how well that bathroom scale is designed. It is not enough that a measuring instrument be well made or reliable. For any measuring procedure, you need to be assured that the device you are using can provide the kind of data that you seek to obtain. Language tests used in schools are no exception. These assessment tools should also be appropriate for educators' intentions and have the capacity to provide the type of data which educators are interested in gathering.

When educators claim that a test is invalid, they argue that it does not yield the data which they seek to obtain. Can a test be reliable without being valid? The answer is: yes. A highly reliable, well-constructed test can in fact be invalid. Just as a well-made and accurate bathroom scale is not suited for use in a pharmacy or a science lab, some reliable tests are ill equipped for measuring human intelligence or academic achievement or language proficiency.[5]

Consider the following analogy. An educator compared the use of reliable but invalid tests when assessing children's learning to measuring how high the dancer can leap with the help of a sophisticated device and then claiming that the obtained measurements tell all we need to know about this performer's artistic prowess.[6]

Evaluating Test Validity. Unlike test reliability, test validity is not quantifiable. There is no simple number that can express the test's capability to provide users with the kind of information that they are seeking to obtain. The job of assessing test validity is performed by teams of competent experts. Qualified, experienced language educators alone can say whether tasks contained in a test can really measure language proficiency or language attainment of language learners.

Limitations of Standardized Tests and Alternative Approaches to Assessment of Young English Language Learners

Problems with Standardized Tests. Standardized tests (both language proficiency and high-stakes achievement ones) have been the target of criticism by classroom teachers and assessment experts. First of all, educators have some concerns about reliability of these testing instruments.[7] Critics point out that a single measurement performed at the end of a school year is unlikely to yield accurate information about a child's language proficiency and academic attainment. Detractors of standardized testing also remind us that a young language learner may be nervous when taking a standardized test or have difficulty understanding test directions; these problems commonly experienced by children diminish test accuracy or reliability even further.

While reliability of standardized tests has been brought into question, it is the validity of these assessment instruments that educators criticize most bitterly.[8] Those who object to the use of standardized tests with English language learners point out that these instruments are misleading and not suited for their intended purpose—in short, they cannot provide the kind of data educators seek to obtain.

Limited validity of standardized tests has a lot to do with their make-up. This is the case because standardized language tests use inauthentic, artificial language tasks. Take the example of standardized English language proficiency tests meant to ascertain how well somebody can speak, read, and write English. Children who take these tests are not asked to use language in the way that they would if they spoke, read, and wrote English in real-life situations. Instead, language learners must fill in blanks, match words with their definitions, and do transformation exercises to demonstrate their command of a grammatical item. Because takers of standardized tests use language outside meaningful contexts and deploy strategies not found in real-life communication (e.g., filling in bubbles or matching words), because standardized test tasks tend to be discrete points rather than *integrative*, because their language is fragmented rather than whole, these tests do not create realistic models of language use or in the words of a language testing researcher "do not accord well with what people do when they process text or discourse in normal ways."[9]

Critics of standardized tests argue that because language proficiency tests are made of tasks that are unlike the tasks language users perform in everyday life, these tests do not necessarily say much about children's linguistic performance in real-life situations and do not really measure the true extent of their language proficiency. Numerous studies describe young children who appear baffled when taking a test and are later observed speaking, reading, and writing in English with both confidence and competence.[10]

Just as standardized proficiency tests, high-stakes tests used with language learners have limited validity.[11] When content knowledge tests are administered in English, limited second language proficiency often prevents children form demonstrating the true extent of their content knowledge. A child may know a concept in science or mathematics but be unable to handle a test task because it is coached in complex English.[12] In some states, children may take content tests in both their home language and English. This measure is only helpful, however, if students are literate in their home language. So far there is no evidence whether the use of home language translations helps increase validity of high-stakes tests.[13]

Cultural Bias of Standardized Tests. Another problem with the use of standardized tests for the assessment of English language learners is the *cultural bias* of these testing instruments. Researchers have pointed out that test tasks included in standardized tests are based on the situations, norms, or lifestyles with which young English language learners may be culturally unfamiliar.[14] Children may have difficulty performing a test task simply because it presumes familiarity with a scenario not to be found in the student's home culture. Today, when young language learners must take language tests alongside native speaking children, concerns about the cultural bias of standardized tests have become particularly keen.

An elementary school teacher from southern California made the following comment on the attempt of test writers to reduce test bias by making token references to immigrant children's experiences:

> The test tries to make up for that [cultural bias] by writing stories about Carlos. You know, they put these ethnic names in these stories ... like Carlos in the kitchen with his mother setting the table when the car drives up into the driveway and honks the horn. It cracks me up that they're trying to take a test and adjust it to these kids, like "Oh well. Maybe they'll listen and pay attention because it says Carlos or because it says Juan and Maria."[15]

High-Stakes Testing Driving Instruction. While both language and high-stakes tests have been criticized for their insufficient reliability, low validity, and a cultural bias, there is an additional problem which is associated specifically with the use of high-stakes testing. While the measure was originally conceived to enhance the quality of teaching available to language minority students, in effect, the impact of standardized assessment on instruction may be negative. In their efforts to raise test scores, teachers find themselves engaged in so-called *test-driven instruction*. In the test-driven classroom, instead of implementing intellectually exciting, meaningful projects, language teachers spend an increasing amount of time coaching children to take standardized tests. Drilling young language learners to answer text comprehension questions replaces authentic conversations about books; training students to use test-taking strategies replaces exciting explorations.

A study of the effect of high-stakes testing on the quality of second language teaching in elementary school reports a typical situation. Teachers in the study have profound reservations about the impact of testing on the quality of their teaching. This is how a teacher describes her classroom which succumbs to test-driven instruction:

> This year, I think all I care about is, "OK, am I using the vocabulary that the kids will see on the test?" All I think about [is], "OK, let's see what's on the test, and let me teach to the test.[16]

Persistence in the Use of Standardized Tests. Even though validity of standardized tests is limited, even though they are criticized for their cultural bias, even though these tests' limiting impact is well documented, the use of standardized testing is unlikely to stop any time soon. In the words of a second language assessment expert "Testing is here to stay."[17]

There are multiple reasons why standardized assessment instruments have become entrenched in the United States' educational system. Proponents of standardized tests point out that these assessment instruments provide a *common yardstick*, or a means of evaluating and comparing students from vastly diverse educational backgrounds. These tests provide the means to compare children and subdivide them into groups in accordance with the test results. Second, standardized tests are popular because of their efficiency; they are relatively cheap and easy to administer and score. Further, standardized tests are appealing to the public and policymakers, because they express performance of educational institutions or individual academic attainment in terms of a simple number. Last but not least, standardized tests are touted as an effective means of rendering schools *accountable* to the public.

Improving Assessment of English Language Learners. Reckoning with the fact that standardized tests are deeply ingrained in the educational system of the United States, educators who work with English language learners look for ways to increase reliability and validity of the assessment system currently in use. TESOL educators strive to make assessment of language learning more reliable and valid, and look for ways to diminish the cultural bias of standardized tests.

One of the most commonly made recommendations is taking classroom teachers' appraisal into account when evaluating language development[18] and academic attainment[19] of language learners. "Whose judgment counts?" ask second language educators[20] dismayed by the fact that their perspective is not taken into consideration in the evaluation of language learners.

Researchers also recommend that the context of student learning and students' educational backgrounds should be factored in during the assessment process. According to this scenario, language learners' home background, previous educational experiences, and the students' current classroom environment should be taken into consideration in the assessment process.[21]

Given that classroom teachers observe their students speak, read, and write English on a daily basis and in a natural communication context, researchers and classroom practitioners argue that including classroom-generated data in the evaluation of language learners can render language learners' assessment both more accurate and more valid.

What evaluative instruments do teachers use in the classroom? The answer to this question is contained in the next section of this chapter.

Teacher-Made Assessment Instruments

Classroom assessment is traditionally subdivided into two categories, known as formative and summative assessment. *Formative assessment* is informal evaluation which teachers implement on an ongoing basis to make sure that students are mastering the concepts and the target language items which they explore in class. For the formative evaluation of their students' progress, language teachers use *journals, observations, questioning,* and *portfolios*.[22]

The different kinds of formative assessment instruments mentioned above are best suited for different purposes.[23] Journaling, that is, written exchanges between the teacher and her students, works best if the teacher wants to make sure that her students are able to connect the concepts explored in class to their personal experiences. For instance, upon teaching a lesson that focuses on wild and domestic animals, the teacher may ask her students to draw a picture or write a story about their experience with animals. Similarly, upon reading a book that deals with an unusual childhood experience, children can describe or draw a picture of a similar experience in their own lives. When students and teachers engage in journaling, teachers offer feedback by writing personal, individualized comments to language learners' journal entries. Aside from providing teachers with valuable information about student learning, these written conversations help build a bond between the teacher and language learners.

Observation, or kid watching, is helpful when the teacher is interested in finding out whether her students have the know-how needed to complete a certain task or whether they can help themselves while dealing with the challenges posed by a language learning activity. Whereas some children know how to use picture dictionaries and graphic organizers, or put together an outline or a semantic map, others do not have these important skills or—as language educators put it—do not possess *strategic competence* essential for completing certain tasks. By observing how her students resolve the challenges presented by the acts of speaking, reading, or writing in a second language, language teachers can learn the extent of their students' strategic competence and ascertain what type of help would benefit language learners.

Portfolios have caught the attention of educators as a way of evaluating students' progress through an extended period of time. Portfolios are purposeful collections of students' work which document student learning or in a word of an assessment researcher "produce a portrait" of a student.[24]

Portfolios are an effective means of assessment, because they build students' *metacognitive awareness* in that they help children recognize their own strengths and weaknesses. Portfolio experts recommend that a teacher and a language student have individual *portfolio conferences* to decide which samples of students' work should be included in the portfolio. During the conferences, the teacher works with the student to help him or her identify the areas in need of improvement. For instance, a young language learner may need to work on capitalization, or punctuation, or elements of text grammar, such as a closing or introductory sentence. Portfolio experts recommend that teachers develop portfolio contracts or other forms to document students' needs and to raise students' metacognitive awareness. In portfolio contracts, a student and a teacher jointly describe a skill on which the student needs to focus.

While formative assessment is an ongoing process, teachers use *summative assessment* at the end of an instructional unit or academic year. *Teacher-made tests* and *showcase portfolios* are common means of summative assessment. Teacher-made tests are traditional assessment instruments which often include close-ended tasks, such as matching words with pictures or answering questions.

Showcase portfolios are collections of the best pieces of work which students have produced in the course of an instructional unit. Showcase portfolios may include pieces of writing created by students, photographs of student's participation in role-plays, or artifacts that document students' involvement in hands-on science projects. It is important that portfolios be comprehensive, but not overloaded with artifacts, and that all the pieces included in the portfolio be provided with captions which explain to potential portfolio viewers (such as children's parents and administrators) the nature of an activity which took place in the classroom.[25] It is also important that students be able to describe activities represented in their portfolios.

Both formative and summative assessments play an important role in teaching. Data provided by classroom-based assessment provides teachers with feedback regarding students' learning. These data help teachers set realistic goals for their lessons, letting educators know which instructional strategies work best.[26]

Just like other assessment tools, teacher-made assessment instruments need to be reliable and valid. If the teacher realizes that language learners did worse than she had expected on a teacher-made test, she might question the reliability of her own assessment instrument. When after the test children cry out "Not fair! We never studied this," they question the validity of a teacher-made test.

While it is important that teacher-made assessment instruments be reliable and valid, second language educators know that the quality of a teacher-made assessment tool cannot be reduced to its reliability or validity. Nor is the most innovative assessment tool inherently effective per se. The usefulness of assessments administered in the language classroom has everything to do with the quality of instruction. If instruction challenges and stimulates young language learners, assessment tools are likely to be conceived in the same intellectually challenging and stimulating spirit.

Main Points

- Good assessment instruments used with young language learners need to be reliable (accurate) and valid (produce the kind of data that educators seek to obtain).

- Second language educators question reliability and validity of standardized proficiency and high-stakes tests used with young language learners.

- Suggestions have been made to take teacher judgment into account when evaluating language proficiency and academic attainment of young language learners.

- Some of the innovative assessment instruments used by second language teachers include journals, observations, and portfolios.

Notes

1. J. Abedi (2002), "Issues and Problems in Classification of Students with Limited English Proficiency." Paper presented at the 2002 *Annual Meeting of the American Educational Research Association.* http://www.cse.ucla.edu/products/overheads/aera2002/abedi.ppt.

2. A. Kindler (2002), *Survey of the states' limited English proficient students and available educational programs and services: 2000–2001 summary report.* Washington,

DC: The George Washington University National Clearinghouse for English Language Acquisition and Language Instruction Educational Programs. www.ncela. gwu.edu.

3. Abedi, http://www.cse.ucla.edu/products/overheads/aera2002/abedi.ppt.

4. F. Genesee and J.A. Upshur (1996), *Classroom-based evaluation in second language education*. New York: Cambridge University Press.

5. A detailed discussion of language test parameters is contained in F. Genesee and J.A. Upshur (1996), *Classroom-based evaluation in second language education*. New York: Cambridge University Press.

6. A. Karp, Personal Communication, 2006.

7. J. Bordie (1979), "Report of the Committee for the Evaluation of Language Assessment Instruments: Winter and Spring," Austin, TX: Texas Educational Agency, Division of Bilingual Education. Cited in B. McLaughlin (1985), *Second-language acquisition in childhood, vol. 2: School Age Children*, 2nd ed. Hillsdale, NJ: Lawrence Erlbaum Associates.

8. For example, R.P. Duran (1988), "Testing of Linguistic Minorities." In R. Linn (Ed.), *Educational measurement*. New York: Macmillan, pp. 573–587.

9. J. Oller (1992), "Language Testing Research: Lessons Applied to LEP Students and Programs." In *Proceedings of the second national research symposium on limited English proficient student issues: Focus on evaluation and measurement*. Washington, DC: United States Department of Education, pp. 43–124.

10. For example, H. Stefanakis (1998), *Whose judgment counts? Assessing bilingual children, K-3*. Portsmouth, NH: Heinemann.

11. E. Rosansky (1981), "Future Perspectives on Research in Oral Language Proficiency Assessment." Paper presented at the *Airlie House Conference on Language Proficiency Assessment*, Warrenton, VA. Cited in McLaughlin (1985), *Second-language acquisition in childhood*, vol. 2, 2nd ed. Hillsdale, NJ: Lawrence Erlbaum Associates.

12. M. La Celle-Petersen and C. Rivera (1994), "Is it Real for All Kids: A Framework for Equitable Assessment Policies for English Language Learners." *Harvard Educational Review*, 64(1), 55–75.

13. M. Neill (2005), *Assessment of ELL students under NLCB: Problems and solutions*. http://www.fairtest.org/nattest/NCLB_assessing_bilingual_students.pdf.

14. A.M. Padilla (1979), "Critical Factors in the Testing of Hispanic Americans: A Review and Some Suggestions for the Future." In R.W. Tyler and S.H. White (Eds.), *Testing, teaching and learning: Report of a conference on research on testing*. Washington, DC: National Institute of Education, pp. 219–243.

15. W.E. Wright (June 5, 2002), "The Effects of High Stakes Testing in an Inner-City Elementary School: The Curriculum, the Teachers, and the English Language Learners." *Current Issues in Education*, 5(5), 16. http://cie.ed.asu.edu/volume5/number5.

16. Ibid., p. 10.

17. B. Law and and M. Eckes (1995), *Assessment and ESL: On the yellow big road to the withered of Oz*. Winnipeg, CA: Peguis Publishers Ltd., p. 41.

18. Stefanakis, *Whose judgment counts?*

19. Neill, *Assessment of ELL students under NLCB.*

20. Stefanakis, *Whose judgment counts?*

21. N. Cloud (1991), "Educational Assessment." In E. Hamayan and J. Damico (Eds.), *Limiting bias in the assesment of bilingual students.* Austin, TX: Proed, pp. 219–245.

22. J.M. O'Malley and L.V. Pierce (1996), Authentic assessment for English language learners: Practical approaches for teachers. Chicago, IL: Addison Wesley.

23. F. Genesee and J.A. Upshur (1996), *Classroom-based evaluation in second language education.*

24. R. French (1992), "Portfolio Assessment and LEP Students." In *Proceedings of the second national research symposium on limited English proficient student issues: Focus on evaluation and measurement.* Washington, DC: United States Department of Educxation, pp. 249–279.

25. S. Moya and M. O'Malley (Spring 1994), "A Portfolio Assessment Model for ESL." *The Journal of Educational Issues of language Minority Students*, 13, 13–36.

26. F. Genesee and E. Hamayan (1994), "Classroom-Based Assessment." In J. Richards (Ed.), *Educating second language children: The whole child, the whole curriculum, the whole community.* New York: Cambridge University Press, pp. 212–240.

Index

About the Author

TATIANA GORDON is Associate Professor in the School of Education and Allied Human Services and the Director of the TESOL (Teachers of English to Speakers of Other Languages) program at Hofstra University.

CPSIA information can be obtained at www.ICGtesting.com
Printed in the USA
BVOW01*2135070514

352758BV00007B/416/P